T0064256

PRAYER
TEMPLATES

Simplified Requests
for Messy Times

❖

Kandy Persall

WESTBOW
PRESS®
A DIVISION OF THOMAS NELSON
& ZONDERVAN

WestBow Press books may be ordered through booksellers or by contacting:

WestBow Press
A Division of Thomas Nelson & Zondervan
1663 Liberty Drive
Bloomington, IN 47403
www.westbowpress.com
844-714-3454

ISBN: 978-1-6642-2340-0 (sc)
ISBN: 978-1-6642-2342-4 (hc)
ISBN: 978-1-6642-2341-7 (e)

Library of Congress Control Number: 2021902860

Print information available on the last page.

WestBow Press rev. date: 03/18/2021

To Noah, Joshua, Judah, Felicity, Kaiya, and Leah
who the Father has chosen to be a
new generation of prayer warriors

Contents

Introduction

"Every attempt to begin to write has been frustrated, and even now, one is conscious of a strange reluctance to do so. There seems to be some mysterious power restraining the hand. Do we realize that there is nothing the devil dreads so much as prayer?" (The Kneeling Christian).

I resonate with this anonymous author. Although my work bears no resemblance to his classic, I understand his frustration and reluctance to publish a book on prayer. How can our inadequate words stimulate others to pray? Yet, the Father lovingly urged both him and me forward despite our misgivings and hesitancy.

Personally, the idea of a written prayer began thirty years ago in response to prolonged overseas living. The needs of friends and family often burdened me, but distance kept me from ministering face-to-face. Since these years were before the day of video chats, email was my best connection with home.

My mentor, Bobbie Trull, often hand-mailed her prayers to me. Filled with wisdom and references, she often used the apostle Paul's prayers as her guidelines when she interceded for me. Bobbie's words still encourage me when I reread her yellowed pieces of correspondence.

Fellow missionary Kay Chandler also aided me in this prayer journey. She regularly gave her seeking neighbors printed prayers of salvation, encouraging them to read these daily until truth became life. I admit her example shook my theology at first, but Kay helped me bridge my upbringing against rote prayers with the desperate need to plant truth in the heart.

Following the examples of Bobbie, Kay, and nineteenth-century author Andrew Murray, I began typing out my intercession for family and friends. I'm still surprised at how many respond that they are saving these "letters" (and now texts) to guide their own times of prayer.

This book is an archive of those personal prayers. I admit that the difficulty of generalizing a specific prayer has often immobilized me. The need to omit names to expand effectiveness proved a five-year struggle. Sheltering in place gave me plenty of time "to finish doing it also, just as there was the readiness of desire it" (2 Corinthians 8:11). And when I look at today's world, maybe the timing is perfect, after all. Now more than ever, it's time to pray, even if we must borrow someone else's words to get us started.

You will find this compilation messy. The topics aren't exhaustive but are launchpads for deeper prayer. Personal petitions lie attached to intercessional prayers. Some prayers seem too short and others too long. You may discover a longing for additional days on some themes, while other themes do not currently intersect with your life. When you desire to go deeper, I've included a thirty-day devotional reading in part II. If you want reassurance from His Word, write me at Kandy@hungryformore.org for your free e-copy of *His Perspective*.

You may never read this book cover to cover. Most will use this as a reference to jump-start your biblical prayers, especially when you can't articulate those requests with words. If my wording isn't yours, change it. If the situation doesn't resonate, skip that sentence and keep praying. If the whole prayer doesn't match your heart, try another. The real nuggets of gold lie in the parenthetical references to His Word. Meditate on them and personalize them into your prayers. Yes, this book is a mess, but His truth is not. Let this book guide you into the depths of His clarity.

After arranging 85,000 words into this volume, I will be the first to admit that prayer doesn't consist of syllables. Prayer is the pixel point of the heart seeking to converge with God's desire. We wait before Him until we know a glimmer of His thought and then offer that back to Him so that He can release it upon the earth. The words included here cannot do that without His Spirit's prompting. Yet don't let that keep you from praying, for nothing is too difficult for Him (Jeremiah 32:17).

"Now to the One who constantly loves us and has loosed us from our sins by His own blood, and to the One Who has appointed us as a kingdom of priests to serve His God and Father—to Him be glory and dominion throughout the eternity of eternities! Amen!" (Revelation 1:5b–6 The Passion Translation).

That part is finished! I lay down my pen,
And wonder if the thoughts will flow as fast
Through the more difficult defile. For the last
Was easy, and the channel deeper then.
My Master, I will trust Thee for the rest;
Give me just what Thou wilt, and that will be my best!
How can I tell the varied, hidden need
Of Thy dear children, all unknown to me,
Who at some future time may come and read
What I have written! All are known to Thee.
As Thou hast helped me, help me to the end;
Give me Thy own sweet messages of love to send.
So now, I pray Thee, keep my hand in Thine;
And guide it as Thou wilt. I do not ask
To understand the "wherefore" of each line;
Mine is the sweeter, easier, happier task,
Just to look up to Thee for every word,
Rest in Thy love, and trust, and know that I am heard.

—Excerpt from Frances Ridley Havergal, *Kept for the Master's Use.*

PART I

PRAYER TEMPLATES

Addiction

Day 1

Father,

You are the only wise God (Romans 16:27). Your wisdom is unsearchable and Your ways unfathomable (Romans 11:33). Why You reach out to us for a relationship is beyond my comprehension, but I thank You that You have chosen us as the beloved bride for Your Son (Revelation 21:9).

Despite my foolishness and weakness, You call me to intercede on behalf of the situations You lay before me (1 Corinthians 1:27; Isaiah 62:6–7). I feel inadequate most of the time. But I'm reminded by Your Word that You don't condemn me for that weakness (Romans 8:1). Instead, You exchange Your life for mine and grant me the mind of Christ, which flows His wisdom into me (1 Corinthians 2:16; 1 Corinthians 1:30).

In Proverbs 12:18, You promise that the tongue of the wise brings healing (Proverbs 12:18). Somehow, out of Your extravagance, You have given curative power to the words of a wise person. So I come boldly to Your throne with confidence (Hebrews 4:16), using the powerful tongue of Jesus within me to speak out Your words of health and freedom to (*name of person under addiction*). Your purpose in (*name's*) life is to heal from the inside out.

You sent Your Son to destroy the works of the devil (1 John 3:8). (*Name's*) addiction to _____ is one of those reasons. I align my desires for him with Your desires, asking that Your purpose comes into reality in his life (Matthew 6:10). I know You hear this request, and You have promised to grant any request that is according to Your will (1 John 5:14–16). I expect You to act, for that gives us plenty of reason to praise You more. You are his help. You are his God (Psalm 42:11). Hallelujah! In Jesus's name, amen.

Day 2

Father,

Thank You not only for being the God who releases captives (Isaiah 42:7) but also the God who sent Your Son specifically with the key (Luke 4:18; Revelation 3:7). Your desire has always been that humankind is fruitful and subdues the earth rather than the earth defeating us (Genesis 1:28).

I come to You today on behalf of one of the captives. (*Food, drugs, alcohol, pornography, narcissism—you fill in the addiction*) is holding (*name of individual*) prisoner, and I come to You on behalf of this enslavement.

Breaking this addition is like a dream to him right now, but You are the bondage breaker. You are stronger than any "strong man" of addiction that has (*individual*) bound and guarded (Luke 11:21–22). Spirit of addiction, in the name of Jesus Christ, I demand you prostrate yourself before Christ as I press my foot down upon your neck (Joshua 23:10). I turn the tables on you, spirit of addiction, commanding that you become captive and obey Christ (2 Corinthians 10:4–5). God of peace, come quickly to crush this enemy as I pin him underfoot (Romans 16:20). Arise, oh Lord, and shatter the teeth of this enemy until it loses its bite (Psalm 3:7). May I persevere in prayer over this addiction until it resembles dust in the wind (Psalm 18:42).

Lord, because of my weakness in understanding spiritual foes, I ask that You do the fighting on (*individual's*) behalf while I merely trust You (Exodus 14:13–14; Psalm 138:7–8).

I ask Your Kingdom to come fully into (*individual's*) life so that Your desire will be done within him, according to the pattern You planned for him in heaven (Matthew 6:10; Ephesians 2:10; Exodus 26:30). Lead him out of this captivity by Your very hand (Psalm 126:1). How joyful he will be when he looks back one day to see Your work (Psalm 126:2). We look forward to the day when he can help others find freedom from oppression by saying, "It was the Lord that did this marvelous thing. It was all His work" (Psalm 126:3)!

Reset (*individual's*) life back to that time when he was more excited about life than craving this addiction. May Your work pour out abundantly like a rushing stream pervading his whole life (Psalm 126:4). There may be days of tears ahead, but grant him the insight to see that You are collecting every tear (Psalm 56:8). As these fall, help him know how these tears are like precious seeds encapsulating life. I claim Your promise that cries will sprout up as joy (Psalm 126:5–6).

Father, grant holy anger toward this addiction to take hold of (*individual's*) heart. Grant him the ability to hate the habit more than he desires it. It is only through the death of a seed that real-life sprouts (John 12:24). When tempted to cheat, may he call Satan out for the liar he is and desire You more than the substance (John 8:44). Reveal to him the littleness of the addictive morsel and the largeness of abundant Life You offer.

Granted, when we try to control ourselves, there is little control. But I am asking You to be his self-control. You promised that You would give self-control as evidence of Your Spirit, so do what is necessary to bring this to pass (Galatians 5:22–23). Even if this first includes bringing him to salvation.

I stand with the abundant claim check You have promised. Fulfill this order according to Your bounty, as I believe in You. In Jesus's name, amen.

Anger

Day 1

Holy Father,

Thank You for being near to all who will call upon You in truth (Psalm 145:18). You are the One who blesses with every spiritual blessing as I live inside You (Ephesians 1:3). Thank You for adopting me to be Your child and for freely giving me Your forgiveness and grace (Ephesians 1:5–7). I appreciate You.

You have created me with a passionate character, complete with intensity and vigor for life. But sometimes, my zeal expresses more force than necessary. My passion is no surprise to You, as even the apostle James struggled with these same tendencies. His entire epistle speaks of quarrels, conflicts, and the effect of tongues (James 1:26; 3:6, 10; 4:1, 11). He stresses that the anger of man never achieves Your righteousness but that we are to be quick to hear, slow to speak, and slow to anger (James 1:19–20).

Being slow to speak and slow to anger isn't easy for many of us. But You encourage me to lay aside my old self, especially when it is quick to speak angrily (Ephesians 4:22). Continue renewing me in the spirit of my mind and clothe me in the well-fitting garments of righteousness and holiness (Ephesians 4:23–24). Reveal how I can be angry without sinning, so the devil has no opportunity to wound others through my words (Ephesians 4:26). Show me how to unleash violent prayers against the evil one instead of upon those who disappoint me (Matthew 11:12; Psalm 144:1). Turn every unwholesome word I think into one that edifies (Ephesians 4:29).

May my bitterness and anger be replaced with kindness, tenderheartedness, and forgiveness (Ephesians 4:31–32). Even when others use inappropriate words, may I be thankful instead (Ephesians 5:4). Teach me how to evaluate evil and counteract in the opposite spirit. When I see anger, may I act and speak in love. When I see division, may I work and communicate in unity. When I see hatred, may I act and speak in kindness and love.

I want to walk like a child of light who pleases You (Ephesians 5:8–10). Fill me with Your Spirit, Lord, so that my speech includes psalms, hymns, and spiritual songs rather than rants, raves, and rebellion. Overflow my heart with melodies that praise Your name so Your name is glorified (Ephesians 5:18–19). In Jesus's name, amen.

◆ ◆ ◆

Day 2

Holy Father,

Thank You for being a God who grants endurance, for I need forbearance (Romans 15:5; Hebrews 10:36). I tend to react rather than respond, but I realize that reactive anger is not sourced within You. You desire that I pause more, breathe more, and be still (Zechariah 2:13). Live the life of Your Son through me.

Fleshly anger doesn't achieve Your godly righteousness, so I must purpose You to act through me before an infuriating situation occurs (James 1:20). Any self-control on my part requires Your Spirit walking patiently, not my flesh responding reactively (Galatians 5:22–23).

Transform me, both internally and eternally. Nipping my anger isn't a once-and-done process. Although the deliverance for renewal has already happened, the decision for results is a daily occurrence (2 Corinthians 5:17; Colossians 3:10). I am willing for You to make me ready to be transformed. I will continue to press forward toward this goal, no matter how long it takes (Philippians 3:12).

Thank You for planting Yourself, the Living Word, within me (James 1:22). Active and rapidly growing, You expand to fill every place where You are invited (Acts 12:24). Help me to welcome You moment by moment.

Separate my thoughts and words to produce spiritual fruit and not worthless, fleshly weeds (Jeremiah 15:19). Help me sort through the words that I think, obeying only the ones You speak (John 8:28). Allow me to see myself through the eyes of others and use this humiliation to turn again to Your strength.

This is a tall order, but You are a big God. Show Yourself strong today (Psalm 68:28). In Jesus's name, amen.

Anxiety

Day 1

Holy Father,

I admit that I don't understand why Your children have to deal with anxiety. You are the only Sovereign, the King of kings and Lord of lords (1 Timothy 6:15), yet there are times when Your children still find themselves weighed down with fear.

I ask, "Are You not God in heaven? And do You not rule over all the kingdoms of the nations (as well as the kingdoms of darkness) (2 Chronicles 20:6)?" Yes, I know that You do.

Didn't You, oh God, drive out the inhabitants of the land of Israel and give it forever to the descendants of Abraham, Your friend (2 Chronicles 20:7)? Yes, I know that You did.

Didn't You restore the demon-possessed man to peace so that he sat at Your feet "clothed and in his right mind" (Luke 8:35)? Yes, I know that You did.

Wasn't the healing always complete and final, even when You were exhausted and had to grant a second immediate touch (Mark 8:23–25)? I know that it was.

Wasn't it You Who granted others the power to pray down healing, to such an extent that You saw Satan fall from the heavens like lightning (Luke 10:18)? Yes, I know that You did.

Didn't You say that those who believe in You can expect to do things even more remarkable than what You did while on earth (John 14:12)? Yes, I am sure that You promised this.

Your Life is living within me and is mightier than the power of the world (1 John 4:4). You promised that if evil comes upon me, I can stand before You for Your salvation (2 Chronicles 20:9). You empower by giving strength for all things (Philippians 4:13). Even in my physical weakness, I can know powerful divine strength (2 Corinthians 12:10). So, will You please send the superhuman energy of Your Spirit to spring up within me (Colossians 2:29)? I need a continuous spring of Your promised living water (John 7:38).

Father, these are all promises of Your Word. I didn't make any of them up to prove my point. I recall them to mind as You direct. If all these things are so, and I believe they are, then repel Satan away from me as fast as the lightning shoots from the sky. I do not ask on behalf of my own righteousness. "There is no human who does not sin," and I fall into the human being category (2 Chronicles 6:36). But remember, You now view me as Your righteousness. I traded You my sin for the nature of Your Son (2 Corinthians 5:21). Do this for His sake.

You commanded that if anyone is sick, they should call the elders to pray over her and anoint her with oil (James 5:14). Reveal if I am to follow through with this anointing. I am willing if You so lead. I confess my weakness and now ask that You restore me to a full life in mind and heart (James 5:16).

You are the God who comforts and encourages and refreshes and cheers the depressed (2 Corinthians 7:6). Do so for me, O Lord. Grant me peace and restful sleep tonight, for I am Your temple (2 Corinthians 6:16). May I be not only Your house of prayer but also a place where everything cries, "Glory!" (Matthew 21:13; Psalm 29:9). May the temple of my body be restored to its intended beauty (2 Chronicles 24:12–13). I ask this in Jesus's name, amen.

◆ ◆

Day 2

Father,

Thank You that You are the unmovable rock of my salvation (Psalm 18:2), far more significant than my anxious and quavering heart (1 John 3:20). You tell me over and again in Your Word, "Do not fear," but I forget quickly, allowing worry to weigh down my heart (Luke 21:34). I'm tired of this cycle.

My emotions can be like the storms of the sea, tossing this way and that. Yet I remember that you are greater no matter what is within my own heart (Isaiah 55:9). In the very depths of my own weakness, I bow before You, knowing that somehow my frailty is the very thing that initiates Your power (2 Corinthians 12:9). My feebleness launches Your ability to descend in strength (2 Corinthians 12:10). You tell me that You must increase and I must decrease (John 3:30), so getting comfortable in my weakness must be a prerequisite for seeing Your power (2 Corinthians 11:30). Selah.

Spirit of fear, you have no place in my life because anxiety never originates in God (2 Timothy 1:7). Jesus has given me all authority over the spirit of fear and your henchmen of despair, hopelessness, and worry (Luke 10:19; Mark 16:17–18).

Father, bind up the evil one as he calls the rulers of darkness onto the court of my mind and emotions (Mathew 16:19). Thank You, Lord, for giving Your angels charge concerning me, to guard me in all my ways (Psalm 91:11). Thank You for sending out Your heavenly warriors as ministering spirits to help me in this area (Hebrews 1:14). Your invisible messengers bear me up every time I am about to trip (Psalm 91:12). Grant me boldness in prayer to tread upon the lion of doubt and the serpent of anxiety, treading them down until they are dust under my feet (Psalm 91:13; Psalm 18:37–42).

Grant me a glimpse of You every day, Lord (Psalm 17:15; 1 John 3:3). As You reveal Yourself, my focus will be riveted to Your splendor and fixed upon Your glory (2 Corinthians 3:18). May my eyes become so accustomed to seeing You that all else is undecipherable. Seeing the God of all peace is the best way to know peace (2 Thessalonians 3:16). In Jesus's name, I pray. Amen.

◆ ◆ ◆

Day 3

Holy Father,

Even within my mother's womb, You bore and cared for me (Isaiah 46:3). Now that I am Your child, You encourage me to ask whatever I desire in Your name and promise that You will do it (John 14:13–14). That's risky on Your part, yet You open the door wide and encourage me to ask.

So, in Your name, I ask for great peace to descend upon my heart. Station Your military guardian angels to defend the entire perimeter of my heart and mind (Philippians 4:6–7). The stress of (*situation*) has stirred up the winds and waves of my emotions, but if You get into my boat, the wind will stop (Mark 6:51). I am claiming this divine intervention. May I yield to courage and recognize You despite the ongoing storm (Mark 6:50).

You encourage me to breathe with an untroubled heart. I do believe in You. Now I take the next step and actively believe in Christ's Presence within me (John 14:1). May that trust extend out from me at home as You become my compassion and patience.

I'm not asking that You take me out of the situation but that You keep me from the evil one despite it (John 17:15). Yes, that is what is needed. I resist the devil's workings, no matter his form. He is always on the prowl, and I reject his dealings with me and this situation (1 Peter 5:8). Keep my heart and mind constant on You while You strengthen my soul and stabilize my emotions to rest in You (1 Peter 5:10). In Jesus's name, amen.

◆ ◆ ◆

Day 4

Holy Father,

There are times in prayer when I genuinely don't know what to say. My mind is spinning. My emotions are reeling. And the whole situation honestly seems far more extensive than either You or me. This situation is one of those. Somewhere in the recesses of my spirit, I know that You have this situation under control and that nothing can snatch us out of Your hand (John 10:28). I choose to believe that with You, nothing is impossible (Mark 10:27).

Yet my prayer is more anguish than words. I am comforted knowing that You are well acquainted with these kinds of prayers. When I don't know what to say, You take up the intercession on my behalf (Romans 8:26). You are the very best prayer partner I could ever ask for (Romans 8:34). Thank You for that.

While Your Son was on earth, He asked two blind men, "What do you want Me to do?" (Matthew 20:32). Could it be that You would ask me that same question as well? "What do I want?" Well, I want _____, ultimately, entirely, wholly, and miraculously. That's what I want. You said, "Ask, and it shall be given," so I start there, by merely asking that You step in (Matthew 7:7).

You said, "If two of (us) agree on earth about anything that they may ask, it shall be done for them" (Matthew 18:19). Well, I know that there are at least two of us talking to You about this, so I'm sure we've fulfilled that prerequisite. You said that You would accomplish whatever we ask for in Your name so that You may receive the glory (John 14:13). As I stand here with Jesus praying alongside me, I know that this surely counts toward that purpose. Your Word says, "Mountains melt like wax at the Presence of the Lord" (Psalm 97:5), so I ask that You melt away the mountains of distress and exhaustion in this situation.

I don't understand what form the result will take. It could be instantaneous, but You may choose to allow a process. Regardless of Your method, this situation needs the peace that passes all understanding (Philippians 4:7). I need a heart that is confident in You without fear (Psalm 27:2–3). Grant that, will You? Flood souls with the comprehension of Your Love and fill me up with Your goodness (Ephesians 3:18–19). Renew my mind daily so that I can see past the situation into the depths of the spiritual (Ephesians 4:23; 2 Corinthians 4:18). Give rest of soul.

Hear the voices of those crying out on behalf of this situation. Be gracious and answer (Psalm 27:7). You have instructed me to seek Your face, so I've come to do so (Psalm 27:8). Remind me to keep on asking (Luke 18:1–8). As my feeble heart seeks, be my help, for I have no one else to count on but You (Psalm 27:9; 121:1–2).

I've submitted all of these requests onto Your spiritual work order just as You have asked me to do. I now push the work order across the table to You. Release the resources. Discharge the supplies and meet the needs. Please note that this work order doesn't have my signature but the authority of Jesus's name. So be it.

Day 5

Holy Father,

Praise You that, by one sacrifice, You regained for humanity all that Adam gave away (Hebrews 10:12–13). As I come boldly to Your throne today on behalf of _____, I realize that my power in prayer comes as I align myself with Your holy will (Matthew 26:39). I do so now, asking that Your Kingdom and Your will come into my life, in the same way that these are unfolded in heaven (Matthew 6:10).

By no merit of my own, You have given me the authority to tread upon all the power of the enemy without injury (Luke 10:19). _____ 's enemy right now is insecurity, negative self-talk, and low self-esteem. You, my holy Joshua, have called me to put my foot on the neck of this adversary of insecurity, pinning him down until You deal the final blow (Joshua 10:24).

I confess to You that I have been a fearful warrior, recoiling from taking my victorious position over this defeated foe. I have forgotten that You, the Holy One within me, are greater and stronger than our opponent in this world (1 John 4:4). Forgive me, Lord.

Surge Your power within me by bringing all Your promises back to my memory (Colossians 1:29; John 14:26). Do this for _____ as well. Thank You for sending Your Son to free us from fear and destroy all of the enemy's works (Luke 1:74; 1 John 3:8). Praise You for being faithful to strengthen and protect us from the evil one (2 Thessalonians 3:3). Reveal Your accomplished work that together, we may faithe You into experience.

Now, I put my foot down upon the enemy's work in _____. Cover her, O Lord, in this day of battle (Psalm 140:6). Thank You for training our hands for war and our fingers for battle (Psalm 144:1). The evil one has acted the victor too long. Spirit of (*insecurity*), spirit of (*hopelessness*), spirit of (*anxiety*), you have dominated lives in this family long enough. In the name of Jesus, defeat the work of (*fear*) in her life. I demand you obey the Stronger Man, Jesus, and once and for all leave _____ alone (Luke 11:21–22). Go to where the Lord Jesus Himself sends you.

Realizing that the evil one will try to block prompt delivery of Jesus's provision, remind me, Lord, to pray persistently until the emancipation comes (Daniel 10:12–13). I'm not moving my foot off the evil one's neck until You crush him underneath (Romans 16:20). Strike the evil head of (*insecurity*) that comes against her and slit him open from thigh to neck. Turn the source of this pain against evil instead of against her (Habakkuk 3:13–14).

In the physical realm, she and I don't look like warriors, but in Your Spirit, that is who we are. Just one of us can put to flight a thousand of the enemy, for it is the Lord our God Who fights for us (Joshua 23:10). Come even now, Lord Jesus, to redeem _____'s soul in peace from the battle, which is against her (Psalm 55:18). In Jesus's name, amen.

◆ ◆ ◆

Day 6

Holy Father,

Thank You that I have a hideaway of safety inside of You. I can flee for protection there and find that Your wings are outstretched, waiting for me. May I never be reluctant to escape into Your refuge (Psalm 71:1).

If I depended on my actions to achieve a connection with You, I would be continually discouraged. In Job's day, he despaired by realizing there was no arbitrator between You and him (Job 9:32–33). But now, because of Jesus, this problem is solved (1 Timothy 2:5)! You exchanged my sin for Your righteousness (2 Corinthians 5:21). All I need do is faithe You (Romans 4:5).

Today, I claim Your righteousness, not mine, asking that You deliver me, rescue me, and listen to my fears about (*situation*) (Psalm 71:2). Be the garrison of my mind, where I can continually come for safety when my thoughts want to weigh me down. Thank You for mandating Yourself as the refuge city for my life and being the strong castle into which I can run (Psalm 71:3).

Rescue me out of earshot of the evil one, who continually whispers discouraging thoughts to my mind. Hide me away from the tongue of this liar who desires only to execute, embezzle, and exterminate me (Psalm 71:4; John 8:44; John 10:10). The minute those anxious thoughts begin, I ask Your consolations to flood me with delight (Psalm 94:19).

You alone are my Hope (1 Timothy 1:1). You alone are my confidence (Psalm 71:5). You have sustained me since birth, and I am overwhelmed. Thank You, Lord (Psalm 71:6). When I think of all You have done, my mouth is filled with praise all day (Psalm 71:8).

Even though my strength is decreasing, I can thank You, knowing that You are renewing my inner self day by day (2 Corinthians 4:16). You will never throw me out of Your Presence or abandon me just because I age (Psalm 71:9). The evil one whispers, "You are _____!" or "_____" (Psalm 71:10–11). But You say, "My power is made perfect in weakness," turning my weakness into one more opportunity for displaying Your strength (2 Corinthians 12:9–10).

You promise never to leave me or forsake me (Hebrews 13:5) because You will carry me throughout my graying years (Isaiah 46:4). Use my weak vessel to testify of Your strength even when I am old and wrinkled (Psalm 71:18). May I still yield fruit in my old age, full of the sap of the vine and very green (Psalm 92:14; John 15:4–5).

Fasten my thoughts onto Your righteousness and Your salvation (Psalm 71:15–16). Keep my attitude fixed onto Your hope (Psalm 71:14), for when I attach my hope onto You; I am cleansed and made new (1 John 3:3).

I have seen much distress in my lifetime, Father. Now, I ask that You show me revival, blessing my latter days more than those of my youth (Job 42:12). Lift Your people from the depths that worldly pleasures have taken them (Psalm 71:20). Comfort us by sending renewal (Psalm 71:21).

Thank You, Father, for hearing my prayer (Psalm 65:2). Praise You for being a God who is for me, not against me (Romans 8:31). Thank You that Your truth is everlasting and permanent, the total opposite to my apprehension (Psalm 100:5; 1 John 4:4). Help me recognize the devil's lies instantly and turn my thoughts into praise (Hebrews 13:15). May my lips be set aside for shouts of joy, and my thoughts and emotions reserved for singing Your praise (Psalm 71:23–24).

This prayer is authorized by the blood of Jesus and signed in His name. Hallelujah!

◆ ◆ ◆

Day 7

Holy Father,

Thank You not only for existing as the God who is love but for also revealing that there is no fear in Your Love (1 John 4:16, 18). Seeing true love is the only thing that can genuinely eject fear from our hearts (1 John 4:18). Our capacity to live without fear always sources in Your Love toward us (1 John 4:19).

You desire us to serve You without fear (Luke 1:74). But sometimes, we are overwhelmed with the distractive enemy (Psalm 55:2–3). _____ is living in this anguish of heart right now (Psalm 55:4). So, I lift her to You, the only One who can redeem her soul in peace from the battle against her (Psalm 55:18).

Clothed with Christ as my armor, I stand to war against the spirits of fear, anxiety, depression, and despair on behalf of _____. In Jesus's name and because of the work of His cross, I can expose fear and his underlings as a defeated foe (Colossians 2:14–15). By Christ's authority, I demand fear to release forever his grip on _____. Jesus has sovereignty in both heaven and earth (Matthew 28:18). Fear has none. Thank You, Jesus, for rendering these spirits powerless and delivering all who are afraid (Hebrews 2:14–15). Hallelujah!

Father, reveal to _____ that You are the supreme and final ruler who cancels out all of the enemies' plots and strategies. You have the final say because everything is under Your dominion (1 Chronicles 29:11). Wrap Your Presence around her so safely that she feels enveloped in You (Psalm 125:2 TPT).

Open her eyes to see the energizing power of Your righteous right hand (Isaiah 41:10). When she goes limp, scoop her up into Your protective arms (Psalm 54:4). Come in power with Your mighty gushing, outpouring love to fill and surge into her entire being (Romans 5:5). Turn any fleshly thoughts of fear into Spirit thoughts of life and peace (Romans 8:6). When Satan accuses of inability, may she rejoice to know that this accusation is her glory since weaknesses are the best places to display Your strength (2 Corinthians 12:10).

_____ is already aware that her flesh holds nothing good (Romans 7:18). Yet she can glory in this fact, knowing that in You there is no condemnation (Romans 8:1). Open her eyes to see that although her "husband," the law, wouldn't release her from his grip, the death she died with You grants her entry into a new dimension of life (Romans 7:1–4). She now lives alongside You in the heavenlies (Ephesians 2:6). This is not a one-day reality but a current Kingdom reality (Revelation 1:6). Open her eyes to see.

Thank You for already securing her salvation (John 14:20). Make way for her where there seems to be no way, so that she may live by faith rather than feelings (Isaiah 43:16–19; 2 Corinthians 5:7). Reveal how far above all rule and authority, power, and dominion she is—all because of trading her life for Christ's (Ephesians 1:21). May _____'s spirit settle down where You are the Architect and Builder (Hebrews 11:10). Even so, Lord Jesus, come!

I pray these things by the authority that Jesus gave to me as His child (Matthew 16:19). Amen.

◆ ◆ ◆

Day 8

Holy Father,

Praise You that Your name is a strong tower. We can run into You and find ourselves safe (Proverbs 18:10). Now that You placed us inside Christ, we desire to remain there every single moment (Colossians 3:3).

As I come to pray for _____, I realize that just because we are in You doesn't mean we won't have trouble (2 Timothy 3:1). Indeed, all who desire to live godly in Christ Jesus will be persecuted (2 Timothy 3:12). And so, before I even pray for her safety, I ask first that You would reveal Yourself to her.

Despite how hard it seems, You say it is good for us to endure affliction, for that's how truth becomes a reality to us (Psalm 119:71). Whatever trial _____ faces today, I plead with You to comfort and revive her with Your Word (Psalm 119:50).

Pour out Your lovingkindness to her, Father, so that she can have an answer for anyone who reproaches her (Psalm 119:41). Walking in Your liberty comes only by walking where Your Spirit directs (Psalm 119:45). Stir within her a desire to seek Your visits and delight in Your voice (verse 45).

Stir her with boldness as we join others who are praying for her (Acts 12:5). Send Your angel to protect her with light and instruct her movements (Acts 12:7–8). Rescue her from all that the evil one would throw against her (Acts 12:11). And in the midst of it all, crush Satan under the feet of Your ever-present peace (Romans 16:20). In Jesus's name, amen.

Change

Day 1

Holy Father,

Thank You for being the God of peace (Hebrews 13:20). As I come before Your throne today, I am struggling to find composure in this change. As I center my thoughts on You, I ask that You grant me Your serenity.

As the God of peace, I ask that You crush whatever works the evil one plans against me (Romans 16:20). May the details be a testimony of Your work, accomplished as I faithe You (John 6:29). Grant me evidence of Your concern by seeing the particulars performed flawlessly by Your hand (Ephesians 2:10). Grant me insight to know what is necessary and what can be left undone. Thank You that the quality of my actions doesn't depend upon me but on You, the Merciful One (Romans 9:16).

As I encounter physical limitations through this change (like back, heart, exhaustion, stress, etc.), enable me to labor according to Your power that works mightily within (Colossians 1:29). May I reckon any sufferings as a share in Your Son's afflictions (Colossians 1:24). Bring others alongside to help and bear burdens as needed so that we achieve together the unity of Your perfect law (Galatians 6:2).

Cause me to increase and abound in love as You establish my heart without blame in holiness (1 Thessalonians 3;12–13). May I not be troubled but able to believe You wholeheartedly. Thank You for preparing my future for me. I want boldly to go where You lead (John 14:1–3). In Jesus's name, amen.

Day 2

Holy Father,

Thank You for enabling me to hear Your voice (John 10:27). When You called, I answered, even if I was aware of the feebleness of that response (Genesis 12:1). Thank You for being my shield and generous compensation. Keep me faithful so that You may reward with Your magnificent Presence (Genesis 15:1).

Increase my trust and keep me steadfastly faithful to listening to You carefully. Thank You for rewarding all who faithe You by allowing us to house the Presence of Christ (Hebrews 11:6). Remind me often that You consider me righteous because of Your Presence, not because of what I do (Genesis 15:6; 2 Corinthians 5:21).

Often, while seeking You, things get dark, and I fear what lies ahead (Genesis 15:12). Continue speaking so that I may know the fulfillment of all Your promises and see Your salvation (Genesis 15:17; 2 Corinthians 1:20; Psalm 91:16). Show me once again that You are the God who sees (Genesis 16:13).

Be my strength so that I may walk blamelessly before You (Genesis 17:1). May I experientially know nothing is too hard or too wonderful for You to accomplish (Genesis 18:14). Reveal all that You are going to do so that I may teach others just how to keep Your ways (Genesis 18:17, 19). In Jesus's name, amen.

◆ ◆ ◆

Day 3

Holy Father,

Thank You for taking the time to create and form me (Isaiah 43:1). I was not something that You just threw together but a project that You detailed with care. You planned me and did the math to decide just how my environment would best fit my needs. Down to each minute detail, You formed each portion of my body. You didn't stop with creation; You watched my sin and then stretched out to redeem me. You have even given me a name and taken me for Your possession (Isaiah 43:1). Thank You.

Now, as I pass through the rough waters regarding (*situation*), I know that You are with me, not that You *will* be but that You *already* are (Isaiah 43:2). Although this uncertainty seems like a raft amidst river rapids, You have promised that I will not be capsized (Isaiah 43:2). I know the outcome. I may get wet, but I won't lose the raft! I'm clinging to this promise.

I remember that You promised that the fire wouldn't touch me when I walk through it (Isaiah 43:2). Although this is a big decision, I can know that granting my choice to You gives this fiery trial no power (Daniel 3:27). May I come out of this, not even smelling like smoke!

Thank You that You are not only the God who made me but the God who is still smoothing my edges. I am Your precious, treasured child. Because You value, honor, and love me, I can rest assured that You will arrange the details (Isaiah 43:4).

Strengthen my faith even now to see that You are in charge (Isaiah 43:5). You are the Savior (Isaiah 43:11). May I stop mulling over the past (Isaiah 43:18). Instead, may I perceive what You are doing and grant You room to work (Isaiah 43:19). In Jesus's name, amen.

◆ ◆ ◆

Day 4

Holy Father,

Thank You that You are a God who fights for us while we keep silent (Exodus 14:14). Despite our tendency to give up easily, You teach us how to remain at rest while still moving forward (Exodus 14:14–15). We desperately need Your endurance (Hebrews 10:36).

As I begin this new task, there are many enemies close at my heels. Distractions, lack of commitment and contentment, past failures, and being overwhelmed on the one hand and quickly bored on the other all dog me with doubts. Yet it is You who has called me out of the bondage of fear (Exodus 6:6). Lead me to see the salvation that You will accomplish (Exodus 14:13).

Position Yourself between me and this strong army (Exodus 14:19). Even when I don't want to follow through, fight for me and grant me the faith to stop worrying and move forward in Your power (Exodus 14:14–15). Enlighten me with Your Presence even when all others see only darkness, and part the waters as I press forward to completion (Exodus 14:20, 22).

Up until this time, I tend to be quick to start but slow to finalize. Hurl these enemies of unfocused diversion into the sea (Exodus 15:1), and so prove to be my strength and song (Exodus 15:1–2). Guide me by Your power into daily habitation with You (Exodus 15:13) so that no matter what changes, I am aware of Your indwelling (Exodus 15:17; 1 Corinthians 3:16). May I diligently listen to Your voice and be led to moment-by-moment obedience (Exodus 15:26). May Your Word be my daily food portion (Exodus 16:4) and my great delight (Jeremiah 15:16). In Jesus's name, amen.

———————————◆ ◆ ◆———————————

Day 5

Holy Father,

This time of shaking has been good for me (Hebrews 12:26–27). While every structure of support crumbles away, this world shift has forced me to analyze better how I've built upon the foundation. I have all sorts of building materials available: the wood of activity, the hay of busyness, and the stubble of good deeds.

You have rocked all of these. And as in many earthquakes, after the quaking comes the fire. "Our God is a consuming fire" (Hebrews 12:29). The fire of Your love tests the quality of my work (1 Corinthians 3:13). Only the gold of love, the silver of faith, and the precious gems of hope will remain once the dust clears.

As I look around the rubble of my life, I sense You saying to look up. Your voice calls me to step out of the debris and explore this newly discovered portal of silence. Cautiously, as I step over the fragments, I want desperately to pick up my favorite pieces of life and rebuild my structure of comfort.

Yet, You urge me forward.

Drawing me with Your magnetic power, You beckon me to the doorway of stillness. You specifically designed my solitude to attract me to this threshold. Like the apostle John who peered into the empty tomb, I stand at the entrance and wonder. But rather than sending me out to tell the brethren, You beckon me to enter and know (Revelation 22:17).

Even as I press forward, my thoughts swirl, and my mind surges with a tangle of distractions. How do I quell this hive of bees within this holy portal of silence? From somewhere within this realm of light, You take control by personally commanding all fleshly thoughts into silence. You stand in Your holy habitation and beckon me near (Zechariah 2:13).

My inadequacy freezes me in my tracks.

This portal of silence leads to Your Presence. Even as I fearfully hug the wall upon entry, I'm aware that this is the place where my mountains will melt like wax (Psalms 97:5). Herein, I glimpse the fulness of joy for which I've longed (Psalm 16:11). Oh, show me Your glory (Exodus 33:18).

The shaking of my world has uncovered a dimension I've never seen before. My solitude has granted me the opportunity to hear Your still, small voice. As I hesitate to move by faith rather than sight, forgive my blind groping. Don't allow me to turn back. I'm trembling with the fear of the unknown, yet Your silent Presence draw me like a lamb, O Shepherd (John 10:4). Entice me after You that I may experience You more fully through this entryway of quietude. Selah.

Depression

Day 1

Holy Father,

Thank You for being our Rock of Escape when we are overwhelmed (2 Samuel 22:2). Praise you for being our Deliverer and Rock of Refuge.

I'm coming to You today with a request. I need to experience You as my Refuge. My emotions are so volatile right now that I can't see You clearly. I know that I would know healing if I could just see truth (Matthew 20:32–34). Show me Your glory (Exodus 33:18). Reveal to me precisely what it feels like to have the Rock of Refuge under my feet to stabilize me from the dark violence that pounds my emotions (2 Samuel 22:3).

I call upon You as the One worthy of praise. You alone can save me from these enemies that depress me (2 Samuel 22:4; Luke 1:71). I confess that these include the enemies of negative self-talk, depression, low-esteem, and the thief who steals my joy and ability to laugh. How often I have succumbed to these destructive forces (2 Samuel 22:5).

It seems that I'm not the only one with this problem. Even King David felt like hell and death were breathing down his neck (2 Samuel 22:6). When he was at the end of his rope, he cried out to You, and You listened. Despite my unworthiness, I can claim that I do have Jesus living within me, while David did not. Hear my prayer, God, not because I am good but because You are (2 Samuel 22:7; 2 Corinthians 3:5).

I spin in and out of these fears, Lord. I'm asking that next time—before I go to the depths with my thought life—You come to my rescue. Do so before my downward spiral. Even now, take hold of me and draw me out of the water (2 Samuel 22:17).

Give me faith to believe that You are always greater no matter how mighty my fear (2 Samuel 22:18; 1 John 4:4).

Thank You in advance not only for delivering me but also for delighting in me (2 Samuel 22:20). Let me know Your delight experientially.

I can't say that I have always remained loyal to You, but since You made me Your child, You remain loyal anyway (2 Timothy 2:13). When I look in the mirror, I am often disappointed in myself. Help me to stop looking at me and look at You. You have made me righteous from the inside out (2 Samuel 22:25; 2 Corinthians 5:21). Because of Jesus, I am currently blameless and upright whether I feel like it or not (1 Corinthians 1:8). Let me see those qualities from Your perspective (2 Samuel 22:26).

In the name of Your Son, Jesus, I rebuke the spirit of depression, insecurity, and anxiety. They are defeated foes and have no authority over my life (Colossians 2:15; Luke 10:19). I will stand against them in the full armor of God by prayer and perseverance (Ephesians 6:11). I will not be afraid of the terrors that stalk me at night or of the piercing thoughts that fly at me by day (Psalm 91:5). Come, Lord Jesus, and dissolve these thoughts.

Reveal Your purity to me, Father (2 Samuel 22:27; 1 John 3:3). Be my lamp, lighting my way in every dark pathway (2 Samuel 22:29; John 8:12). I want to turn from focusing on the visible and envision Your invisible power (2 Corinthians 4:18). May I leap over these dark thoughts and emotional walls into bright health (2 Samuel 22:30). Your way is perfect, and Your Word is tried and trustworthy (2 Samuel 22:31).

Focus me in Your truth, not just my feelings about Your truth. You alone are my strength and power. In You alone is my perfection (2 Samuel 22:33; Hebrews 10:14). I will believe. In Jesus's name, amen.

Day 2

Holy Father,

Thank You for being the One who hears prayer. Thank You that everyone (even me!) can come before You with their requests (Psalms 65:2). As a part of Your family, I know that You will never leave me or forsake me (Hebrews 13:5). You are the God of Love and have placed Your Holy Spirit within me as my ever-present, gushing, overflowing fountain of Love (1 John 4:8; Romans 5:5).

Yet sometimes the voice of the evil one is much louder than Your very own distinctive voice. Right now, the accuser's voice is loudly reminding me of my worthlessness (Zechariah 3:1). Lord, I ask that You rebuke this evil voice and close the mouth of the evil one (Zechariah 3:2–5).

I ask that Your loving words wash over me, reminding me that Your full-time job is to transform sinners. No evil action is ever more massive than the covering of Your purity. You came to earth to take away sins, even my sin of (*deceit, hatred, adultery, pornography, suicide, etc.*) (1 John 3:5). This responsibility puts You in the middle of sinners every single day while Your Love covers over a multitude of sins (1 Timothy 1:15; 1 Peter 4:8).

Enlarge my understanding to see that Your power is big enough to transform any life. In the same way that no darkness is more powerful than the sun, there is no sin bigger than You, the light (Genesis 1:2–3). Reveal Your omnipotence and omnipresence. Pierce the words of 1 John 3:20 into my heart, that God is greater than my heart (and all my hidden sins as well)!

Open my eyes to know the hope of Your call, to see Your hidden riches, and to believe in the greatness of Your power (Ephesians 1:18). In Jesus's name, I pray. Amen.

◆ ◆ ◆

Day 3

Holy Father,

I come before You today, knowing that within me lies no good thing (Romans 7:18). In and of myself, I am inadequate to consider that I have any wisdom concerning _____ (2 Corinthians 3:5). But this doesn't deter my desire to pray.

In my weakness, You do not condemn (Romans 8:1). You merely say, "Call upon Me, and I will show you great and mighty things which you do not know" (Jeremiah 33:3). "Come to Me, all you who are weary and heavy-laden, and I will give you rest" (Matthew 11:28). "Present your case; bring forward your strong arguments. Let us reason together" (Isaiah 41:21; 1:18).

As I stand before You, I thank You for seeing Christ in me. Despite my cracked vessel, You look within to see the light of the knowledge of the glory of God in His face (2 Corinthians 4:6). What a miracle!

Secondly, my desperate weakness is of great value to You. Human helplessness is a given, whether I want to admit it or not. You are practical and can see all truth. As long as I dupe myself into thinking I can handle my problems, I believe a lie. You cannot answer a prayer built on deceit no matter how well constructed.

So, let's start there, shall we? I am powerless before the multitude of (*these fears, this attitude, this negativity, these parenting difficulties, etc.*). I do not know what to do, but my eyes are upon You (2 Chronicles 20:12). I accept my helplessness. No well-crafted prayer on my part will defeat these enemies. So I look to You.

Somewhere within me, You have planted a measure of faith (Romans 12:3). I admit to You (as You already know) that mine is minuscule. Yes, I know You are bigger than any problem, but I may or may not act on that knowledge. Locate that pixel of faith, then enrich, energize, and enlarge it (Luke 17:5). May it be that when Your Word says, "Is My Hand so short that it cannot ransom or have I no power to deliver?" (Isaiah 50:2), my heart will answer with a resounding, "No!" When I hear You say, "I will pluck your feet out of this net and keep you from stumbling" (Psalm 25:15; 37:24), I will say, "I believe!"

I desire to overwhelmingly conquer through Jesus, the One who loves me (Romans 8:37). My hope is not found anywhere within myself. You didn't tell me to "be strong" but to "be strong in the Lord" (Ephesians 6:10). You didn't ask me to be powerful but that the "working of the strength is brought about in Christ" (Ephesians 1:19–20). I have been looking in the wrong direction for strength.

You remind me what Watchman Nee said: "God will not give me humility, or patience, or holiness, or love as separate gifts of His grace. He is not a retailer dispensing grace to us in packets, measuring out some patience to the impatient, some love to the unloving, some humility to the proud, in quantities that we take and work on as a kind of capital. He has given only one gift to meet all our needs: His Son Christ Jesus. As I look to Him to live out His life in me, He will be humble and patient and loving and everything else I need—in my stead. Remember the word John's first epistle: 'God gave unto us eternal life, and this life is in his Son. He that hath the Son hath the life; and he that hath not the Son of God hath not the life' (1 John 5:11–12). The life of God is not given us as a separate item; the life of God is given us in the Son."

Herein is a glimpse of glorying in weakness (2 Corinthians 12:9). Teach me how to source life out of Your Life instead of asking You to patch up a weak part of (*my patience, my attitude, my love, etc.*) (Luke 5:36). You are my (*patience*). You are my needed (*attitude change, energy, parenting wisdom*) as I keep my eyes fixed on You (Hebrews 12:2). Selah.

"Oh, the depth of the riches both of the wisdom and knowledge of God! How unsearchable are His judgments and unfathomable His ways! For from Him and through Him and to Him are all things. To Him be the glory forever. Amen" (Romans 11:33, 36).

Employment

◆

Difficult

Holy Father,

I come to You on behalf of _____. You've promised that You will care for him like a shepherd does his sheep (Isaiah 40:11). He feels scattered and hopeless, but You saw this ahead of time. You have a plan and a way through this choppy sea (Isaiah 43:16). You promised never to leave or forsake him, so we may confidently assert, "The Lord is _____'s helper! He doesn't have to be afraid! What can man do to him?" (Hebrews 13:5–6). Hallelujah. You reign.

Granted, his strength is currently powerless, leaving him confused. He feels brokenhearted and crushed, but You promised to come near and save this specific type of individual (Psalm 34:18). _____ qualifies, don't You think? Deliver him from whispers of defeat (Ezekiel 34:12) and quench his thirst and hunger with living water and good pasture (Ezekiel 34:14). Grant him rest as he waits on You (Ezekiel 34:15) and open a door no one can shut (Revelation 3:8). He has kept Your Word, Father. Keep Your promise.

You promised that You will *always* lead us in triumph in Christ (2 Corinthians 2:14), so keep his eyes fixed on You and Your provision (2 Chronicles 20:12; Hebrews 12:2). Reveal Yourself in his midst. If discipline is necessary, then I ask that You reveal how it will be for good, that he may share in Your holiness (Hebrews 12:10). All discipline seems awful at the moment, but allow _____ to see beyond now and into the future. There, he will possess the peaceful fruit of righteousness (Hebrews 12:11). Strengthen his hands today, granting his feet straight paths (Hebrews 12:12–13). Bind up any bitterness between him and his family that would only cause more trouble and defile Your purposes (Hebrews 12:15).

Your ways are different from ours, and we often don't understand (Isaiah 55:9). Yet You said that Your promises wouldn't return to You void. You accomplish what You desire (Isaiah 55:11). Please remind _____ of the last thing that You promised him. May he have the strength to stand not only on the promise but also on the Promiser (Romans 4:19–20). Fully assure him that what You promise, You can perform (Romans 4:21).

Thank You for always hearing our prayers (Psalm 65:2). You hear even our groanings, counting them as prayers (Romans 8:26). Intercede personally, O Lord, for _____ according to Your will and allow him to conquer this trial as he trusts in You (Romans 8:37). May he soon be able to testify that the very thing the devil meant for evil has changed into a victorious and excellent result (Genesis 50:20).

We come before You with the name of Jesus on this work order. Notice this request is not signed by man but by Your Son. In Jesus's name, amen.

◆ ◆ ◆

New

Holy Father,

Thank You for being Jehovah, the Lord God, who is compassionate and gracious (Exodus 34:6). Indeed, Your lovingkindness abounds toward us. We bless Your holy name.

As _____ has this interview, I ask that You grant him the favor of Your best choice (Exodus 33:13). I pray that You show him Your glory by revealing Your decision regarding this opportunity (Exodus 33:18). If Your Presence is not going with him, I ask that he knows not to accept this position, regardless of what the perks may be (Exodus 33:15). Show him clearly what to do and which way to turn (Psalm 5:8).

I ask that You set his heart to study Your Word and put Your truth into practice, no matter where You lead (Ezra 7:10). I pray that he would discern between humankind's word and Yours, not influenced by the most popular idea but always looking toward You as the Author and Perfecter of his faith (Hebrews 12:2). May he be a man who longs for the pure milk of the Word over someone else's interpretation of who You are (1 Peter 2:2). May _____ follow Christ rather than entrusting himself to humankind's wisdom (John 2:24) and be a man like those of Berea who received the Word with eagerness and examined the scriptures daily (Acts 17:11). In Jesus's name, amen.

Encouragement

Day 1

Holy Father,

I praise You that You embody strength (1 Chronicles 16:27). As I study Your strength, I notice that You are strong because You know that we are weak (2 Corinthians 12:10). It seems that allowing us to experience extreme weakness is an essential part of Your plan (Psalm 102:23). Otherwise, we would never cry out to You as we do now.

I confess my strength feels wholly dried up (Psalm 22:15). Not only is my flesh tired, but my heart is now failing me too (Psalm 73:26). Now I know what King David meant when he said that his weakness hurts (Psalm 38:10).

You make a big deal about Your promises, Lord. You promise to give Your people strength, literally blessing Your children with peace (Psalm 29:11). You guaranteed that You would not only be our strength but that You would also be our shield to ward off the emotions and doubtful thoughts that inevitably come (Psalm 28:7).

So today, I come before Your throne boldly (Hebrews 10:22). I am fulfilling my part in seeking (1 Chronicles 16:11; Psalm 105:4). Don't forsake me during this time when my strength is low (Psalm 71:9). Be a very present help in this time of trouble (Psalm 46:1). Command strength to rise within me (Psalm 68:28).

I know You are a God who calls things into being that didn't previously exist (Romans 4:17), so summon faith to live within me. This will help my heart and enable me to move into thankfulness (Psalm 28:7). Incline Your ear to me so that I can say, "I have never been ashamed at believing in God" (Psalm 31:1–2)!

Lord, when You adopted us as Your children, You became our dwelling place (1 Corinthians 3:16). Your Kingdom is actually within me now (Luke 17:21). May I see the strength and beauty within me that You see (Psalm 96:6). May everything within me cry out, "Glory!" (Psalm 29:9). Take my eyes off the situation and place them onto You. Only in this way can I see "the joy of the Lord" as my strength (Nehemiah 8:10). In Jesus's name, amen.

◆ ◆ ◆

Day 2

Holy Father,

Thank You for being greater than my heart (1 John 3:20). I confess to You that sometimes my life feels bitter, and my emotions lash out like a wild animal (Psalm 73:21–22). You are well aware of how often I fail. Thank You that despite being intimately acquainted with all my ways, You never leave me (Psalm 139:3, 5, 8). My heart and my flesh fail often, but You are the strength of my heart (Psalm 73:26).

Deep within me, there is an obedience lever that seems to toggle on and off. My emotions influence the switch one way and my intellect the other. Neither of these is faithful. My feelings are too volatile, and my thoughts too selfish. How can I get off this roller coaster (Romans 7:24)?

You reveal that reliance on Jesus is my only way to deliverance (John 14:6; Romans 7:25). You are my only hope, so shine the light of Your truth again into my heart (2 Corinthians 4:6). Come, Lord Jesus, and capture my little lever for Your purposes. Take my thoughts, emotions, desires, and ego captive, so they obey You (2 Corinthians 10:5). This request comes not from emotional surge or intellectual reasoning but from the depth of my spirit, where You already abide (Romans 8:9; 16).

Thank You for continuing to pray for me, Jesus. Knowing that You are praying from the heavenlies and that the Holy Spirit is praying from within me encourages greatly (Romans 8:34, 26). What better prayer partners could anyone have?

From the heavenlies as well as from my innermost being, You are at work (John 5:17). Carefully mold me from the outside and well as the inside. Overpower the straggling holdout of guilt while increasing the victory of my faith (1 John 5:4). Thank You for not holding my faults against me (Hebrews 10:17–18). You make me smile. In Jesus's name, amen.

Day 3

Holy Father,

Thank You for being the God of all Comfort (2 Corinthians 1:3). You are the One who comforts us in *all* our affliction, whether it is a (*cough, cold, or wayward child*) (2 Corinthians 1:4).

I have recently been burdened excessively with (*health, family, employment, etc.*) issues. I haven't despaired of life, but this has dragged me down and sapped my strength (2 Corinthians 1:8). Praise You that I not only have You but also know You. Thank You that I have a place in You on which to set my hope (2 Corinthians 1:10). Thank You that every one of Your promises is for me (2 Corinthians 1:20). Show me the depths of life in Christ as I seek to experience each promise by faith.

Continue to lead me forward to triumph. In this time of crushing, release the aroma of Christ amid this pressing (2 Corinthians 2:14–15). Despite many stressors, encourage me to speak for Christ in the sight of God (2 Corinthians 2:17). Granted, I don't feel adequate to do this, but remind me daily that my sufficiency is in You (2 Corinthians 3:5).

Continue Your work within me and remove any veil of misunderstanding, that I may know You fully (2 Corinthians 3:16). Your comfort is often found in Your nearness, rather than a change in my situation. Thank You for the liberty You offer as I rest in You and open my spiritual eyes to see You more clearly (2 Corinthians 3:17). Make it obvious how near You are, inside my spirit, reflecting Your glory (2 Corinthians 3:18; Luke 17:21). Slow me down to find time to stare daily at Your Presence so that I may know Your heart. Selah.

Day 4

Holy Father,

You are the God who harkens to our prayer (Jeremiah 29:12). We are so thankful because _____ needs someone mighty and robust to hear her cries.

Your Word says, "Whoever believes in Him will not be disappointed" (Romans 10:11). We know that if our hope is in our situation, there is always a good chance of being disappointed. But we've learned not to trust in others because their motives are no better than our own (John 2:24–25).

But just because _____ has no cause to be disappointed in You doesn't mean that she isn't anxious. I'm sure that there are all kinds of emotions raging that I can't even understand. Yet I come to You on her behalf.

First, I ask for comfort. You are the God of all Comfort (2 Corinthians 1:3). Not just a bit, not only for religious stuff, not just in death but *all* comfort. Whether our need is large or small, You are the place to go when we need encouragement. So, I come boldly to the gates of the heavenlies to pick up just the right amount for _____ (Hebrews 10:19).

Secondly, I'd like to ask for peace. Grant _____ the peace that is superior to what she has ever experienced before. May she have peace that sets up a military-type guard in her soul from the hostile invasion of anxiety (Philippians 4:7). As she awaits Your direction, may peace be the dominant characteristic of her home.

You can do this, Father because peace and comfort are Your specialties. You know just where the weak places are in our minds and emotions. Double Your guard there in any unfortified areas. Disallow negative, doubting thoughts to loop through her mind. Instead, may she find great defense in thankfulness every time a negative emotion or thought attacks.

Thirdly, I specifically ask that You grant her an answer this week. I'm sure I'm not the only one she has asked to pray. We all stand before Your throne, joined together with this one request. You promised that where two or three are, You are there in our midst (Matthew 18:18). Here we are standing united. Open a door that no one can shut (Revelation 3:8). We collectively reach out our hands, gripping the hem of Your garment, and expect You to act (Matthew 9:20). We cling to You until she is secured. We will not let go until You bless her (Genesis 32:26). Remind us to pray often in this vein.

Thank You in advance for Your comfort and peace. You can do exceedingly abundantly beyond what I can come up with (Ephesians 3:20). One translation even says that You "will achieve infinitely more than (our) greatest request, (our) most unbelievable dream, and exceed (our) wildest imagination! (You) will outdo them all, for (Your) miraculous power constantly energizes" (Ephesians 3:20 TPT). Hallelujah! I bring this work order to Your throne and ask that You notice it is signed in the name and blood of Jesus. So be it, Lord.

Faith

Day 1

Father,

Thank You for giving heed to my prayer (Psalm 66:19). You, the Creator of the universe, hear my prayer. No matter my concerns or how inefficiently I utter them, You hear my prayer (Psalm 17:6). "Call to Me," You command, "so that I can rescue you" (Psalm 50:15). "Call to Me," You encourage, "and I will answer you and tell you great and mighty things which you do not know" (Jeremiah 33:3). "Ask anything, using My Name, and I will do it" (John 14:14). You empower me boldly with everything I need about life and godliness (2 Peter 1:3). My only part is to believe.

And yet I falter, tremble, and hesitate.

Maybe my belief has been in the (*miracle, healing, change of situation, etc.*). But that's not my calling, is it? You ask me simply to believe in You (John 11:25–26). Whether my requests are for my family, my future, or my friends, my prayer must focus on the person, not the predicament. You, O Lord, are the place where my faith must rest. On the who, not the what. "Yes, Lord; I have believed that You are the Christ, the Son of God" (John 11:27). And because I believe in the who rather than the what, I *can* have great faith because greater is He who is within me than he who is in the world (1 John 4:4).

I lift my eyes to the mountains, wondering from whence my help will come. But I realize that help won't be in the form of prescriptions or politicians, in paychecks, or paid vacations. No, my assistance will always and only come from just one source—and that source is You (Psalm 121:1–2).

I can faith You with (*the ICU*). I can trust You despite (*the grief*). I can believe You amid fear. For even when I am faithless, You remain faithful (2 Timothy 2:13). Hallelujah! You promise to accomplish what concerns me (Psalm 138:8). I will believe. You promise to strengthen and protect me from the evil one (2 Thessalonians 3:3). I do believe. May it be done according to my faith, not according to my doubt (Matthew 9:29).

O Lord, increase my faith (Luke 17:5). Show me more of Your resplendent glory so that I can stretch to believe You more (Exodus 33:18). I lie exhausted in Your faithfulness. Selah.

Day 2

Holy Father,

Thank You that You reign high and lifted up over all the nations (Psalm 47:8). Your reign covers the countries here on earth as well as all principalities in the heavenlies. You even rule over those stubbornly resisting You (Ephesians 6:12). You, O Lord, are the Ancient of Days, the One who is above all with thousands upon thousands in attendance and myriads upon myriads standing before You as judge (Daniel 7:9–10). Praise You for sending Your Son to live my life and die my death that I might be faultless before You, my Judge (Jude 1:24). With confidence, I enter within the veil by the blood of Jesus and speak out my requests (Hebrews 10:19–20).

Father, enlarge the influence that the tent of my body represents. Reveal what it means to lengthen my cords and strengthen my pegs (Isaiah 54:2). Indeed this is not something I can do but is Your work alone (Philippians 2:13). Thank You that, even now, You are busy bringing it to pass (1 Thessalonians 5:24).

Place upon my "loins" (that inner depth of emotion and desire—Psalm 51:6) Your belt of truth (Ephesians 6:14). May Your truth so electrify and purify me that I resemble Your Son, burning as with fire (Ezekiel 1:27). May this blazing passion for truth extend into my actions, affecting not only my intentions but also my feet (Philippians 2:13).

You affect my outer person; may You also burn an intensity within me for prayer (Colossians 4:2). Like Your Son, may I have feet of fire (Revelation 1:15; Ezekiel 1:27) that I plant upon the very neck of my enemies (Joshua 10:24). While I love humanity, may I demolish all demonic forces that stand against knowing You (2 Corinthians 10:4–5). After all, my enemies are not flesh and blood but spiritual forces of darkness (Ephesians 6:12), the very prince of the power of the air (Ephesians 2:2).

Since the battle is fierce, teach me to pray with boldness (Hebrews 4:16; 10:19). May I pray with the authority that You freely give Your children (Luke 10:19)—the power to take back what humankind lost in the Fall. You are my consuming fire (Hebrews 12:29). Consume all within me that is not of You (Malachi 3:1–4). May my prayers, indeed my very life, resemble Your brilliance so that when people look at me, they glorify only You (Matthew 5:16).

Set my heart and mind aglow with the radiance of who You are (Ezekiel 8:2). Grant insight so clearly that I begin to resemble the very brightness of heaven's expanse (Daniel 12:3). May You, my light, lead many to see that righteousness is sourced only and always in You (2 Corinthians 5:21).

Thank You for giving me the very mind of Christ (1 Corinthians 2:16). Hallelujah. May I use it to comprehend Your love and so be filled up to the fulness of God (Ephesians 3:19).

Grant me to be strengthened with power through Your Holy Spirit in my inner self (Ephesians 3:16), so that I may display strength and take action in the coming months (Daniel 11:32). May I be a source of understanding to many and never fear the repercussion of speaking truth (Daniel 11:33).

Thank You that Your Kingdom has come down to live within me (Luke 17:21; Colossians 1:27). Reveal to me how to keep unlocking the heavenly doors onto the earth (Matthew 16:19). May my prayers be powerful to see Your Kingdom increase upon the earth, in the same way that Your Kingdom is divinely supreme in heaven (Matthew 6:10). In Jesus's name, amen.

Day 3

Holy Father,

Why am I so opposed to going through the fire?

You promised that You would never fail me or forsake me (Joshua 24:20), but somehow I still have my doubts. I confess that when I look back on my life, I see Your complete faithfulness. But then again, there is tomorrow. What's the deal?

It's that trust thing, isn't it?

Faith is a gift from You (Ephesians 2:8). You have divvied up trust for each of us, giving each just the right amount (Romans 12:3). But I guess I tend to be more like the father with the sick child in the Gospel of Mark. I believe in You—to an extent—but, whew, I need a fresh portion of faith for the next challenge (Mark 9:24).

Faith is like manna, huh? We can't stockpile it but only get just enough for the current need.

You have promised to rain faith from heaven for us. Every day, we are to go and gather one day's portion (Exodus 16:4). Every day. It's so simple, but I think I forgot to ask You for my share this morning. Maybe that's the reason I'm hungry.

Can I start over?

Can I have my allotment of faith for this day? You can see how hungry I will be. You know how much I will need.

Paul talked about the faith of the Thessalonians being greatly enlarged (2 Thessalonians 1:3). Could you do that for me?

But maybe I need a bigger container to receive it in. Perhaps You'd better enlarge my heart while You are at it (Psalm 119:32). Make me a person who makes You proud. And in the meantime, get me through today. I love you. In Jesus's name, amen.

Family

General Parenting

Father,

Thank You for implanting Your Word within us through Your Son, Jesus (James 1:21; John 1:1). Although we don't understand it, from that first day until now, Your Word grows within us, accomplishing what You purpose to do (Acts 19:20: Isaiah 55:11). When we believe in this miracle, we watch Your Word perform a great work within us (1 Thessalonians 2:13). What an encouraging thought!

As I bring our family before Your throne, I ask that You cause us to increase and abound in love for one another, despite our individual personalities (1 Thessalonians 3:12). Establish our hearts without blame in holiness, even as we interact with attitudes we don't understand (1 Thessalonians 3:13). May our whole family walk in a manner pleasing to You while we take one step at a time (1 Thessalonians 4:1).

As our children grow and mature, may they have the strength to abstain from sexual immorality and know how to possess each of their own vessels in honor (1 Thessalonians 4:4). May purity be the call upon their lives, rather than the immorality of the world. I pray that they would be young individuals whose ambition is to focus on what You put before them so that they will know how to behave amid a crooked world (1 Thessalonians 4:11–12).

Fasten their hearts with the breastplate of faith and love. Place a helmet of salvation on their minds (1 Thessalonians 5:8). May they see their salvation as a personal reality, not just a parental umbrella (1 Thessalonians 5:9).

Give them a desire to know truth, for this is the way to keep their way pure (Psalm 119:9). May the Word they have hidden in their hearts become their greatest treasure, as their lives increase in eternal value, not temporal (Psalm 119:14–16; 2 Corinthians 4:18). May they fix their hope on You, the living God, and be an example to others who know them (1 Timothy 4:10, 12).

In any area that our children are in opposition to You, send someone who can correct them with gentleness, so that they can come to the knowledge of the truth (2 Timothy 2:25). In kindness, bring them to their senses, Father, so that they can escape every trap the evil one lays (2 Timothy 2:26). Indeed, don't allow them to be led into temptation and deliver them from the evil one (Matthew 6:13).

I am convinced that You can guard these precious ones (2 Timothy 1:12). We already entrusted them to You. Make a hedge about our children on every side, teaching them daily what it means for You to be their dwelling place (Job 1:10; Psalm 91:1). We ask that Your work be revealed to us Your children and Your great majesty to our children (Psalm 90:16).

I pray all these things in the mighty name of Jesus. Amen.

For Specific Child

Father,

Thank You for being not only our Lord but also a secure refuge during times of adjustment (Psalm 91:2). You are our strength and very present help in trouble, even when it seems that the earth around us is falling apart (Psalm 46:1–3).

I come to You lifting up (*child's name*). He is facing a new situation and desperately needs to see that You are his help in this change (Psalm 46:5). Reveal Yourself so brightly that he will no longer focus on this seeming disaster but upon You, the One who can save him from his (*loneliness, stress, confusion, consequences, etc.*). Show him how You look rejoicing over him as an individual, as well as a picture of You, bent over, writing a song about Your love for him (Zephaniah 3:15, 17). May the effect of Your righteousness result in peace and confident trust in Your faithfulness (Isaiah 32:17).

Lead (*child's name*) to cast all his cares upon You so that he will see Your affectionate care for him (1 Peter 5:7). After this little bit of suffering, may he find that he is both completed and settled (1 Peter 5:11). Bring him several good friends who know the right things to do and encourage one another to follow through to do them (James 4:17).

I pray that we would be an example of what it means to set our minds on You, despite uncertainty (Colossians 3:2–4). May we continue to be gentle and forbearing with one another, letting Christ's peace settle all questions that arise (Colossians 3:13, 15). As we wade through this new direction together, may everything be done for You and not for humans (Colossians 3:23). In Jesus's name, amen.

Education

Holy Father,

Thank You for choosing us and crediting Your obedience for our own (1 Peter 1:2; Isaiah 53:12). How thankful we are that our holiness doesn't source from our actions but the life of Jesus Christ within us (Colossians 3:3). Because of Your life within us, we are already holy, just like You are (1 Peter 1:15–16). We are perfect in the same way You are, by nature, not by works (Hebrews 10:14; 12:23). Fasten our faith and hope on Your living Presence within us (1 Peter 1:21).

As our children (*grandchildren*) return to school, I think of them often. Urge my every thought to be lifted into prayer so that my love for them is like burning incense, whose fragrance continually reminds You of their needs (1 Thessalonians 5:17; Psalm 141:2).

Give each of our children (*grandchildren*) a craving for Your Word (1 Peter 2:2). For those who are not yet Christians, I ask that they may grow in respect to salvation toward Your perfect timing. You have called each one to Yourself (2 Peter 3:9). Grant them a lifetime of opportunity to display Your perfection (1 Peter 2:9).

You choose Your children to be a blessing (1 Peter 3:9). I ask that I be that blessing to my child (*grandchild*) this year so that they, in turn, become blessings. You have promised to keep Your eyes upon them while listening attentively to their prayers (1 Peter 3:12). What a great promise from the

Omnipotent One! Grant them the desire to always acknowledge You as first place in their hearts (1 Peter 3:15).

School can be a confusing place, Father. A place of worthless thoughts and deceitful traps (1 Peter 3:10). Protect them from the evil one, so that even if they must suffer in some way for the sake of righteousness, they will recognize Your hidden blessing (Matthew 6:13; John 17:15; 1 Peter 3:14). May they not fear intimidation or anxiety but always be aware of Your hope within them (1 Peter 3:15).

Whatever challenges this year brings about, may my children (*grandchildren*) have a good conscience because of Christ's resurrection (1 Peter 3:21). Teach them how to rest as children of God who incline to please You rather than themselves (1 Peter 4:2). Urge them toward an intense and unfailing love for others, as this is the path to forgiveness and freedom (1 Peter 4:8). May they cast all of their anxieties upon You each day as they leave for school. Thank You for caring for each detail affectionately and watchfully (1 Peter 5:7). In Jesus's name, amen.

Summer Vacation

Holy Father,

Summer is pending, and my schedule is about to change. Children need full-time care again. I'm excited but know from experience that this creates its source of challenges. I'm glad You are my source to run to when I don't know what else to do (Psalm 31:1 The Message).

First, I ask that this be a summer that I don't lean on what I perceive with my reasoning. Instead, may both my children and I find ways to acknowledge You daily. Straighten out my paths as I entrust these months to You (Proverbs 3:5–6). Sometimes, when we are all together, boredom can set in, making the dark seem blacker. May our pathway as a family get brighter and brighter as we walk in the light You provide (Proverbs 4:18). Thank You that when we have just a little of Your light, You promise that we are on the way for more (Psalm 39:6).

Focus our eyes to look into ultimate reality, where You reign supreme over the details (Matthew 10:29). Give me the energy to do one thing at a time, carefully considering how I teach my children. I can't do this on my own, Father (Jeremiah 10:23 ESV). Establish my footsteps into Your pathway so that I can lead my children into the future You have planned (Proverbs 4:25).

Reveal to me how I can still spend time in Your Word this summer. With limited alone time, I ask that You stir up the Word already within me (Psalm 37:31). Grant me recall with the Word that's already in my heart. You are my Holy Rememberer (John 14:26). Guide me while I do chores, watch over me while I sleep, and speak to me first thing in the morning (Proverbs 6:22). Thank You that Your Word is light to our family (Proverbs 6:23). When I have spare time, remind me to seek Your Presence rather than the latest social media. Knowledge of You is where I will get understanding for my day (Proverbs 9:10).

As I relate to my family, I ask that You bind up nitpicky words from our mouths. Although I seldom feel wise, I know that You have made me so in Christ Jesus (1 Corinthians 1:30). Faithing this, I know my tongue can bring healing (Proverbs 12:18). Reveal to me how I can help my children fulfill the desires You have put within them without spoiling them rotten (Proverbs 13:12, 24). It's a delicate balance.

Even though you have made me wise in Christ Jesus, I still want to ask for wisdom today (James 1:5). Grant me understanding to speak words that encourage, not words that tear down (Proverbs 14:1). Teach me how to use my words to soothe and be like a robust life-giving tree (Proverbs 15:4). Weigh my motives and direct me on how to see myself as You do (Proverbs 16:2). I commit my parenting plans to You, Lord. Fulfill Your promise and organize them for our best (Proverbs 16:3).

May the training that my children receive be straight from Your heart. Despite my exhaustion and questions, be the foundation that allows them to grow into Spirit-led adults (Proverbs 22:6). Grant me strength and remind me daily to ask for it. I'll need it, especially in the unexpected times of trouble (Proverbs 24:10). Thank You that even when my flesh and my strength fails, You are still the strength of my heart (Psalm 73:26). Give us a vision as to where You are taking our family (Proverbs 29:18).

As I work out what Proverbs 31 means for me, remind me that parenting success is not through my works but faith in Your works (Romans 11:6; Ephesians 2:10). May I someday hear my children say, "My mom is a woman worthy of praise!" (Proverbs 31:30). In Jesus's name, amen.

◆ ◆ ◆

Wayward Child

Holy Father,

You promised that You would not break off a battered reed or put out a smoldering wick (Matthew 12:20). But right now, we feel broken and snuffed out. We realize that Your ways are higher than our ways, and Your thoughts much higher than ours (Isaiah 55:9), but we are having a hard time finding comfort when our hearts are breaking for our child (*grandchild*).

Jesus, I remember that many times Your prayers consisted of loud crying and tears (Hebrews 5:7), so as You look down upon our wordless cries, we ask that You remember and have mercy. You are the God of all Comfort, so we ask that You reveal that part of Your character to us (2 Corinthians 1:3). Although each day seems like a thousand years, I claim that Your action's slowness *must* be because of Your patience (2 Peter 3:8).

Asking that the situation change is not the place to start, is it, Lord? So, our first cries are not only for comfort but also for strength. Send an angel to strengthen us, just as You did Your very own Son during His agony (Luke 22:43). This experience is sifting us like wheat, but I ask that our faith not fail. May this experience bring us strength so that we may one day strengthen others (Luke 22:32).

Indeed, it is faith that we need most right now. Ours has been dramatically shaken. Faith is that quality that allows us to see You clearly and know that You are working everything to our good (Romans 8:28). Granted, this is something we cannot see right now. So, hold up our arms when we feel too weak to hold them up ourselves. Send us friends to support us in prayer, one on one side and one on the other (Exodus 17:12).

Increase our faith (Luke 17:5). Allow this time of seeking You to create a refreshing in our lives as we tremble to stand in Your Presence (Acts 3:19).

Before I bring my child's rebellion to Your throne, I ask that You search within me to reveal my own. Convict me about anything that would hinder these prayers.

Rebellion runs rampant in our society. The wicked are in our midst, and (*name of child*) has been entrapped by society's sly deceit (Jeremiah 5:26). It is as if he has fallen under a deluding influence, enticing him to believe that which is false (2 Thessalonians 2:11). But we won't allow him to go under without a fight.

Right now, the strong man of deceit and rebellion is fully armed and guards (*name of child*) carefully. Yet, in Your name and Your righteousness, we come against those spirits with One who is far more potent. In the name of Jesus, we bind up rebellion, deceit, and anger (*other characteristics may be mentioned here*) within (*child's*) life. We demand that these spirits go to where the Lord Jesus Himself would send them. Jesus, we ask that as You attack, Yours would be the overpowering victory.

In Your name, we push back these adversaries, and through Your name, we trample down those who rise against us (Psalm 44:4–5). In Your name, we ask that You take away the armor on which these spirits have relied so long, leaving (*child*) deceived. I pray that You will even take the very things that the enemy is using against (*child*), purify them, and return them to him so that one day he can use them as plunder against the evil one (Luke 11:21–22). We claim this not because we have the power within ourselves but because You have given us authority to tread upon these slimy serpents, without injuring our faith (Luke 10:19).

Bind up a quarrelsome spirit from our tongues so that we may always correct with gentleness. Please, O Lord, please, grant (*child*) repentance leading to the knowledge of the truth as You bring him to his senses (2 Timothy 2:24–26).

We pray these things because of Your holiness and not our own. Comfort, heal and refresh because of who You are. In Jesus's name, amen.

Grandchildren

Holy Father,

Thank You for adopting me into Your family to call You Father (Romans 8:15). As divine Father, You know just how to parent my children and grandchildren. Today, I bring them to Your attention, asking that You awaken them with awareness to Your truth (Daniel 9:13). Draw them with Your holy magnetism and prepare their hearts to receive Your Word in great eagerness (John 6:44; Acts 17:11). Betroth them to Yourself as pure virgins in Spirit, revealing their need to submit any fleshliness to You (2 Corinthians 11:2; John 17:2). Release Your Word to perform Your work and will in their lives (1 Thessalonians 2:13).

Bring other Christians alongside to supply whatever is lacking in their faith (1 Thessalonians 3:10). Reveal to me my lack of confidence so that I may press forward to pray with power. Cause them to increase and abound in love for others, establishing their hearts without blame in Your holiness (1 Thessalonians 3:12–13). You were their parent before I was (Isaiah 46:3), so, as Abba Father, preserve their life and don't let their feet slip (Psalm 66:9).

Plant them firmly in Your dwelling place to thrive in Your Presence (Psalm 92:12–13). Grant them roots that seek deep living water so that they will yield spiritual fruit even in the dry season (Jeremiah 17:8). Shine the brilliant light of Your Son upon them with ever-increasing intensity until the day of Your return (Proverbs 4:18; 2 Peter 1:19).

Equip them to do Your will in everything (Colossians 3:17). May Your Spirit actively grow within them so that they may please You (Hebrews 13:20). Grant me the insight to see Your will for them, even when it differs from my particular desire. Open Your heavenly storehouse for them, raining down Your goodness, especially in the form of Your Spirit (Deuteronomy 28:12; Luke 11:13). Reveal the particular path You have for their life and fill them with the joy of waiting before You (Acts 2:28). In Jesus's name, amen.

Sending a Child to College

Holy Father,

Thank You for blessing our family with God-sourced knowledge and intelligence (Daniel 2:21). You are the One who reveals the profound and hidden things and knows just what is in the darkness. You have always been our light in the dark times (Daniel 2:22). Thank You that You never change and that we can rely on You as we make this new adjustment (Hebrews 13:5).

As we send (*child's name*) to college to glorify Your name, I come asking that You grant us the specific requests we have laid at Your feet (Daniel 2:23). You, O Lord, know all things, including just how to manage these details so that Your name will be glorified. As we separate into different locations, walk with us, whether in the midst of calm or amid fire (Daniel 3:25). Work signs and wonders so that (*child/children's name*) will remember Your dominion from generation to generation (Daniel 4:3).

Lord, I ask that You give (*child going to college*) wisdom and insight as she seeks Your will in her relationships. May there be no mistakes as she relates to her classmates. Guard her against deceitful and propaganda-pushing tongues. Instead, give her a deep understanding of Your plan for her life. Even when the way gets difficult, may she trust Your heart for her best. Be her patience as she waits and set her default coping mechanism to prayer. May she always seek You wholeheartedly so that she sees You quickly (Jeremiah 29:11–14).

For our children still at home, may they have an in-depth knowledge that You are going before them into this year (Deuteronomy 20:4). They, too, will feel the void that will result when their sister goes to college. May this year be characterized by walking in Your ways, keeping Your statutes, and listening to Your voice.

Thank You that each one of our children is already Your treasured possession. Continue the consecration process that You have already begun in their lives (Deuteronomy 26:17–19). In Jesus's name, amen.

Intercession for Christian Parents

Father,

Thank You for being just that—a good Father (Psalm 103:13–14). You surpass the best of all fathers. Your care for us is more profound than anything we can imagine here on earth (1 Peter 5:7).

I know that _____ and _____ are good parents. They love their children with all that they are. It's not just something they talk about but something they enact for their children. They protect them from harm, grieve when they are sick or sad, and struggle with decisions of what is best.

Knowing this, how much more are You a good, good Father?

Because You are Spirit and not flesh (John 4:24), Your first desire is to give us spiritual gifts, not physical ones. Foremost of all these gifts is Your Holy Spirit (Luke 11:13). I know that _____ and _____ have often prayed that You would pour out Your Spirit upon them. But when the messiness of life presses in, we honestly admit many other things take precedence over the Holy Spirit. Particulars like a (*steady job, a dependable car, and a safe place to live*).

You remind us that "your heavenly Father knows that you need all these things" (Matthew 6:32). Sometimes it's hard to believe that. Sometimes You seem so busy doing heavenly business that I feel that my needs are at the bottom of Your priority list. Maybe _____ and _____ are feeling that way now.

With this weakness in mind, I come asking that You give us a glimpse of Your fatherly heart. May we become so convinced of Your goodness that we wholeheartedly believe that seeking You first supplies our needs (Matthew 6:33). I pray that You give us eyes to focus on the unseen (2 Corinthians 4:18) and let You deal with the physical, especially our children. Faith always deals with the invisible, huh, Father?

Show us Your glory (Exodus 33:18). As we fix our eyes on You, may our ears hear Your response: "I Myself will make all My goodness pass before you, and will proclaim the Name of the Lord before you; I will be gracious to whom I will be gracious and will show compassion on whom I will show compassion" (Exodus 33:19). Choose this family for Your gracious favor. Choose them for Your abundant compassion. Let us all see Your hand daily, renewing us in our inner person (2 Corinthians 4:16) and granting us peace in every circumstance, even parenting (2 Thessalonians 3:16). In Jesus's name, amen.

◆ ◆ ◆

Intercession for Christian Parent Sending Child to College

Holy Father,

As I bring (*parent of the college-aged child*) before You, I'm so glad to remember that You are hers and she is Yours (Psalm 95:7). You promised to make known to us the path of life and light, even when we can't see one foot in front of another (Psalm 119:105). Grant (*parent*) awareness that You are near so that she can know Your fulness of joy despite her child's absence (Psalm 16:11).

Having part of the family living away from home is quite an adjustment. Some days, (*parent's*) heart will be quite heavy, and the adjustment will seem unbearable. Living these days in Your comfort is the only way to endure them. Remind her often that she can rejoice because You have never left her and are still very near to both her and her child (Philippians 4:4–5).

Raising (*college-aged child*) to adulthood has been (*parent's*) goal, but a mother's heart still grieves in the separation. Thank You that You will never leave either mother or (*daughter/son*). Lead them to remember confidently that You are their Helper. Neither of them has to be afraid (Hebrews 13:5–6).

I ask that You equip her (*daughter*) in every good thing so that she can do Your will and make room for what pleases You (Hebrews 13:21). Thank You for her (*son*), who will remain at home for these next couple of years. May (*parent*) be prepared to watch him take flight when his time comes. Grant this family the strength to walk by Your Spirit and not by their flesh (Galatians 5:16). We await Your fulfillment in Jesus's name, amen.

Intercession for Non-Christian Parents

Holy Father,

You, O Lord, are the _____ family's Father (Acts 17:29). A Father to the fatherless (Psalm 68:5), You know better than any parent on earth what it is like to have mischievous children. How comforting to know that You don't only want to be their Father but to show them what that means to step in and redeem their situation (Isaiah 63:16).

Draw them with the peace available in Jesus Christ (Romans 5:1). Their lives are filled with pressure and tediousness right now. You have said that if any of us lacks wisdom, we can ask You for it (James 1:5). The _____ family definitely needs that wisdom. You have promised that You will give Your wisdom to all people generously and without reproach (James 1:5). That is excellent news when they are so tired and not sure how to handle their current situation.

You see things differently than we do (Psalm 92:5). We desire that this situation change immediately for the better, but sometimes You allow it to continue to parent us. You say that You disciple us for our good (Hebrews 12:10). Reveal to _____ and _____ a glimpse of how You are doing that and why.

I ask and will continue to pray that You grant them relief in these challenging times (Matthew 7:7). You are not a harsh disciplinarian but a Tender Parent who is loving and kind. As these parents wait upon Your solace, blossom patient, unswerving endurance within their hearts (Romans 5:3). Open their spiritual eyes to see how patience leading to mature hope is the very best for their children as well as for themselves (Romans 5:4). Thank You that Your hope never disappoints those of us with Your Spirit because You are always a God of increase (Romans 5:5).

When the children demand their own way, I ask that You give _____ and _____ strength. After all, You promise to provide strength to the weary and power to the weak (Isaiah 40:29). Your Word also says that You are an ever-present help in trouble (Psalm 46:1). I'm holding You to Your Word on this one too.

Parents have great need of You, Father. Teach all of us Your fatherly ways. In Jesus's name, amen.

Finances

Day 1

Holy Father,

Thank You that You are utmost in power and greater than the evil one who rules this earthly realm (Colossians 1:6; 1 John 4:4). Thank You for abiding within us so that we can come to know Your voice (Colossians 1:27; 1 John 4:12; 10:4). Your nearness is our good (Psalm 73:28).

You knew that we would have a hard time seeing into the heavenlies, even though Jesus, as a man, had a clarity of vision (Matthew 14:19). So immediately after His resurrection, He took the time to appear to His disciples in various forms, getting them accustomed to recognizing You by faith and not by sight (John 20:15, 20; 21:7; Luke 24:31). You wanted all of Your disciples to understand that You guide with spiritual eyes, not physical ones (2 Corinthians 5:7).

Knowing that the spiritual is foremost to You, humanity still has physical needs. When Your Son included the request for bread in His prayer teaching, He gave me the authority to bring even physical needs to You (Matthew 6:11). So, I come to You with my financial condition.

The entrapment of this economic web seems impossible to untangle. Honestly, this feels like a bear trap has seized me by the heel and snapped shut on me (Job 18:9). Yet You promise that Your eyes are continually toward me to pluck my feet out of this net (Psalm 25:15). You are the One who delivers from the snare of the trapper, so I ask that You break this trap, allowing me to escape (Psalm 91:3; 124:7). Show Yourself strong.

Granted, I sometimes beat myself up in situations like this, feeling partially at fault and undeserving of an escape. Yet this is not how You see the circumstance, for my thoughts are not like Your thoughts (Isaiah 11:8–9). The realm in which we live is only a shadow of the reality in the heavenlies (Hebrews 8:5). You can see both domains and give me grace for living in this copy of existence while I await the actuality of truth (Hebrews 9:24). Pull back the veil that lies before me, just like You did for the servant of Elisha (2 Kings 6:17). Show me Your kindness so that I can relax in Your compassion, rather than stress in the disappointment (Hebrews 12:2; Colossians 3:2).

When I see You, Your image transforms my mind and heart (1 John 3:2; 2 Corinthians 4:18). Lord, give me understanding into the fantastic gift You have provided, the very mind of Christ Himself (1 Corinthians 2:16). Teach me how to set my mind on things by Your Spirit while You provide for my needs (Romans 8:5; Galatians 5:16). I bring these things before You with the signature of Your Son on the request. In Jesus's name, amen.

—————————————◆ ◆ ◆—————————————

Day 2

Holy Father,

Praise You for being God and that there is no One like You (Isaiah 46:9). You are the owner of everything, from the beast in the forest to the cattle in the field (Psalm 50:10). The silver is Yours, as is the gold (Haggai 2:13).

Although owner of all, You are also a God who loves to give (1 Chronicles 29:14; John 3:27). You do not provide sparingly but abundantly and lavishly toward Your children (Romans 8:32). Indeed the God who loves a lavish giver is One Himself (2 Corinthians 9:7). Thank You for being present and at hand and allowing me to come to You for every need (Luke 17:21). Already I can see what blessing it is for me to know affliction and seek Your face on behalf of this need (Philippians 4:14).

You knew I would be in this situation, needing (*specific item*) yet without the means to acquire it (Psalm 139:15). You've brought me to this place so that I would seek You, which is what I am doing (Acts 17:27). I'm not only seeking You personally but also asking others to seek You on my behalf (Romans 15:30). This need has caused many to seek Your face.

Providing (*specific item*) is not out of Your realm of ability. You establish Your purpose, and You will accomplish all of Your good pleasure (Isaiah 46:10). My portion is to ask and wait upon Your particular answer (1 Kings 3:5).

Show me how to open my mouth wide so that You can fill it (Psalm 81:10). Reveal how I can best align my desire to Yours so that You can either fulfill that desire or change it to Your purpose. Most of all, bring me near to Your heart (Psalm 145:18–19).

May I patiently wait on Your provision in whatever form You choose and pray often without losing heart (Luke 11:13; 18:1). I rejoice now for the promises that You are already bringing to pass. Thank You for providing all that I need according to Your riches in Christ Jesus (Philippians 4:19). Grant me faith to seek You wholeheartedly (Hebrews 11:6). In Jesus's name, amen

———————————— ◆◆◆ ————————————

Day 3

Holy Father,

Thank You for choosing us as Your royal priesthood (1 Peter 2:9). When You beckoned us toward You, our entrance into Your Presence is what sets us apart. Yet this distinction wasn't just so that we could sit on a shelf and look good. No, we've been chosen as people who would "obey and be sprinkled with Your blood" (1 Peter 1:1–2). What depth of meaning such words hold.

Although I can't fully understand it, the sprinkling of Your blood always cleanses (Romans 5:9). Because You have sprinkled me, I am now free from guilt (Leviticus 7:2–5; Hebrews 10:14). Because You have forgiven me, I don't have to keep worrying about making amends for my sins (Hebrews 10:18). How blessed I am that You have taken care of my guilt forever (Romans 4:8).

Sure, I can do nothing to gain more of Your favor, but I must still die daily to my thoughts, emotions, desires, and ego (1 Corinthians 15:31). Just like a vessel, tilted to pour out its contents, my soul must daily be tilted and poured out before You (1 Samuel 1:15). If everything remains settled inside of me, I become stagnant. But when I lean Your way, all of the surging feelings and anxieties can spill out and be absorbed into You. I guess that is why I am so often overwhelmed by my weakness. Frailty makes it that much easier to cascade into Your arms.

How beautiful that Your Love, like water, rushes to the lowest-lying spot. As I descend, You rush in. Thank You for flooding Your love into my heart (Romans 5:5). What a terrific trade: my spinning thoughts for Your unmeasurable concern.

In the coming days, as I make decisions about the tedium of life, I ask that You remind me to keep bending low. May tension flow out of me so that Your intimacy can replace it. Grant me wisdom to spend the right amount of time on each task, as I aim my attention to You (Hebrews 12:2).

Praise You, O Lord, for revealing that in Your emptiness I find true filling. Keep me focused on the fulness of Your hope rather than the lack of my desires. In Jesus's name, amen.

God's Presence

Day 1

Father,

Thank You for never giving up on us (Hebrews 13:5). You are always drawing us toward Yourself with an everlasting love and bending down to feed us personally (Jeremiah 31:3; Hosea 11:4). Even when we are distracted or busy, there is a magnetism about You that draws us back (John 6:44). Thank You for never abandoning us.

I realize that the way to keep my way pure is to keep it according to Your Word (Psalm 119:9). Yet, life happens, and I find myself wandering away from waiting in Your Presence (Psalm 119:10). I ask that Your Word be a treasure to me, not only to keep me from sin but also as my delight (Psalm 119:11; Jeremiah 15:16). May I find great rejoicing in Your testimonies and meditate daily upon Your precepts (Psalm 119:14–15).

Open my eyes, Lord, that I may find new things in Your Word every time I open Your Book (Psalm 119:18). May I experience Your Word as an extension of Your life, not just as words on a page (Deuteronomy 32:47; Hebrews 4:12). When I am sad, strengthen me according to Your Word (Psalm 119:28). When I am joyful, lead me to praise (Psalm 119:47). When I am busy, enlarge my time to include You (Psalm 119:32). Grant me Your lovingkindness, O Lord, so that I will have an answer to all those who doubt Your goodness (Psalm 119:42). In Jesus's name, amen.

Day 2

Holy Father,

I desire to see the glory of Your Presence. "Show me Your glory!" is my frequent cry, and I often don't even understand the One whose beauty I want (Exodus 33:18). As I pause to wait for You, I hear You say, "Behold, there is a place by Me, and you shall stand there on the rock" (Exodus 33:21).

O glorious Father, thank You for revealing that the rock is Christ (1 Corinthians 10:4). He is the radiance of Your glory and the exact representation of Your nature (Hebrews 1:3). I cry to see You, and You answer, "(*Your name*) have I been with You such a long time, and yet You say, show me the Father?" (John 14:9). When I fix my eyes on You, the revealed God, I can drink in the essence of the invisible One as well. Hallelujah!

You have already put me in the cleft of the rock and covered me with Your hand (Exodus 33:22). Although no one has seen You, O God, You sent the Word made flesh into the world that He might explain You (John 1:18). You consecrated me as a priest in Your Kingdom, so I have ready access to You, my King (Revelation 1:6; Hebrews 10:22). Such knowledge is too excellent and glorious for me; I can't attain it (Psalm 139:6).

Even so, reveal how I am to use my spiritual eyes to see all that You have prepared for me (1 Corinthians 2:9). I have already received Your Spirit and have Him sealed within me. Hallelujah! You cannot leak out! (1 Corinthians 2:12; 2 Corinthians 1:22).

Guide me into Your invisible ways so that I may grow accustomed to living there (2 Corinthians 4:18). I want to be well acquainted with who You are even before You transfer me to heaven one day. Being in Your Presence allows Your Spirit to seep into me and enlarge my heart. Yes, Lord, may it be. In Jesus's name, amen.

Day 3

Holy Father,

Thank You that You are the light of the world (John 8:12). How blessed we are that Your life is the light of humanity. No amount of darkness can squelch Your light, for You dwell in unapproachable light (John 1:4–5; 1 Timothy 6:16). You can see in the dark just as well as in the light (Psalm 139:12). What a blessing to have You lighting my way.

You pass this spark of light to Your children so that now we are light in this dark world (Matthew 5:14). My task is to glow in the locate You place me. I can't help radiating when I hold fast to the Word of life (Philippians 2:15–16). Show me how to glorify You as I emanate who You are (Ephesians 5:8–10).

Enlighten the eyes of my heart, so I may live in Your hope, Your greatness, and Your strength as I walk this earth (Ephesians 1:18–19). May my eyes adjust to everlasting light as I gaze on Your glory so that my transition to heaven one day will be seamless (Isaiah 61:19). There will be no need for the sun or moon in the new Jerusalem, for You will illumine everything therein (Revelation 21:23). Hallelujah! In Jesus's name, amen.

Growth

Day 1

Holy Father,

How can it be that Your power lies within our hearts? Your provision for me is quite mind-boggling. You chose me in Christ before creating the world and now have given me everything I need for life and godliness (Ephesians 1:4; 2 Peter 1:3). You even chose me as a wife for Your Son and as a priest for Your Kingdom (Ephesians 1:22–23; Revelation 21:9; 1:6). Wow!

So, why don't I faithe Your Word more? You granted me understanding into the mysteries of the Kingdom of God, so open my eyes to see the Word You have implanted within me (Luke 8:10; James 1:22).

My habit is to believe for a while, then grow lax in my faith (Luke 8:13). Fleshly anxiety occupies more of my thoughts than following You. I'm ashamed to confess that most often, I disregard Your Word by seeking my gratification through entertainment and amusements. But fleshly indulgence brings me no peace and effectually strangles evidence of Your ongoing work within me (Luke 8:14).

Remove any rocks and thorns that keep me from growth (Luke 8:14). Till me and even fertilize me so that my heart's soil may be ready for germination. Grant me the moisture of Your Spirit and Your gentle watch care, O Faithful Farmer. Give me good soil that welcomes the infinite root system of Your Spirit. I stand before You, ready for Your hand. In Jesus's name, amen.

Day 2

Holy Father,

Thank You for Jesus Christ, our Lord, who strengthens Your children to do all things (1 Timothy 1:12). You tell me more than once in Your Word that

I have power through You to do all things (Colossians 1:11; Philippians 4:13). Conversely, apart from You, I can do nothing (John 15:5).

As I consider my activities, I realize that You have gifted me in many ways. My natural talents come quickly and tempt me to achieve in my power. Yet, I've noticed that when I attempt to accomplish anything in the flesh, I take my eyes off You and put them on myself. I begin to worry and fuss to improve so that others will notice my accomplishments. Soon, I am empty and dry, wondering why I no longer feel the sense of Your nearness.

You bring me to this place often. I must be reminded that as long as it is my idea and my work, it will profit nothing (John 6:63). Even religious activity attained in the flesh never counts for Your Kingdom (1 Corinthians 3:13).

Remind me that everything I do apart from You has no value. Even Jesus did nothing on His initiative but only what He heard and saw the Father doing (John 5:19, 30). Show me how to walk in this same manner. As I face upcoming challenges, may I walk not according to selfishness and spend time uselessly. This is exhausting. Instead, may I efficiently allow Your Spirit to live Your life through my body, mind, and emotions. Your life is my only hope. In Jesus's name, amen.

◆ ◆ ◆

Day 3

Holy Father,

Thank You for granting us everything we need for life and godliness (2 Peter 1:3). You've given us knowledge of who You are and have drawn us to Yourself by a glimpse of Your excellent glory. So, when I request to grow in grace, I know this is a request You will grant because it is Your will (2 Peter 3:18; 1 John 5:14–15).

How exciting to know that You have not only put this desire within me but that You are already bringing it to pass (1 Thessalonians 5:24). Not one of the good promises You made has ever failed. Every single one of them has always come to pass (Joshua 21:45). Hallelujah!

Of course, as with all Your promises, I must grow into them. I desire to grow in (*writing, time management, promise-keeping, direction, and discipline*). Despite all external proof to the contrary, You not only have already delivered me from distraction, but You are delivering me at this moment and will continue to do so (2 Corinthians 1:10).

You promise that You will accomplish all that concerns me, so I stand at the gates of heaven with the key to the Kingdom that You have given me (Psalm 138:8). I ask that You unbind the blessings of obedience and discipline already stored in heaven for me. Indeed, how great is the warehouse of Your goodness (Psalm 31:19)!

Bind up all distraction, laziness, and discouragement from affecting my follow-through (Matthew 18:18–19). Push back the enemy from his destructive strategies and reestablish my boundaries in beautiful places (Psalm 16:6). Give me eyes to see the evil one fall like lightning, as my faith remains strengthened in You daily (Luke 10:18). In Jesus's name, amen.

———————— ◆ ◆ ————————

Day 4

Father,

What is real revelation? In Greek, it is called *apokalypsis*—the laying bare, making naked or uncovering of that which was unknown. Could this be the pathway to humility?

I desire for You to reveal Yourself to me. I've asked that the eyes of my heart be enlightened and that I might know the mystery of Your will (Ephesians 1:18, 9). But when You begin to pull back the veil, I'm made aware of my own nakedness. I know how Eve felt, as I, too, want to run and hide. Bared, I look much less spiritual.

You don't condemn me for this (Romans 8:1). Your x-ray eyes have always seen through my ruffles and lace. You aren't shocked (1 Corinthians 13:12), yet I'm ashamed, as I thought spiritual Spanx hid my flaws. Sigh.

Therein lies a big part of the problem, huh? Looking for goodness just because I primp. This is not real purity. No, any good that I wear comes from standing unadorned in You (2 Corinthians 5:21).

Seeing myself naked in the mirror of Your eyes makes me more readily forgive the faults of others. When I see my imperfections, I can more easily love others through theirs. Each of us stumbles in many ways (James 3:2).

You've turned on the light in the darkest closet of my heart (Luke 2:32). Exposure is simply part of light's quality. Yet You reveal that standing in the light cleanses me. Your ultraviolet rays destroy both flesh-borne and soul-borne pathogens. Your light-emitting diode heals, renews, and energizes me from the inside out.

I'm encouraged to know that even the infected syringe can become clean again by just resting under the light. This, then, is my response as well. Not guilt, not agony, not shame. Just relaxing and allowing Your rays to penetrate my facade. You restore and transform me while I stare wide-eyed at Your beauty (1 John 3:2). Positioning myself before You is what purifies me, not merely changing my actions (1 John 3:3). By Your grace that I am what I am (1 Corinthians 15:10).

Thank You that I don't have to shrink away from Your revelation, despite my faulty image (1 John 2:28). As I look into Your eyes, I do not see my reflection but Your own. What a blessed certainty.

Truths like these purify my soul (1 Peter 1:22). I ask that You remind me to feed more upon Your Word than upon the propaganda of the world.

"Search me, O God, and know my heart; Try me and know my anxious thoughts and see if there be any hurtful way in me and lead me in the everlasting way" (Psalm 139:23–24).

◆ ◆ ◆

Day 5

O Father,

We've been like babies, awaiting strained food from pastors and personalities rather than feeding directly from Your hand. We've subsisted on spiritual smoothies blended from tweets, sound bites, and media reports. So, in Your longing for us to grow, You've pushed time aside to begin our meal training.

You desire that we increase in wisdom and favor (Luke 2:52). You offer us a fork and set before us bite-sized portions of Your Word (Isaiah 55:1–2). We bobble in the highchair, unsure how to ingest Your Word without having it puréed via podcast or devotional (1 Corinthians 3:2).

Many of us have tube-fed upon spiritual quips for so long that we find difficulty biting into substance. Yet, as corruption intensifies and society panics, we will desperately need discernment between the premasticated and the meaty. O how we need Your insight to separate truth from deceit. Only Your life is real food (John 6:55). Show us how to grip the utensil and maneuver meat into our mouths (2 Timothy 2:15). Self-feeding is going to take some practice (Hebrews 5:14).

I'm ready to feed solely on Your Word, Father. Put me in the booster seat of Your Presence and be patient when I make a mess. Set me in the kitchen with only the divine person of Your Holy Spirit to guide my hand and heart (John 14:26). Take away what distracts me from solid food and grant me a hunger for Your righteous satisfaction (Matthew 5:6).

You have food to offer that I can't even imagine, so I yearn to value Your Word more than breakfast, lunch, or dinner (John 4:32; Job 23:14). I want to be a healthy eater, not a picky one, so introduce me to a variety of Your truths. As You feed me and I chew this Book, may Your Word become my joy and heart's delight (Ezekiel 3:1; Jeremiah 15:16). I've tasted and know that Your Word is not only useful but, if savored, is sweeter than the honey drippings of the honeycomb (Psalm 34:8; 19:10).

Your Book reveals Your heart. Time in the kitchen with You will both satisfy and stimulate me to hunger for more. Thank You for granting me a taste of Your kindness and for having a plan for my growth (1 Peter 2:2–3). Tie on my bib; I'm ready to eat. In Jesus's name, amen.

Guilt

Day 1

Holy Father,

How is it that every single day You manage to amaze with Your love? I know that You are love but can hardly comprehend just all that encompasses (1 John 4:16). Instead, I deal with daily guilt and shame.

Despite asking Your blood to cleanse me from all sin, I have a problem believing it is accomplished. Although You said that You perfected me continually from all past, present, and future sin with one divine offering, it seems too good to be true (Hebrews 10:14; 1 John 1:7). I say that I believe that You delivered me at the time of salvation, but then for some reason, I still try to please You by what I do. I start in the Spirit and later try to get better by my own effort (Galatians 3:3).

Then, I reread that You offered one sacrifice for the sins of all time (Hebrews 10:12). You sat down in heaven because You finished the whole work (John 19:30). I don't have to try to be sanctified because You made me perfect with a decision of Your will (Hebrews 10:10). Amazing!

Unfold the presence of Your vast love to me and help me understand what it means to have a God who doesn't take my wrongs into account (1 Corinthians 13:5). If You expect this kind of love from me, then surely You are this kind of love! You've removed my sin as far as the east is from the west (Psalm 103:12). Even by the fastest jet, I can never get those two distances into the same locale.

Grant that I rest in Your abundant peace as You overflow into my spirit (Romans 5:5). My life is no longer about me and my mistakes. It's about You, Christ in me. You are the hope of my glory (Colossians 1:27).

May I stop being so spiritually narcissistic, always looking over my shoulder to wonder how I am doing. Instead, keep me focused on looking at You. Grant that I comprehend the breadth, length, height, and depth of Your love (Ephesians 3:18). Remind me not only of Your patience, kindness, and lack of arrogance but also reveal how little I can provoke You (1 Corinthians 13:4-5). Hallelujah! In Jesus's name, I pray boldly. Amen.

❖ ◆ ◆

Day 2

Holy Father,

I'm struggling with understanding Your idea of perfection. I confess that my perspective is based more on report card grading than Your Word's truth. I tend to look for an ideal score instead of looking to You, my Perfect Core.

Your law is perfect (Psalm 19:7), and somehow that confuses me to think that I should adhere to Your law with flawless precision. I read Your challenge to "be perfect" like You are, so I scurry immediately toward my understanding of that reality (Matthew 5:48). I try to act right, even though You continually repeat that activity can never make me flawless (Hebrews 7:19; 10:1).

I've got to stop leaning on my understanding of all of this (Proverbs 3:5). Will You help me? My only hope for perfection is Your perfect life within me. Live Your life through me.

My spirit is already perfect (Hebrews 12:23), but that doesn't include every jot and tittle of my actions. My behavior will never be excellent according to my standard during this lifetime, but that's okay with You (Hebrews 9:9)). A clear conscience comes from relaxing into Your arms (Hebrews 9:14). Perfection is a pass/fail class. Do I have the life of Jesus or not (1 John 5:11–12)? My job is to show up for the lab course (James 1:4).

Help me to stop thinking about what I look like and focus upon You (Hebrews 12:2). Herein lies the key. Your Son kept entrusting Himself to You daily (1 Peter 2:23). Why do I think I should get a shortcut?

At this moment, I trust You. At this minute, I believe You live in me (Galatians 2:20). I am perfectly willing at this moment, and You are satisfied. Let's go from this place together. In Jesus's name, amen.

Day 3

Father,

Thank You for sending Your Son as our mediator between You and me (1 Timothy 2:5). Since Jesus is Your exact replica (Hebrews 1:3), the more I know Him, the more I know You as well. Even so, since Your ways are higher than mine, there is still much I don't understand (Isaiah 55.8). Send Your Spirit to pray through me.

I thank You that I may use Your name as the signature on all my requests (John 14:13). You promised that anything that I ask according to Your desire would be granted (1 John 5.14–15). So, I come before You to receive the promises that You already have stored up for me.

Create within me the desire to know You (Psalm 73:25). Often, because of failures, I feel too downcast to desire You. Remind me that You have separated my transgressions from me as far as the east is from the west (Psalm 103:12). Allow me to see Your perspective of who I am, rather than looking at myself through Satan's lens of defeat. May I look into Your face, lost in Your Presence, rather than into the feebleness of my temporary dwelling (1 Chronicles 22:19).

In Your name, deliver me from the evil one (Matthew 6:13), binding and loosing my experience into the ways of the heavenlies (Matthew 18:18). Your Word is forever settled in heaven (Psalm 119:89), so settle Your Word in my heart as well. May what You say be the way I judge myself, not how my situation looks. Stir faith in my heart each time You speak (Proverbs 3:6 The Message).

The evil one has a habit of accusing me. This is no surprise, as the accuser is the meaning of his name (Zechariah 3:1). But in Your name, I ask You to rebuke all accusations of failure, covering my mind with clean thoughts because of Your salvation (Zechariah 3:5). Remind me often of the turban You created for me to wear—the one engraved saying, "Holy to the Lord" (Exodus 28.36). Thank You that You are my High Priest, seated now in the heavenlies to cleanse my conscience from the "should have's" (Hebrews 8.1; 9.13–14). May I please You daily, without worrying about other people's rules.

Refute the accuser so violently that he is cast away from Your Presence with lightning force whenever he mentions my name (Luke 10:18). Don't allow him to point his finger at me. Instead, I ask You to point Your finger at the adversary on my behalf (Luke 11.20). Grant me the obedience necessary to hear Your Word and follow through to do it (Luke 11:28), without looking back (Isaiah 43:18). I ask all these things in Your name. So be it.

<hr />

Day 4

Father,

Today, I bring before You my tendency to judge emotionally. Admittedly, my wavering feelings are no more difficult for You to calm than wind or waves, but I need an extra measure of faith to conquer my attitude (Luke 8:24; Romans 12:3). Open my eyes to see Your power despite the storm of my feelings (Acts 16:14).

For a time, I managed to continue to live by law even after You released me from it. I'm ashamed to admit this, but You accomplished so much for me that I felt impressed to do something for You in return. But, You continue to remind me that religious rules never result in perfection (Romans 3:20).

Honestly, religion (and even church) has only increased my transgressions (Romans 5:20). I followed the rules to look impressive. Admitting this doesn't surprise You but merely reveals the largeness of Your grace) (Romans 5:21). Religious methods have led me to the feet of Your Son (Galatians 3:24). Hallelujah. I see now that religion won't give me a satisfying life, for rules can never make the worshippers perfect (Galatians 3:21; Hebrews 10:1–2). So, what can?

This provision is not a what but a who. When Your Son walked on earth, His personality had emotions and desires. Your will and His feelings were not always the same, but the Spirit within Him kept Him holy (Matthew 26:39). Rules didn't keep Him pure. His connection with You did. He followed Your will, not by predeciding what He would do but by submitting His will to Yours, moment by moment (Hebrews 10:5–7).

Now, this very same Spirit lives within me (John 14:17). The Spirit who prompted Jesus with both anger and gentleness will direct me as well. The Spirit's intent has not changed. "Jesus Christ is the same yesterday and today, yes and forever" (Hebrews 13:5).

So, I can boldly say that the same power that kept Jesus in submission can sustain me too (Romans 8:11; Ephesians 1:9–11). As He is, so also can I be in this world (1 John 4:17). The significance is mind-boggling. Teach me how to hear and obey Your still, quiet prompting (1 Kings 19:12).

Letting go of the prescribed order of conduct is very scary for me. Reveal what it's like to have Your power mightily working within me instead of societal expectations (Colossians 1:29). This released life causes me fear and trembling, so I ask that Your power flow through me as I remain submitted (Philippians 2:12–13; 2 Corinthians 12:9–10).

Thank You, Jesus, not only for being crucified in weakness but for now living in power. Remind me that when I am weak, power is the promised result (2 Corinthians 13:4–5). Legalism is not of faith (Galatians 3:12). Trying to please others can't possibly satisfy You (Hebrews 11:6). If I try to please others, I can't be Your bondservant (Galatians 1:10). And whatever is not of faith is just plain ole sin (Romans 14:23).

I used to think that my job was to believe. But You reveal that is merely shifting the emphasis from works to faith. Wow. Confidence is Your job too (Romans 10:17; Philippians 1:27). Thank You for not only making me right through faith but for faithing the faithe for me (Ephesians 2:8–9). Even trusting isn't something I can do myself! You do it all (Romans 8:2–4).

Thank You for putting an end to the law, in whatever form I translated it to be (Romans 10:4). Do that for friends who struggle with legalism as well. Thank You that our lives no longer have to be based on pleasing someone in a church or administrative position over us. Thank You that instead, we are now under Your grace (Romans 11:6). You have set us free from religious law and into the vast, unconfined space of Your Spirit (Romans 8:1). Hallelujah! You completed the requirement (Romans 8:4). You were serious about setting us free into liberty (Galatians 5:1). Minister truth today, so that we can live in Your freedom (John 8:32). We take our hands off the old pump of effort and stand cleansed in Your fountain of living water (John 7:38.) In Jesus's name, amen.

Day 5

Holy Father,

Thank You for revealing Yourself to us through Your Son, Jesus (Galatians 1:12; Hebrews 1:2). He is the best gift ever! Through His obedience here on earth, You took care of all of our disobedience, whether past, present, or future (Romans 5:19). How amazing is this? You saved us not because of any virtuous deed we did but according to Your extravagant favor (Titus 3:5 TPT). You gave Yourself for us so that we are now redeemed from every lawless deed to do what is passionate in Your eyes (Titus 2:14 TPT).

I come from a background that included much right training. Thank You for this groundwork and praise You for those teachers who led me to Christ (1 Timothy 1:5). Now, as I stand before You, may I understand the fulness of being in Your Son (Colossians 1:27). You, O Christ, have settled within me to allow me to know who You are, realize my right standing with You, glimpse the process You are using to make me holy), and understand how much You paid for me—1 Corinthians 1:30 AMP). Open my mind and heart to fathom the completeness of Your work (John 17:4).

What does it mean to have the law's requirement already fulfilled for me (Romans 8:4)? All that I could do, should do, can do, can think, or can act—*all* is taken care of by You (Ephesians 1:10). This life I live is genuinely no longer mine but Christ's Life within me (Galatians 2:20). When You came into my heart, I became the living residence for the personal Spirit of God.

Your life, centered and established within me, is now the energy that animates me (Colossians 3:4). I don't have to try to be virtuous. I *am* good because You are good (1 John 4:17). Open my eyes that I may live in this freedom; that's the whole reason You gave liberty in the first place (Galatians 5:1). Teach me what it looks like day by day to walk in Your inside-out life (Galatians 5:25).

This work request is signed by the blood of Jesus and is therefore legal. Amen.

Day 6

Holy Father,

Thank You for being the God who accomplishes what You begin (Psalm 57:2). I have a high value for follow-through because I desire to be that kind of person myself. As such, I tend to have high expectations for myself and those around me.

Recently, however, You have been emphasizing that there is "not a righteous man on earth who continually does good and who never sins" (Ecclesiastes 7:20). I have successfully moderated my behavior in many ways, but You gently remind me that You aren't as interested in my actions as You are in my heart (1 Samuel 16:7). You are more concerned that I put aside "the pointing of the finger and speaking wickedness" and allow Christ to live His life through me (Isaiah 58:9).

Father, I agree with You. You encourage me not to judge, lest I am judged (Matthew 7:1). How I view others could easily be how You see me (Matthew 7:2). I wouldn't want You to exchange Your abundant grace toward me for a critical, exacting viewpoint. Yet, I tend to have a high standard for others while desiring grace for myself.

Making little rules for myself isn't the answer, Father. These self-regulations look impressive but only lead to indulging my self-love (Colossians 2:23). Heal me from unrealistic expectations. Untangle my feet from the net of judgment and keep my eyes focused on Your perfection, not everyone else's lack (Psalm 25:15; Hebrews 12:2). Lead me into paths of righteousness for Your sake, not my own (Psalm 23:3). Keep me looking up from my unfinished state as You fill me with hope (Philippians 3:12–14). I humbly ask in Jesus's name, amen.

Healing

Intercessory

Day 1

Holy Father,

Praise You for being the One in whom are hidden all the treasures of wisdom and knowledge (Colossians 2:3). We are daily in need of understanding, and we appreciate knowing that You are the Strong Tower that we can run into for all wisdom (James 1:5; Proverbs 18:10). When we look into our past, we remember that You have accomplished many amazing things for us. If we try to make a list of them, we will become overwhelmed. There are too many blessings to count (Psalm 40:5).

Yet, as we stand here together in spirit, looking into _____'s future, her news is scary. When this family thinks about the what-ifs, they could find themselves in despair. Help them follow David's example, looking past the current situation and into Your face instead. Be the help of their emotions (Psalm 42:11). I pray that You will bring the souls of this dear family into peace from the battle raging against them (Psalm 55:18).

Take each family member into Your Presence, that they might live there in spirit and truth. Remind them that:

- Mountains melt like wax before Your Presence (Psalm 97:5).
- There is fulness of joy in Your Presence (Psalm 16:11).
- Times of refreshing come from Your Presence (Acts 3:19).

I claim each of these for _____'s family. Melt away their fear and give them a time of peace as You crush the efforts of Satan against this little girl (Romans 16:20). Completely heal her body, mind, and emotions so that the whole family may know a time of refreshing.

As we all pray these requests, we do so in the very name of Jesus, the Author and Perfecter of our faith (Hebrews 12:2). It is as if Jesus Himself has signed this petition. It is upon His righteousness that we stand, able to make this bold request (2 Corinthians 5:21). We stand at the right hand of Your throne, joining the very prayers Jesus Himself is praying for _____ (Hebrews 7:25). We are part of Jesus's bride and desire to pray just like Him. Remind us to come before You on their behalf often and importunately (Luke 18:7). So be it.

◆ ◆ ◆

Day 2

Holy Father,

You are our light and our salvation. We must remind ourselves of this often because otherwise, we see much of which to be afraid. But with You as the defense of our lives, whom shall we dread (Psalm 27:1)?

I come today to intercede for _____. Her condition has come upon her to weaken and devour her flesh (Psalm 27:2). She must be experiencing days in which she feels that all is against her. I ask that she remain confident in Your provision despite all of her emotions and pain (Psalm 27:3). Without you giving her Your perspective, it will be easy to sink into her own.

As I come before You on her behalf, we ask this one thing from You: each day, as she fights this disease, may _____ remain steadfastly aware of her position in Christ. Thank You for choosing her. May her thoughts dwell on the fact that she is a temple of the Holy Spirit, not a residence of disease (Psalm 27:4). I pray that she may see Your beauty amid this trial and be able to meditate upon Your glory (Psalm 27:4).

Don't forget, Lord, that You promised to conceal her within Your life by hiding her away in Your secret place. Be especially evident in those days that life is just too much to bear (Psalm 27:5). May _____ see many days in which she knows that You have brought her out of hiding so that she stands upon the rock of Your salvation (Psalm 27:5).

Specifically, I ask that you take her every thought captive, lifted away from enemies who desire to damage her body (Psalm 27:6). I pray that her mind and heart would be able to offer sacrifices of praise with shouts of joy, something You alone can do within her (Psalm 27:6). May all who pray for her be able to join with her in praise to the Lord as we see You heal.

Hear our voices as we cry out on her behalf. Be gracious and answer (Psalm 27:7). You have instructed us to seek Your face, and so, we come before You doing so (Psalm 27:8). Now that our feeble hearts search, we know You will not turn Your face from us. You will be our help, for we have no one else to count on but You (Psalm 27:9). Good thing You are faithful (1 Corinthians 1:9).

Teach us Your way and lead _____ on a level path. Her body has many foes right now, so don't deliver her over to this disease (Psalm 27:11). Therein is despair. Instead, give her the strength to wait on You (Psalm 27:12–14). Yes, may she wait on You and find that her heart takes courage as she is silent before You. This is our cry that she can wait silently and watch You push the disease out of her body (Psalm 27:14). In Jesus's name, amen.

——————————— ◆ ◆ ———————————

Day 3

Holy Father,

I rush into Your Presence regarding _____. Thankfully, her situation is not a surprise to You. Your eyes miss nothing, neither this situation nor this threat (Hebrews 4:13). We are so thankful that we have someone far stronger and more powerful to turn to as we struggle to know how to pray (1 John 4:4).

You are the Author of life and love to give life (Acts 3:15; John 14:6). I remind You that You came to give abundant life and to destroy the works of the evil one (John 10:10; 1 John 3:8). I believe this includes _____.

Because You not only believe in life but actually *are* life, I come to You, Jesus Christ, the life-giver, to rebuke the evil one's dealings in _____ 's body (Jude 9). As one of Your mighty warriors, I put my foot down upon the neck of this enemy of disease (Joshua 10:24). Fill all who are praying with Your great power to crush the evil one underneath us (Romans 16:20).

As we pray, we take a stand to say no to this infirmity as it tries to create havoc. You have given us authority to pray in this way (Titus 2:11–12; Luke 10:19). Thank You that the kingdom of this world is on its way to becoming the kingdom of our Lord and Christ (Revelation 11:15).

You, Jesus, are already the victor and have already disarmed the rulers and authorities (Colossians 2:15). You sit at the right hand of the Father, awaiting Your enemies to be made a footstool of Your feet (Hebrews 10:13). We drag this disease captive (along with the thoughts and fears of what he might do) and bring him to Your feet (2 Corinthians 10:4–5). May the kingdom You have already set up in heaven come with power into _____'s body (Matthew 6:10).

I recognize that my prayers feel inadequate. My prayer for _____ sounds more like a groan than a request (2 Corinthians 3:5; Romans 8:26). But, I *do* have the life of Jesus within me (1 John 5:12). And so I come boldly to Your throne, asking on behalf of both _____ and her family (Hebrews 10:22).

Banish this disease by a point of Your finger (Luke 11:20). Fill this family with peace in such a powerful portion that You displace all doubt. Hallelujah for who You are. Hallelujah, for Your power is working this very instant mightily (Ephesians 3:16). "Now to Him Who is able to do exceeding abundantly beyond all that we ask or think, according to the power that works within us, to Him be the glory in the church and in Christ Jesus to all generations forever and ever. Amen" (Ephesians 3:20).

◆ ◆ ◆

Day 4

Father,

I come to You today on behalf of _____. You are the Spirit that gives life (2 Corinthians 3:6), so I ask that You flow energy through _____'s (*stomach, heart, liver, etc.*). You are her strength during this time when she is frail, and we call upon You to be her healer as well (2 Corinthians 12:10; Exodus 15:26). Lead her to Elim, where she can rest beside the springs of Your living water (Exodus 15:27).

During her time in the hospital, may Your love control her. Even in her weakness, may she prove to everyone nearby that You live through her (2 Corinthians 5:14). May the words that come from her weakness prove Your strength, which can do mightily works within her (Colossians 1:29).

As I mention all of these promises that You have made on _____'s behalf, I ask that You allow me to pick them up at the doors of heaven for her, delivering them to her through my prayers. Make grace abound to her so that she will have all sufficiency in everything (2 Corinthians 9:8). We depend totally upon You, for You are our life (Colossians 3:4). In Jesus's name, amen.

◆ ◆ ◆

Day 5

Holy Father,

Thank You for being our daily burden bearer and the One who not only makes promises but also keeps them (Psalm 68:19; Hebrews 10:23).

As I come to you today on _____'s behalf, I claim Your promise to restore health (Jeremiah 30:17). I come before You to join all those who are praying for her. Thank You for choosing her surgeon. Guide his hand as he operates. May there be no mistakes.

May the outcome bring her a new life without any rebound or complications. Arise over and within _____, so that she may have another experience to testify that completeness is within You. I pray that her healing will result in such joy that she goes forth with skipping (Malachi 4:2)! In Jesus's name, amen.

◆ ◆ ◆

Day 6

Blessed Father,

Thank You for being our Healer (Exodus 15:26). As You well know, it's very easy for me to despair when I hear news like that of _____'s recent (*seizure, accident, fall*). Yet, our hope remains in You. We watch expectantly, waiting on You to hear our prayer because You are the God of salvation (Micah 7:7). Anything is possible when we catch a glimpse of Your face and find our faith activated (Mark 9:23). You are always a help to our countenance because You are our God (Psalm 42:11).

Restore _____ to health (Jeremiah 30:17). I know that You love her with everlasting love. May she be like a tree firmly planted by streams of water that yields fruit. May she prosper even in these days (Psalm 1:3).

May this scary event draw _____ and her family closer to You, rather than wedging You apart. Reveal Your abundant lovingkindness to each member of her family (Jeremiah 31:3). Deepen _____'s trust in Your guiding hand that she may walk toward You on a straight path without stumbling (Jeremiah 31:9). Remember that those who love Your law have great peace, and nothing causes them to stumble (Psalms 119:165). May this be true of her. Be her peace, Jesus (Ephesians 2:14). In Your name, I pray. Amen.

◆ ◆ ◆

Day 7

Holy Father,

Thank You for being a Lord near to all who call upon You in truth (Psalm 145:18). How very fortunate I am to believe in Immanuel, the God who is not only near but has set up residence within me (Deuteronomy 4:7; John 1:14). When we cry to You, You send from on high, snatch us out of the deep waters, and rescue us onto a broad, spacious place (2 Samuel 22:18–20). All of this just because You actually delight in us (2 Samuel 22:8). Amazing!

As I ponder on who You are, I come before You on behalf of _____ and his family. Since You have promised to be an ever-present Help in trouble (Psalm 46:1), this would be a great time to reveal Yourself as their support. Be their Rock of Strength as they wait on You (Psalm 31:2). May this situation result in their knowing You personally as the Lord, their healer (Exodus 15:26). We ask that You touch (*site of injury*) with Your hand to mend and restore (Job 5:18).

While You are healing the wound, we pray that You would heal his family's fear and broken heart (Psalm 147:3). This tragedy has caused them great grief. Their soul has almost despaired within their hearts (Psalm 42:6). It seems that what they feared came upon them and what they dreaded happened (Job 3:25). Even though they are now walking through the valley of this shadow right now, I ask that You reveal how very near You are (Psalm 23:4). Your nearness can only mean good to them (Psalm 78:23). Grant us additional faith so that we will not fear evil tidings but instead trust You diligently (Psalm 112:8). Heal, so that many can rejoice in the abundant peace and security You provide (Jeremiah 33:6).

Remind me of any fleshliness within me that You need to address in me so that I can pray with effective fervency (James 5:16). Hear and heal not for our glory but according to Your own lovingkindness and truth (Psalm 115:1). In Jesus's name, amen.

◆ ◆ ◆

Day 8

Holy Father,

We read that You are our Light and our Salvation, but honestly, with _____'s diagnosis of _____, we think of much to fear (Psalm 27:1). Yet You have always been the defense of our lives. So indeed, whom shall we dread?

The evil one desires to sift _____ and his family through this. As part of Your body, I join my heart in prayer to block Satan's wishes. I'm sure that it seems like a host has encamped against them, yet in tandem with other intercessors, we ask that their heart not fear. Reveal how much bigger Your forces are than those of the evil one (2 Kings 6:16–17). Despite the warfare against them, allow their confidence to remain steadfast in You (Psalm 27:3).

(When the patient is a Christian)

As we come before You on his behalf, we ask this one thing from You: that each day, as You fight this disease for him, _____ would rest, beholding Your beauty. Thank You for choosing him and promising not to withhold anything good (Psalm 84:11). May his thoughts dwell on the fact that he is a temple of the Holy Spirit, not a residence of disease (Psalm 27:4). Thank You for being especially attracted to those who suffer (Psalm 34:18) and being very near those who walk through the shadow of death (Psalm 23:4).

(Whether or not the patient is a Christian)

Whether this family sleeps, drives, eats, or visits medical personnel, I ask that their eyes see You. Magnetically draw this family to Yourself, concealing them in Your tabernacle and hiding them in the secret place of Your abode. Draw their entire family to You, their rock (Psalm 27:5). I pray that as they walk through these days, especially the (*chemo, surgery, radiation*), You will lift each head above the enemy, not giving the evil one any say in this matter. May the praises of the small victories eject Satan from this situation with power (Psalm 27:6).

Hear my voice as I cry out on _____'s behalf. Be gracious and answer (Psalm 27:7). You have instructed us to seek Your face, and so I'm answering the call (Psalm 27:8). Don't abandon the prayers offered up on his behalf (Psalm 27:9). I know Your character, Father. You do not desire the enemy to have any foothold. Yet, intense times like these are bound to cause fear. The evil one only wishes to kill, steal, and destroy (Psalm 27:12; John 10:10). Overpower him, in Jesus's name.

This disease has made _____'s spiritual foes evident. Teach _____ Your way and lead him on a level path (Psalm 27:11). Don't deliver him over to the despair of this disease, but give him the strength to wait on You (Psalm 27:12–14). Yes, may _____ wait on You and find his heart taking courage. This is our cry. Expectantly, we wait for You to heal (Psalm 27:14). In Jesus's name, amen.

Day 9

Holy Father,

This health journey has sure been a long haul for (*patient*). She has been through so much sifting. First, she had the pitchfork of learning the news, which involved an emotional toss into the air with a hard landing when she discovered the worst. The evil one demanded permission to sift and still seems to do so (Luke 22:32). Had it been me, I think that my flesh and my heart would have failed by now. Thank You that no matter how she has reacted day by day to the strain, You continue to be the strength of her heart (Psalm 73:26).

I'm not sure why endurance is so important to You, but You do testify that each of us needs it (Hebrews 10:36). By this very endurance, we gain mastery over our wavering minds and emotions (Luke 21:19). Knowing this, I come into Your Presence asking that You grant (*patient*) two specific items in spirit: a daily, overwhelming realization of Your love and the very endurance of Your Son (2 Thessalonians 3:5). She is not of "those who shrink back" but has faith in the preservation of her soul (Hebrews 10:39). Thank You that her practice over the years prepared her for such a time as this (Esther 4:14).

Sustain (*patient*) on her sickbed and restore her to health (Psalm 41:3). As You do this, we continue to corporately pant for You just like a deer in need of refreshing water (Psalm 42:1). As we all hope in You, may we arrive at the day that we can praise You in (*patient's*) situation, knowing that the help of Your Presence has proved mighty (Psalm 42:5). In Jesus's name, amen.

◆ ◆ ◆

Day 10

Dear Father,

I come before You on _____'s behalf. Thank You that because of Christ, I can come before You boldly, with the righteousness of Your Son covering me as I enter (Hebrews 10:19). I thank You that You daily remind me of my weakness so that I have lots of practice crying out before You. I am convinced that You alone deliver (2 Samuel 22:2–3).

The news of this (*tumor, lesion, lump*) is indeed scary, as we perceive it in our flesh. We have watched many others endure just such an illness and know the pain that it can cause. Thank You that _____ does not have to face this on her own. Thank You for Your promise that if we cast all our anxieties upon You, You will bear them (Psalm 55:22). Your yoke is easy, and Your burden is light (Matthew 11:30), so we ask that _____ will live to tell of Your works for years to come (Psalm 118:17).

You desire that we see You with increasing clarity, so our relationship with You may deepen. I take this crisis as an opportunity to see You in Your fullness. May this revelation be not only for me, O Lord but also for _____.

In my frequent prayers for her, I have continued to ask that You reveal Yourself (1 Corinthians 2:9). Deliver her from the anxiety she feels as she looks at the situation surrounding her (Psalm 94:19). May she see Your deliverance (Exodus 14:13). Rescue her as You perform signs and wonders, both in heaven and on earth, on her behalf (Daniel 6:26). May she have the eyes of her heart opened to know the things You have already freely given her to use for Your glory and her benefit (1 Corinthians 2:12). Teach her how to ask purely and simply for everything she needs while always increasing her faith (Luke 11:1). Open Your Word to her so that You are her joy and delight (Jeremiah 15:16). May her faith rest in dependence on Your truth, the final reality, not upon the weakness of her ability.

Just as she daily prays to be a blessing, may she see those blessings provided to her through Christ Jesus (Ephesians 1:3). May she be a blessing to the medical personnel ministering to her and a conduit of the benefit that You are pouring out through her (1 Peter 3:9, Romans 5:5).

Hear our prayer, O Lord, because You are our Father. See and hear. I pray these things, not because of my merit, Lord, but because of Your great compassion (Daniel 9:18). In Jesus's name, I pray. Amen.

◆ ◆ ◆

Day 11

Father,

No matter how far we travel into Your depths, we realize that Your path will always include lessons on steadfastness and endurance (2 Thessalonians

3:5; Hebrews 10:36). Yes, You lead us beside quiet waters and trails of righteousness, but those can lead directly into the valley of the shadow of death (Psalm 23:3–4). Even knowing this causes our hearts to fear immediately, but You know our weakness and encourage us to be anxious for nothing because You are near (Philippians 4:5–6). We don't have to fear evil because You are with us (Psalm 23:4).

How amazing it is to know that Your nearness is closer even than the shepherd David knew. You've now set up Your very residence within us (John 1:14; Luke 17:21). As _____ adjusts to his new normal, I ask that You give him a fresh revelation of Your Holy Spirit (Luke 10:13). Every single day, may he be satisfied with Your likeness when he awakes (Psalm 17:15). Indeed, what he sees with his physical eyes cannot satisfy (Proverbs 27:20), but having a vital, living glimpse of You is genuinely all that he needs (Psalm 23:1). Seeing You transforms us from the inside out (1 John 3:2).

Just as radiation worked from within, I ask that Your bright illumination would heal _____ from the inside out. Spill over from his spirit into his mind and emotions, and then overflow into each bodily organ. You are the God of life (1 John 1:4). Refresh _____ with Your life as he waits in Your Presence (Acts 3:19). Indeed, the mountain of this health problem can't help but melt like wax when exposed to Your splendor (Psalm 97:5). "Light is sown like seed for the righteous, and gladness for the upright in heart" (Psalm 97:11). May light continue to manifest itself as reality in _____'s life. I claim this in the name of Your Son. Amen.

◆ ◆ ◆

Day 12

Holy Father,

I wait in silence for You alone because I know You are the only One who can provide salvation (Psalm 62:1). Praise You for being our Rock and our Stronghold. As I come before You on _____'s behalf, I reach my weak hands up and find that Your Spirit lays hold of my hands and directs them with Your very own powerful prayers (Romans 8:26).

Thank You for being a very present Help in times of trouble—not a far off-help who is hard to contact (Psalm 46:1). As I cling to You and You cling to me, settle the _____ family's shaky nerves and refresh their souls (Psalm 62:2).

I come to pick up the abundant rest You have promised. You said that anyone weary could come for it, so I'd like to add my spiritual back to the multitude of others who are bringing rest down from the heavenlies for _____ (Matthew 11:28). Reveal to them how best to "stand by the ways and see and ask for the ancient paths where the good way is." There is where their rest is found (Jeremiah 6:16). I'm asking that just as You heal their emotions and minds (souls), You would do so with _____'s body. Return him to optimum health (3 John 2).

We praise You that (*any good news*). This is indeed an answer to many desperate prayers on _____'s behalf. We do not assume that this is a medical fix but a direct result of Your healing hand. Thank You.

May this family know Your Presence, which melts the mountains of impossibilities like wax (Psalm 97:5). I'm glad that power belongs to You, O Lord (Psalm 62:11). Accomplish each detail that concerns them (Psalm 138:8) and save them with Your amazing right hand (Psalm 138:7). We wait upon You. In Jesus's name. Amen.

◆ ◆ ◆

Day 13

Holy Father,

We confess that we do not know how to pray as we ought. Yet we do understand that Your Spirit stands ready in times like these to grab our outstretched hands of weakness with His hands of strength (Romans 8:26). Reveal Your great promises that we might claim them on behalf of the _____ family.

You promised that Your Presence would go with us and give us rest (Exodus 33:14). How badly they need not only Your rest but a moment-by-moment glimpse of Your face. You say that there is "a place by You" where we can stand protected and wait (Exodus 33:21). I ask that You tuck _____ into that special cleft of the rock and cover her with Your hand (Exodus 33:22).

We know that the Spirit has formed _____, and it is Your breath that gives her life (Job 33:4). Grant her healing that she may live vitally among those she loves. Restore health and heal her wounds by Your great power (Jeremiah 30:17). As You release resources from the heavenlies, I ask that You give strength to both her and her family; invade every fiber of their being with peace (Psalm 29:11).

(For a Christian friend)

You are her life (Colossians 3:4), and Your life is her light (John 1:4).

There are going to be days that her heart and her strength will fail (Psalm 73:26). Thank You that our power is not the measure of success. We rely upon Your strength as she waits upon You (Psalm 27:14). May Your nearness be the best part of her day (Psalm 73:28). Thank You for being near to the brokenhearted and for saving those crushed in spirit (Psalm 34:18). I claim this for her family as well.

As they walk through the multitude of doctors' offices and medical procedures, I ask that their ears will hear Your Word spoken softly into their ears, showing them whether they should walk to the right or the left (Isaiah 30:21). I claim that You will surely be gracious to them the minute You hear their cry (Isaiah 30:19). May they tarry daily before You until clothed with Your power (Luke 24:49).

Show us all Your glory as we wait on You (2 Kings 6:17). We ask this in Jesus's name, amen.

Joy

Day 1

Holy Jesus,

When I received You as my Savior, You gave me the gift of joy. Thank You. Your divine package deal of salvation included spiritual gifts. Although the Kingdom of God consists of righteousness, peace, and joy in the Holy Spirit (Romans 14:17), I confess to You that I don't often access Your rejoicing.

Even though I am skin, bone, and blood, You are Spirit (John 4:24), consisting of love, joy, and peace (Galatians 5:22–23). Joy is as much a part of You as muscles are a part of me. And now I discover that You prayed for me to have Your joy to its fullness (John 15:11, 17:13).

So today, I do not say, "Give me joy." I know this gift has been mine since You became my Lord. Wedges of joy and slices of peace aren't doled out cafeteria-style in Your Kingdom. All joy, peace, patience, and kindness are found only and always inside You. Open my eyes to live Your life so that I may know Your joy.

You repeat the same theme in the parable of the lost sheep, the lost coin, and the lost son. The return of the wayward brings You joy (Luke 15). Teach me how to lead every unruly emotion under submission to You. May I experience Your joy as I capture every thought in Your name (2 Corinthians 10:5).

You said, "These things I have spoken to you, that My joy may be in you and that your joy may be made full" (John 15:11). The emphasis is on divine joy, not natural joy. I often want happiness for my benefit. I want my feelings to be paramount. Yet, to truly have Your joy, I must focus on Your passions, not upon my desires (John 15:8). No wonder I so often ask for blessing and don't receive it. I am asking because I want to be personally happy rather than glorifying You (James 4:3)! Forgive me, Lord.

You love it when believers are united in the same heart and mind (Philippians 2:2). As the Father surges within You, You energize us, setting off another rush of rejoicing in Your heart. May I unite myself with those abiding in You so that we may all rejoice. Grant us the faith to live Your life rather than our own. May it be, O Lord. May it be.

———————◆ ◆ ◆———————

Day 2

Holy Father,

I remain amazed at the way You desire my communication. You never get weary or tired, even when I come to You with the same requests day after day, month after month, year after year (Isaiah 40:28). Because You are the Holy One who hears, I come before You again today, lifting (*this situation*—Psalm 65:2). Thank You for receiving my prayer (Psalm 6:9).

Praise Your name for being the sacred One who is clean through and through (Psalm 22:3). As I boast of Your holiness and righteousness, I find that You inhabit and move Your belongings into my praise (Psalm 22:3). When I celebrate Your fame, You come near to that place of light and sit in my very midst (Psalm 22:3). Indeed, when I began to sing and praise, You set up ambushes against Your enemies (2 Chronicles 20:22). So I sing of Your amazing life, asking that You replace the evil one's plans for defeat with Your purpose for holiness.

When a strong man, fully armed, guards his own house, his possessions are undisturbed (Luke 11:21). But, Lord, that strong man of melancholy has kept me in bondage long enough. I beg You, the Triumphant Victor, to fight for me while I remain silently seeking Your face (Exodus 14:14).

A grand triumph march has already taken place in the heavenlies (2 Corinthians 2:14). In a majestic procession, You have paraded Your defeated foe for all spiritual eyes to see, hear, and smell the victory. Knowledge of Christ has a sweet fragrance. Open my spiritual senses to recognize Your noisy and tumultuous procession.

Show me the rich spoils and the defeated captives that You bring under submission. These demonic captives like (*despair, fear, hopelessness, etc.*) are bound and gagged by Your death on the cross. Thank You that the victory is already mine in Christ Jesus! Death is no longer master over You or those who live in You (Romans 6:9). You granted me rescue from the hand of my enemies because You desire I serve You without fear (Luke 1:74). Thank You that although I am sometimes perplexed, I do not have to sink into despair (2 Corinthians 4:8).

May I not focus on my foes during this procession but onto You, the Exalted Christ. Your entrance completes this glorious parade. Praise You that Your victory is not against flesh and blood but the rulers, against the powers, against the world forces of this darkness, against the spiritual forces of wickedness in the heavenly places (Ephesians 6:12).

At times, I feel as if I am put to death all day long. But truth is not in my feelings; reality is in You, the Conqueror. "In all these things, we overwhelmingly conquer through Him who loved us!" (Romans 8:37). May I live today in Your victory. In Jesus's name, amen.

Day 3

Father,

Thank You for being the God of all flesh, even mine! Indeed, is anything too hard for You (Jeremiah 32:27)? Praise You for being the God who goes with me without ever failing or forsaking me (Deuteronomy 31:6). I find myself once again in a situation in which I need a reminder of Your everlasting love.

Every time I pray, I find that I don't know how to pray. Intercede for me with groaning too deep for words, according to the will of God for my life (Romans 8:26–27). How You can work for good even amid difficulty is beyond me but thankfully not beyond Your ability (Romans 8:28). Thank You that Your dealings are not because of my works but because You are the One who chooses and calls out (Romans 9:11).

Have mercy upon me. Call me out of fear and joylessness for honorable use (Romans 9:16, 21). You specifically choose the weakest things to show forth Your power, so reveal the sanctification that You have prepared for me (1 Corinthians 1:28; 1 Thessalonians 4:3). You came to destroy the works that the evil one would try to accomplish for my destruction (1 John 3:8), so I purposely side with You, believing that You are stronger than the tactics that the evil one uses against me.

You are the God of all Comfort and the Father of Mercy (2 Corinthians 1:3), so I ask that You reveal these characteristics afresh to me. As the God of hope who fills Your children with joy and peace in believing (Romans 15:13), I ask that You show me this side of Your character as I have never experienced before. Since everyone who believes is free from all things (Acts 13:39), free me from these negative, swirling thoughts. Reveal Yourself as the God who is and does. Act on my behalf as I wait for You to do so (Isaiah 64:4). In Jesus's name, amen.

◆ ◆ ◆

Day 4

Holy Father,

I praise You for being near to all who call upon You and saving those who cry to You (Psalm 145:18–19). No matter where I am or what I am doing, You are available to me if I come in humility. Thank You for never despising the prayer of the destitute (Psalm 102:17).

I confess that I feel needy because of (*describe situation* - Isaiah 41:17). Sometimes my spiritual tongue is quite parched. This is not a new feeling, for even the psalmist David confessed that his spirit felt overwhelmed (Psalm 142:3). It seems there is no way out and no escape for my soul (Psalm 142:4).

But, Father, You are the God who sees (Genesis 16:13). You specialize in finding the hopeless ones in the wilderness (Genesis 16:7). You knew that I would feel this way and promised to answer and not forsake me (Isaiah 41:17). I ask that You open rivers and springs in the places where I am dry (Isaiah 41:18).

It's time, Lord. It's time for the fountain of life to begin gushing forth from within me (John 7:38). You promised to satisfy the weary ones and refresh those who languish (Jeremiah 31:25). Release this surge in me.

I realize that spiritual winters have great value in our souls. Just as a tree's icy dormancy extends the tree's life, my spiritual winter is actively stimulating my growth. Although I feel dead inside, Your sap is still vigorously at work there (John 5:17). You always see life within me even when I'm barren of foliage. Grant me patient endurance during this winter season so that You may have Your perfect work (James 1:4).

Give me hope and joy for my pending spring, when warmth will shine upon me after this period of wintery cold. Despite how things look, may I faithe the immanent time of refreshing that You promise from Your Presence, Lord (Acts 3:19). As I wait, remind me to find time for Your Presence to see You again. Even the winter sees the sun. You are my fulness of joy (Psalm 16:11). Saturate me. In Jesus's name, amen.

Loss

Grief

Holy Father,

Among Your many names, we find ones like Wonderful Counselor, Prince of Peace, and God of all Comfort (Isaiah 9:6; 2 Corinthians 1:3). No wonder we run immediately to You when we grieve. We understand so little in life and death, yet when we look to You, we know that You are higher than it all. Thank You that Your thoughts and ways are higher than ours. Otherwise, our hope would indeed be small (Isaiah 55:8–9).

Show us Your great compassion, Lord, for our hurt is real. Give our family a fresh sense of Your Spirit, not only for instruction but for our nourishment in these coming days without (*name of loved one*) (Nehemiah 9:19–20).

In the moments when grief overwhelms us because of a scent or a song or a sound, I ask that Your Presence be real to hold us close. Through our tears, give us a glimpse into the heavenlies and reveal Yourself as the God of all Comfort (2 Corinthians 1:3–4). Despite our pain, may we sink into Your Presence and experience Your rest (Matthew 11:28; Hebrews 4:9).

I ask that every time we read or remember Your Word, You will revive our grieving hearts (Psalm 119:50). You promised that You would be near to the brokenhearted and save those who are crushed in spirit (Psalm 34:18). We all qualify. Thank You for giving us friends to pray for us and touch us often during this time.

Overwhelm our family with Your peace. May this be a time in which we all see You more clearly. For the family members who do not yet believe in Your view of eternity, grant Christians nearby to speak with Your own Words of clarity and hope. Thank You for blessing our lives with this amazing (*mother, wife, and friend*). (*If the individual was a Christian*): Thank You that (*name of loved one*) is now experiencing profound rest and exquisite joy, no longer relying on faithing through a glass darkly but now seeing You stand clearly before her. We, too, long for the day. In Jesus's name, amen.

Grief, Loss of Godly Christian

Holy Father,

You have recently had a great homecoming. Not only did angels rejoice, You and Your Son awaited _____ with open arms. As she walked into Your Presence, glory met glory (2 Corinthians 3:18). This was the purpose of her life. She no longer has to see through the glass darkly, but she now sees You face-to-face (1 Corinthians 13:12).

Your Word says that the death of Your godly ones is very precious to You (Psalm 116:15). I know that this was especially true of _____. She was a rare combination of the set-apart servant and unpretentious student of her Master. She touched many lives by giving them an example of just what kind of Savior You are. _____ grappled with Your Word and exemplified Your insights with simplicity and candor. Even in her visits to receive treatment, she testified of you and encouraged all she touched.

Lord, I pray for the family _____ left behind. As they walk through this dark valley of grief, I ask that You be close beside them, guiding and guarding every step of the way (Psalm 23:4). Because You are the God that promises comfort, have compassion upon them in their sorrow (Isaiah 51:12). Revive their grieving hearts through Your Word, whether in a song or a card (Psalm 119:50). Be near to their broken hearts and renew their crushed spirits (Psalm 34:18). Bring many around them to cry with them in their grief.

I especially ask this for (*close family member*), as no (*mother, husband, wife, child*) expects to be in this place of pain. Thank You that You will never leave her or forsake her (Hebrews 13:5). She needs Your comforting arms and voice in the coming days. I call upon Your faithfulness and know You won't disappoint (2 Timothy 2:13). In Jesus's name, amen.

Grief, Intercession for Loss of Mate

Holy Father,

Thank You so much for being a God that we can call upon when we are in distress (Psalm 91:15). Because You promise to answer when we call, I am coming to You now on _____'s behalf (Psalm 91:14). As she grieves, I ask You to allow me to share her sorrow (Galatians 6:2). Thank You for the wealth of memories that _____ has regarding her (*husband*). You gave them beautiful years together, and all too soon, it is his time to rest. What a relief it is to know he is free from pain.

Although we know that this death is precious to You (Psalm 116:15), it doesn't make it easy for those he left behind. When a wife loses her husband, she feels entirely abandoned. But You've promised Your comfort, something that I am now asking You to bestow upon (*name*) (2 Corinthians 1:4). You are indeed the God of all Comfort (2 Corinthians 1:3), but we don't know the depth of that comfort until we grieve deeply. Like water, comfort always seeks deep emptiness. Thank You that in _____'s lack, You are abundance, and in her dire weakness, You manifest Your strength (2 Corinthians 12:9).

I ask that _____ experientially come to know what it means to collapse into Your arms. As a result, direct the essence of Your power into her heart (2 Corinthians 13:4). Take care of her future without (*name of deceased*) while she waits on You (Psalm 62:5). Fill every broken place with Your fulness (Ephesians 3:19).

May _____ and I both come to value Your lovingkindness as better than life itself, even the life of our dear husbands (Psalm 63:3). In Jesus's name, amen.

◆ ◆ ◆

Grief, Intercession for Loss of Pet

Holy Father,

Thank You for caring about every detail of our lives, even the small ones (1 Peter 5:7; Psalm 37:23 NLT). You said we could pour out our hearts before You because You are a refuge against all storms (Psalm 62:8).

Lean Your ear over and listen to _____, as she cries out to You in a storm of sadness (Psalm 86:1). Take the emotions running through her soul and intentionally lead her to a quiet place (Psalm 23:2). Replace her thoughts of grief with comfort, for after all, You are the God of all Comfort (2 Corinthians 1:3). You promised to comfort us so that we can in turn comfort those in the same affliction (2 Corinthians 1:4). I ask that this would be true for _____.

Your brilliance often becomes brighter and more apparent through the tears. Allow her to see Your face through the grief. Thank You for being near to the brokenhearted and saving those who are crushed in spirit (Psalm 34:18). I believe You will do this for her. In Jesus's name, amen.

Intercession on Behalf of Tragedy

Wow, Lord … how do we begin to pray for this situation? Simple answers aren't adequate.

You said that if any of us lack wisdom, we can ask You to grant it to us. I especially ask that for (*family of victim*) (James 1:5). I pray that You bind further acts of the evil one, destroying all his intentions upon this family (1 John 3:8). Comfort them by implanting Your Word into their hearts, to cleanse and heal their emotions and minds despite this tragedy (James 1:21).

As Christians come alongside to minister to the family, may all prove to be doers of the Word during this time, not just mouthpieces (James 1:22). True religion is when we visit those in distress. We must not shy away just because we don't know what to say (James 1:27). Allow our faith to be made evident through the works You prompt us to do (James 2:18). May we look into the heavenlies to see just what it is that You are moving Your hand to do for this family (John 5:19).

Despite the pain, lift this family's chin gently so they may see how much You care by looking into Your eyes (John 6:5; 1 Peter 5:7). Grant them a tender glimpse of the eternal things above, where Christ is, and comfort by becoming their very life (Colossians 3:1,4). May they not become weak in faith as they contemplate their frailty toward what to do (Romans 4:19) but instead grow strong in faith, knowing that what You have promised is available. You can perform (Romans 4:21).

Remind them daily that Your Spirit is bearing witness with their Spirit in the same way Your Spirit is also praying when they cannot (Romans 8:16,26). Thank You for listening as Your Son sits on Your right hand and intercedes for them (Romans 8:34). We trust in You. Help our unbelief (Mark 9:24). In Jesus's name, amen.

Hospice

Holy Father,

Thank You that Your Word is forever settled in heaven (Psalm 119:89). We know that even as we pray for _____, You and Jesus have already been discussing his case (Hebrews 7:25). Direct us to speak forth that which is already being done in heaven for him, so that You may loose into his life what You deem the very best (Matthew 18:18). May Christ be sanctified as Lord in his heart so that he can testify about the hope within him (1 Peter 3:15).

During this time of suffering, may he rest in the will of God (1 Peter 4:1). I do not want to hold him back in my prayers from the glory You have prepared for him in the heavenlies, but I do ask You to make the transition gentle. Be it done according to Your Word (Luke 1:38).

Thank You that Your victory swallowed up death (1 Corinthians 15:54). The whole sting of death is sin, so we praise You for taking care of _____ 's sin problem through the obedient life of Your Son (1 Corinthians 15:26; Romans 5:19). No matter what _____ has done since receiving You as His life, it's Your life now written in his accounting book.

The law (doing stuff for You) never makes a person perfect (Hebrews 10:1), so You changed the law (Hebrews 7:12). Hallelujah! _____ is now no longer under the law of sin and death. He is under the law of the Spirit of life in Christ Jesus (Romans 8:2). His body is groaning and suffering right now because he is ready for full redemption (Romans 8:23).

I daresay that he is also eagerly awaiting the day in which he will meet You face-to-face. On that day, his perishable body will become imperishable.

On that day, his fleshly body will become a spiritual body. On that day, his weak body will become one of power (1 Corinthians 15:42–44). O Lord, make this pathway smooth and the timing perfect. Thank You, God, who gives us all this hope of victory as we trust in the Lord Jesus Christ (1 Corinthians 15:58). Give _____ that foretaste of glory divine. In Jesus's name, amen.

Anniversary of Death

Holy Father,

Thank You for understanding even when I do not (Psalm 147:5). I come to You on behalf of this precious family that has so much grief to bear. Hear my cry, O God, and give heed to my prayer, although I don't know what to say (Psalm 61:1).

I know _____'s heart is faint. Lead her to the rock that is higher than everything within and around her (Psalm 61:2). You have been a refuge to me many times, and so I call on You to be a tower of strength for her as well (Psalm 61:3). May this anniversary be a time of refuge for the family, where they tuck underneath the tent of Your Presence. Reveal Yourself mightily, so they can huddle underneath Your soft, sheltering, and comforting wings (Psalm 61:4).

Our souls wait in silence for You because You are our only hope for salvation (Psalm 62:1). How long will the questions and difficulties continue, O Lord (Psalm 62:3)? Once again, we firmly say that we will wait in silence for You. Be the rock of their strength (Psalm 62:5, 7). As they pour out their hearts before you in remembrance, be their refuge (Psalm 62:8). Power belongs to You, Father. Use Your mighty power to heal their precious hearts (Psalm 62:11). In Jesus's name, amen.

Love

Day 1

Holy Father,

Thank You for embodying the complete character of love (1 John 4:16). Amid this crazy society, we need desperately to see past the present and gaze into the eternal. As I remember Your everlasting Presence today, reveal the unsearchable qualities of Your love.

* You are patient with me (1 Corinthians 13:4). You wait as I dawdle. You guide me as I hesitate. You carefully urge me along without exasperation over my immaturity (Ephesians 6:4). As I interact with others, may Your patience flow from me to them.

* You are kind to me (1 Corinthians 13:4). You act benevolently, always offering Yourself to me as an ever-present help in times of need (Hebrews 4:16). You comfort me when I hurt (2 Corinthians 1:3). You rejoice when I faith (Zephaniah 3:17). Your kindness always draws me back to You (Romans 2:4). As I communicate with others, may Your understanding extend through me to them.

* You do not boil over with envy, hatred, or jealousy toward me (1 Corinthians 13:4). Your disappointment with me ended when I faithed You (Hebrews 10:17). That is all You expected. You knew I couldn't keep the law (James 2:10). So, You changed me from the inside out and exchanged my spirit for Yours (2 Corinthians 5:17). You put Your God-seed within me so that I no longer enjoy sin (1 John 3:9). It's not my nature now. Even when I mess up, Your forgiveness absorbs the action immediately without condemnation (Hebrews 10:14; Romans 8:1). As I interface with others, may Your forgiveness spill over through me into their lives.

* You've done everything for me through Christ, and yet You remain humble about it (1 Corinthians 13:4). You emptied Yourself for me so that I could understand You (Philippians 2:7). You are not puffed up and braggadocios about Your gifts to me, so I can worship without You getting a big head about it. Instead of narcissistically patting Yourself on the back,

You spend Your time building me up (1 Corinthians 8:1). As I engage others, may Your same humility extend to them through me.

* You never act improper (1 Corinthians 13:5). You do what is fitting and appropriate. Often, even that is hidden away from my view (Isaiah 45:15). How unsearchable are Your judgments and unfathomable Your ways (Romans 11:33)! You are far greater than my imagination or limited understanding (Isaiah 55:8–9). As I interact with others, may I appropriately act just as You would.

* You never demand entrance into my life (1 Corinthians 13:5). You stand at the door of my heart and knock. You request access into my mind and emotions rather than barging in (Revelation 3:20). You call me and lead me but never with a heavy hand (John 10:4). Turn my affections into a willingness to obey (Luke 12:36). As I speak to others, may Your gentleness envelop them.

* You are not irritated or provoked with me (1 Corinthians 13:5). This, I honestly cannot understand. I irritate myself! Yet, You—the God of the universe—are not provoked at me. Amazing. You don't despise me and aren't even sharp with me. Any stabs and jabs I detect are from the accuser (Zechariah 3:1). No, You have given me peace with You (Romans 5:1). You don't just love me, but You like me as well. You are okay with me! Hallelujah. As I deal with others, may I accept them as You receive me.

* Now that You have forgiven me, You no longer measure my faults (1 Corinthians 13:5). You closed that account book. You paid my debts, and there is no outstanding balance on any of my accounts (Psalm 103:12)! You can't even remember what my sins were in the first place (Hebrews 8:12)! Yes, Lord, as I identify with others, may I offer them the same forgetfulness of wrongs that You extend to me (John 20:23).

* Since You can't remember my unrighteousness, You spend Your time focusing on Christ's righteousness within me (1 Corinthians 13:6; 2 Corinthians 5:21). Every time virtue wins a skirmish, You are there, cheering me on (Zephaniah 3:17). You congratulate me when I understand a fragment of Your truth. You take a hands-on approach to share my joy. Teach me to rejoice with others just like You do.

*You bear all my weaknesses, believe in my strengths, hope in my future, and endure all of my past. Your Love is perfect, unconditional, and complete (1 John 4:18). I do not have to fear You because You aren't going to punish me. You took care of the penalty for me (1 Corinthians 15:56; Romans 10:4; Hebrews 10:18; Isaiah 53:4–5). Your Love has a breadth, a length, a height, and a depth that cannot be measured (Ephesians 3:18). May I respond by going forth in this messed-up world to share You, my Mysterious Love.

◆ ◆ ◆

Day 2

Holy Father,

Despite the turmoil around us, You stress unity. You desired that we become one just as You are One with the Spirit and the Son (John 17:11, 21). Indeed, Father, this was the commandment that Your Son gave His disciples before going to the cross. "A new commandment I give to you," He said, "that you love one another" (John 13:34, 15:12).

Love. Unity. Faith. These are Your desires. By uniting to others who love You, we open a more significant channel for You to love the world. Agape love is not acting nicer but bathing in Your character and sharing it. Agape love isn't expressed in religious duties but in trusting Your love to reward us as a body. Unity is the litmus test for our love and faith.

"And I will ask the Father, and He will give you another Helper," Your Son said (John 14:16). Yes, if we are to utilize this body fully, we are going to need assistance! You have already sent the Helper. Thank You, Father! He grants truth, life, and Your constant, abiding Presence (John 14:17, 19). With our great Love-Helper within us, we have the availability to reside in love.

When we abide in You, we can keep Your commands to love and believe (John 15:10).

Unity isn't when the church decides to agree with our minds, is it, Father? No, we become united by sharing the same Spirit. Our voices lift with one accord because our source is the same. It's You (Acts 4:24)! Fellowshipping with Your Spirit, rather than trying to fellowship with one another, grants the union of spirit we desire (Philippians 2:1–2). The focus must be heavenward, not human-ward. The simplicity of intent causes a unity of purpose.

But, Father, I know my tendency. My natural inclination wants to supersede Your spiritual thoughts and words by getting my way. I have an opinion regarding the government, the country, and the church. Grant me the humility of mind to fuse with Your purpose (Philippians 2:3). May Your attitude not remain hidden deep within me but overflow into my thoughts, emotions, and actions (Philippians 2:5).

Encapsulate everything in the church that is against knowing You and dissolve it with Your love (2 Corinthians 10:5). Unite our desires with Yours so that what we do and what we want delights You (Philippians 2:13). May union with You erupt into unity with others. Even so, Lord Jesus, come!

Day 3

Holy Father,

Thank You for listening to messy prayers. You promised to go ahead of us so that we would have nothing to fear (Deuteronomy 31:8). I am holding tightly to Your promise that even when I don't know how to pray, Your Spirit within me is interceding for us (Romans 8:26).

You have promised never to fail me or forsake me (Hebrews 13:5), but honestly, I feel very alone. I need You, the God of all Comfort, to be my strength in this lonely time (2 Corinthians 1:3). I realize that my emptiness may need more than a human relationship, so I am coming to You today asking that You grant me more than I can imagine (Ephesians 3:20). More than asking You to take away my heartache, I ask that You open my eyes to see You.

You are the God of all Comfort (2 Corinthians 1:3). In Greek, *comfort* sources in the root word *paraklesis*—a form of which (*parakletos*) describes

Your Holy Spirit (John 14:26). Comfort, solace, and encouragement are in Your very nature, but somehow I can't sense You now. Come near to refresh me and grant me a new perspective (Acts 3:19). You say that the Holy Spirit is the very best gift of all (Luke 11:13). Reveal Him to me as a Person. Pour out Your encouragement as I seek Him in Your Word, so I too may have hope (Romans 15:4–5).

You, O Lord, have given, and You have taken away. Even in this, I will bless Your name (Job 1:21). Thank You that I can trust You even when I cannot understand You. Increase my faith and give me understanding that I might know You fully (Luke 17:5; 1 John 5:20). In Jesus's name, amen.

Day 4

Holy Father,

As I come before You today, I stand awestruck by Your love. You loved me before I began loving You (1 John 4:19). Not because I was lovable but just because that's how You are (1 John 3:16). Now You encourage me to love in that same way (1 John 4:11). Unfortunately, I have someone in my life who is difficult to love.

I realize that You demonstrated true love by laying down Your life (Romans 5:8). When You sent Your Son, He served, rather than expecting service (Mark 10:45). You stress to me repeatedly that Your Love is patient, kind, undemanding, and not easily provoked (1 Corinthians 13:4–5). But when I look within my heart, I don't want to serve with patience. I'm irritated by the slightest offense.

So here I am, standing before You today, asking You to expand my thoughts and emotions into a deeper, broader, wider, and higher kind of love (Ephesians 3:18). I am in desperate need of You to renew my mind (Ephesians 4:23). To truly be Your disciple, Love must change me (John 13:34–35).

From the perspective of the flesh, this is hopeless. But deep within, I know that You are working (John 5:17). The request for more love is one You will hear (1 John 5:14–15). So, here it is: open my eyes to see this difficult one as You see them. May they become very dear to me so that a spiritual affection flows from me to them (1 Thessalonians 2:8). Complete Yourself within me, taking every natural thought hostage in the process (2 Corinthians 10:5). I sign this request in the name and with the blood of Jesus. Amen.

Day 5

Father,

I will praise You no matter what (Psalm 34:1 TLB). Despite the clouds that are quite evident to our eyes, You reign supreme and glorious in the heavenlies. You have seen difficulties like this through the ages and remain as faithful as ever. Thank You for being more substantial than all our troubles (Jeremiah 32:17).

As I come before You on _____'s behalf, I realize that before we can pour out our hearts, You must tip us over (1 Samuel 1:15). If everything remains settled inside of our souls, then like water, we become stagnant. When we lean Your way, all our anxieties spill out, and You absorb them. I guess that is why we are so often overwhelmed by our weaknesses. Frailty makes it that much easier to fall into Your arms.

I am greatly encouraged to remember that Your love, like water, descends into our valleys. When Your Spirit entered us, Your love followed as well (Romans 5.5). My lowest days actually attract Your highest good. Hallelujah.

As we make decisions and interface with difficulties, remind us to tip in Your direction, allowing intimacy with You to replace our tension. Grant us wisdom to rest in You for each situation and serve You with gladness (Psalm 100:2). I appreciate You and like who You are.

This work order is signed in the name of Jesus. Amen.

Marriage

Day 1

Dear Father,

Thank You that You are exceedingly more powerful than the evil one (John 10:29). In fact, the only power the devil has over us is when we believe the lies that he tells us. We are sick of living with the (*fill in your fear, anxiety, or issue*). He is lying when he says that we will never be free. We're ready to step into the light so that we can be free of this darkness, Lord (John 3:21).

You promised to deliver us from the hand of the enemy. We are ready to begin living in that freedom (Luke 1:74). We claim that promise and know that You are faithful to deliver us. After all, Your name is at stake here.

We more easily resist someone who angers us, so grant us a wave of holy anger against the devil's deceit. For too long, we've lived with only a mild annoyance toward his deeds. Encourage us that, through You, we have the power to stand up to him in Your name (Acts 13:9–10). We want to draw a line in the sand to say that we will serve You, O Lord (Joshua 24:15). You are our deliverance. Now begin untangling our feet from this net (Psalm 31:4).

Make it a habit to fill us daily with Your mighty, gushing, outpouring love (Isaiah 44:3). May we be a couple who refuses to dwell upon our idiosyncrasies. Instead, may we always seek spiritual thoughts of life and peace (Romans 8:6).

We admit that honestly, nothing good dwells within our flesh (Romans 7:18). I know that about myself, but often I want my mate to think differently. Allow us both to rest within You, realizing that since You aren't blaming us, we are free to live without condemnation inside our home (Romans 8:1).

Open our eyes to see the reality of where we really live—alongside You in the heavenlies (Ephesians 2:6). Not a someday fantasy but a present actuality. Grant that we become people who live by the faith of that statement and not the look of our situation (2 Corinthians 5:7). No matter where You take us in life, may our sight always be on that city whose architect and builder is God (Hebrews 11:10). Even so, Lord Jesus, come! We pray these things by the authority that Jesus gave to us as His children. Amen (Matthew 28:18; 16:19).

◆ ◆ ◆

Day 2

Holy Father,

I'm so glad that You use words to change me from the inside out. Hearing that I am precious in Your sight means so much to me. I love knowing that I am honored and that You love me (Isaiah 43:4). Sometimes You exult over me with joy; sometimes You rejoice over me with a shout; then sometimes You are just quiet in Your love (Zephaniah 3:17). No matter the situation, I like knowing that You are verbal with Your love to me. Thanks.

You would think that I could effortlessly lavish love upon my mate, but it's not always so. Show me how to be angry without sinning so that the devil will never have an opportunity to get to my spouse through me (Ephesians 4:26–27). I pray that no unwholesome word would come out of my mouth but that every word I utter would be suitable for strengthening my mate (Ephesians 4:29). Cleanse all bitterness and anger away so that I will not bring it into our relationship. Instead, make me kind and tenderhearted—someone who has the character of forgiveness, just like You do (Ephesians 4:31–32). I pray that while others may be cutting down their spouses, we can be a couple who finds a way to give thanks instead (Ephesians 5:4).

Allow us to walk into our future together as children of light, not only to learn about one another but especially learning what pleases You (Ephesians 5:8–10). Fill us with Your Spirit, Lord, so that we can daily speak to each other with psalms, hymns, and spiritual songs. May our hearts always be filled with a melody that praises You (Ephesians 5:18–19). In Jesus's name, amen.

Day 3

Holy Father,

Thank You for revealing the value and power of the spoken word. With a word, You spoke both light and life into existence (Genesis 1:26-27). With a word, You calmed the stormy sea (Mark 4:39). With a word, You refused temptation (Matthew 16:23). In fact, You haven't just spoken out the word but have revealed Your Son to us as Your very own voice (John 1:1). Teach us to listen intently to what You are saying to us so that we can know what to say to one another.

When we are confused, speak clearly so that our words reflect Your clarity. When we are anxious, speak calmly that our words respond to one another in encouragement. When we are tempted, speak that we cling to one another closely both in word and in deed.

Enlighten the eyes of our hearts to see the roles to which You have called us. We know that You have already made us clean by the Word that You have spoken over our lives (John 15:3).

(Men) Now, as a husband, may my voice spring forth a cleansing fountain that continues what You have begun in my wife. May the world's trash never be allowed to clog her heart. Give me the wisdom to recognize the baggage that has come into our relationship. And give me the delicacy and patience to rinse her gently until she is free from those wounds and fears.

(Ladies) Father, help me to recognize all that he is doing on my behalf and increase my respect for him day by day. Remind me to thank my spouse daily as I recognize You within him.

Teach us to walk together in love so that our lives will reflect the miracle of that love (Ephesians 5:2). In Jesus's name, amen.

Day 4

Holy Father,

I thank You that You are working in us for obedience (1 Peter 1:1–2). We know ourselves, and without You, following Your example is impossible. We really do stumble in many ways. Yet we claim that the power of God protects us through the faith that You have given us (Romans 12:3). Increase our confidence so that we might see how You are saving our marriage (Luke 17:5).

We admit that the source of our quarrels is just our own selfishness (James 4:1). In a single day, we can lift a lofty prayer and then turn around to criticize each other (James 3:9). We ask You to change us from the inside out.

We know that deep within, Your Spirit is within us, crying out, "Glory!" (1 Corinthians 3:16; Psalm 29:9). Come then and overflow our personalities so that we reflect Your characteristics instead of our own (John 4:14). Just as Christ perfectly represented You, we ask that You bring Christ's personality to life within the two of us (Hebrews 1:3). No matter how impossible that may sound to us right now, we claim that You specialize in giving life in barren places (John 5:21).

You have the power to keep us from stumbling (Jude 24). Give us the faith to first believe this and then to watch You do so within our lives. And when we struggle, we ask that You remind us quickly to confess our sins so that You might cleanse us anew. In Jesus's name, amen.

Day 5

Holy Father,

We remain amazed at the way You desire communication. You never get weary or tired, even when we come to You with the same requests day after day (Isiah 40:28). Because You are the Holy One who hears, we come before You again on behalf of our relationship. Thank You for receiving our prayers (Psalm 6:9).

The way You have created us to relate to one another seems almost counterintuitive. Wives influencing without a word and husbands loving without complete understanding? It appears that You challenge us with standards that are too difficult to achieve. Yet, You are our Creator. You know us from the inside out (Psalm 139:3).

Even though the tongue is a tiny part of our bodies, it can do an awful lot of damage (James 3:5–6). We know this by experience. One minute, we speak loving words, and then the next minute, we're lashing out in anger. It's quite a mess.

So, since You know what we are going to say before we do, we ask that You put a buffer in between our thoughts and our expression of them (Psalm 139:4). You called us to be a blessing; now make us sound like one (1 Peter 3:9).

We realize that You created us to speak out what is on our hearts (Matthew 12:34). If we are harboring past pain, eventually, that's what is going to spill out. How distressing to think that the hurt that is bottled inside could explode all over the one we love most.

Heal each of us from past hurts and neutralize the poison. Purify our inner being so that we can no longer hear bitterness, anger, and rejection. Wash us so that we can listen to only joy and gladness (Psalm 51:7–8). We do want to be a blessing to each other. Help me begin to be a blessing to myself.

Teach me personally when to speak and when to be silent. Grant me a tender heart whether I understand my spouse or not. Take this marriage in Your hands and hold it together despite our weaknesses (Colossians 1:17). In Jesus's name, amen.

◆ ◆ ◆

Intercession for Strife-Filled Marriage

Holy Father,

Thank You for being near to all who call upon You in truth. It's comforting to know that You fulfill the desire of those who fear You. I am clinging upon Your promise to hear my cry on behalf of _____ and _____ (Psalms 145:18–19).

You alone intimately understand their backgrounds and want the best for them (Exodus 3:16). Sometimes, they can't even say that about each other, but You desire to bring them through this heartache into a land that flows with milk and honey (Exodus 3:17). Order their steps as You guide their hearts.

Praise You that nothing is too complicated for You (Jeremiah 32:27). Even though the mountains between them loom significant and look insurmountable, You are the God who causes mountains to melt like wax (Psalm 16:11). You said that if we have faith the size of a mustard seed, we can speak to a mountain; "Move from here to there," and it will move (Matthew 17:20). Teach me how to pray that the distance and coldness they are experiencing may melt away.

Dissolve the mountain of emotional separation by the direct intervention of Your hand. I believe that You are faithful, so please guard them against the effects of the evil one (2 Thessalonians 3:3). Block all malicious intent, using their marriage for Your purposes (Genesis 50:20).

Restore the joy of their first love and rekindle their relationship. Grant them time to spend with each other in peaceful reconnection. I will do my part to believe in Your miraculous power. In Jesus's name, I pray. Amen.

◆ ◆ ◆

Intercession for Christian Family

Dear Holy Father,

Thank You for being the One True God and for revealing Yourself as such to us (John 17:3). You gave Your Son, Jesus, authority over all fleshliness (John 17:2), including my selfishness. Forgive me when I act as if I cannot help my sin, as I recognize that You already have authority over all that I am. Hear me as I pray.

Thank You for already accomplishing all that concerns (*husband*) and (*wife*), their (*children*), their (*pets*), their (*jobs*), their marriage, and their future (John 17:4; Psalm 138:8). Open their eyes to see and experience Your hand in everything (John 17:7). Thank You for daily giving them Your Word (John 17:8; John 8:47) as You send them out to live Your truth before others (John 3:34).

Be their joy (John 17:13). As they meditate upon Your Word, may they come to see You as the living, breathing Word (Revelation 19:13; John 1:14). May the very words they read become a reality within them (John 1:17). Indeed, may You become their very life (Colossians 3:4).

As Your truth rests inside them and lives out through them, transform and purify them (Romans 12:1–2). May they become a holy and sacred vessel from the inside out (John 17:17). Thank You for promising that as they are transformed and set apart, they have the authority to pray to see others changed (John 17:19; Luke 7:8). So be it!

◆ ◆ ◆

Intercession for Individual Walking through Divorce

Holy Father,

In my inadequacy, I confess that I don't know how to pray for _____ . Divorce is a messy, sticky, and often an angering situation that no one expects to endure. I am comforted knowing that as I bring _____ and _____'s experience to Your throne room, I find Your Son there, already interceding for them (Hebrews 7:25).

What a relief to know that I don't have to come up with words for prayer. Your Son is already bent over, representing Your will in the heavenlies (Romans 8:34). So, I come boldly before the throne on behalf of this little family (Hebrews 4:16). Release into their lives and heart all that You have already prepared for them (Matthew 16:19). Your will is already being loosed for them perfectly in heaven, and You have already stockpiled love, favor, and completeness for them (Matthew 6:10; Romans 5:5; Ephesians 4:7; Colossians 2:10).

But this treasure has a double-sided door, huh? Your side is already swung fully open, but someone must come with the earthly pass key to open this side (Amos 3:7). So, here I am, Father, inserting the Kingdom key confidently into this request for them, knowing that You have chosen gladly to give them the kingdom (Luke 12:32). Just as Your Son mediates in heaven on their behalf, I represent their case on earth. I have in hand the keys to the Kingdom that You have given me, and I arrange my will into agreement with Yours.

Satan stands opposing the outpour of this blessing. He remains a destroyer (John 10:10), a deceiver (John 8:44), and a disguiser (2 Corinthians 11:14). He makes this look like it is between a man and a woman when it is just about him. But we are not ignorant of his schemes (2 Corinthians 2:11). We recognize that all of this chaos has come from the very pit of darkness.

In the name of Jesus, I rebuke the spirit of anger, the spirit of chaos, and the spirit of pride (*you may add others here*), demanding that each of you submit to bondage underneath my feet (Joshua 10:16–24). Father, You are our Commander in Chief. Through You, I push back these spiritual adversaries, and through Your name, I trample down those who have risen against _____ and _____ (Psalm 44:4–5). I tread upon the dark spirits like enemies in the mire of the streets of battle (Zechariah 10:5). I obey You to bring them under domination, Lord (2 Corinthians 10:4–5). Now, do Your part. As my holy Joshua, strike these spiritual adversaries and put them to death (Joshua 10:26). This war is not against individual people but the rulers of darkness (Ephesians 6:12). God of peace, crush Satan underneath our feet (Romans 16:20).

In all honesty, it must be You who treads down these adversaries (Psalm 60:12).

As these enemies of deceit, anger, and chaos are defeated, stream Your blessing of peace and fulness into _____ and _____'s life. May the Holy Spirit come upon them, and the power of the Most High overshadow them to such an extent that everyone around them realizes that truly nothing is impossible with God (Luke 1:35; 37). As You move this mountain into the sea, replace it with green pastures and quiet waters (Matthew 17:20; Psalm 23:2). Restore _____ and _____'s souls (Psalm 23:4).

Indeed, I don't understand how You will accomplish all of this. It seems impossible, but my eyes are upon You, not upon the problem (2 Chronicles 20:12). In the meantime, while this evil host seems encamped against

_____ and _____, please give their hearts confidence without fear (Psalm 27:3). Cause them to remember You daily (Psalm 27:4). Heal their relationship, first with You and then with each other. Keep our eyes riveted upon You because in seeing You, there is both hope and transformation (2 Corinthians 3:18; Hebrews 12:2; 1 John 3:2–3). Selah.

◆ ◆ ◆

Intercession for Engaged/Newlywed Couple

Holy Father,

How delighted we are that You have brought (*couple's names*) together! It was You who first said, "It is not good for man to be alone" (Genesis 2:18). You will solve this problem once they join their lives together in marriage.

As I think about the final preparations, I ask that You continue to prepare their hearts. They are signing up for a covenant to reflect Your relationship with Your bride (Ephesians 5:32). What a responsibility!

(*Groom*) is saying that he will nourish and cherish (*bride*), even when the going gets tough (Ephesians 5:29). He is committing to giving himself up for her and daily using Christ's love to wash away her negative thoughts and emotions (Ephesians 5:26). He is stepping out to leave his own family and truly become one to her—closer than he's ever been to anyone else in the world (Ephesians 5:30). What an overwhelming task! Thank You that Your Spirit is within (*groom*) and will be the life and strength to his commitment. We rely on You to be the follow-through that he will need on the hardest of days.

(*Bride*) has one task (the hardest any woman ever faces): that of being correctly aligned with (*groom's*) leadership (Ephesians 6:22–24). Some days, she may not feel like he is leading, and on other days, he indeed may not be. Yet, You haven't changed her call. You have called her into the fight for respect, even when the struggle will be within her. For Your full blessing to flow freely from the heavenlies into their lives, You order the need for proper alignment—(*bride*) underneath (*groom*), (*groom*) underneath Christ, and Christ underneath You (1 Corinthians 11:3). What a mystery. Walk this out faithfully within her while growing her in strength, confidence, and fulness. Being his "helpmeet" takes boldness, assertiveness, poise, courage, and often the power to allow him to fail (1 Peter 3:1–2). May she learn how to be who You have made her be, without being frightened by any fear (1 Peter 3:6).

As I lift this couple, Father, I ask that You finish the work that You have begun: a work of faith. This marriage isn't dependent upon their resolves or energy but upon Your abundant mercy (Romans 9:16). Unlock the heavenlies to release Your love through the Holy, Living Spirit who already lives within both of them (Romans 5:5). Thank You that You are before all things (even this marriage), and in You, all things hold together (Colossians 1:17). I rejoice in all You have in store for their future. Yes, Jesus, Yes!

Ministry

Call to Ministry

Holy Father,

You are our Lamp, the One who goes into the dark places of our lives and shines a penetrating light. You know our innermost thoughts and our pre-spoken words (Psalm 139:1–4; John 2:25). You see in the dark, desiring to illumine our darkness so that we can see Your hand (Psalm 139:12; 2 Samuel 22:29). Thank You for searching our hearts to find us blameless, not to find us at fault (2 Samuel 22:31; Luke 9:56).

As I come before You on _____'s behalf, I thank You that You are his Strong Fortress. May he find himself entering Your Presence daily and resting in Your shelter (2 Samuel 22:33). Thank You that because of Christ's divine exchange, he has become the righteousness of God within Jesus (2 Corinthians 5:21). As he continues to discover what it means to be blameless, make his feet like hind's feet so he can walk carefully in the high places of the Kingdom. Set his feet, Lord, familiarizing him with how to move from one glory to another—not merely from knowledge to knowledge (2 Samuel 22:34).

As he prays, train his spiritual hands for battle among the heavenlies so that he can use Your offensive weapon deftly (2 Samuel 22:35). May Your Word always be on his tongue and in his hand (Isaiah 49:2; Ephesians 6:17). May his hands hold the shield of Your salvation ever close to his heart (2 Samuel 22:36).

Enlarge his steps underneath him, that his feet would never slip into selfishness but always walk to please You (2 Samuel 22:37). Gird him with daily strength for the battle and subdue thoughts and emotions against Kingdom principles (2 Samuel 22:40). Deliver him from contentions and complaints and bring many people into the Kingdom through his ministry (Psalm 31:20; 2 Samuel 22:44, 46).

"The Lord lives and blessed be my rock and exalted be God, the Rock of my salvation!" (2 Samuel 22:47). In Jesus's name, amen.

Mission Trip

Father,

Thank You that You not only created heavens and earth but that You still hold the ownership (1 Chronicles 29:11). When we look upon the degradation of the world, we sometimes wonder just who is in control. Today we come remembering that You still hold all authority—both of heaven and on earth (Matthew 28:18). Your dominion is everlasting supremacy (Daniel 4:34), and all governments of the world are upon Your shoulders (Isaiah 9:6). You rule over all the nations (Psalm 22:28). Hallelujah.

As _____ prepares for (*his*) upcoming mission trip, I can pray with confidence, knowing that no matter where (*he*) goes, You will be there (Psalm 139:7–10). Every location and every person on the earth are all under Your control, for You own them (Psalm 24:1). Thank You for being a nearby God, not one who is far away (Jeremiah 23:23).

I pray that as _____ goes, doubt will not consume (him), but that You will convince (*him*) of Your power to save (Romans 1:16). May (*he*) not focus on the problems but You, the Holy Promiser in (*his*) midst (Isaiah 12:6). Gloriously open (*his*) spiritual eyes so that (*he*) relies only on Your divine perception (1 Corinthians 2:12–14).

_____ may have some trepidation about the unknown. (*He*) may feel that (*he*) is going out in weakness and fear (1 Corinthians 2:3). Assure (*him*) that this is (*his*) best quality. Demonstrating Your power rather than showcasing (*his*) own will always be the pathway where Your power shines brightest (1 Corinthians 2:4–5; 2 Corinthians 12:9). May (*he*) rely on Your Spirit voice rather than (*his*) wisdom and intellect (1 Corinthians 2:6–10).

Prepare hearts even now to hear Your Word by softening any hardness and removing the rocks of deceit (Luke 8:13). Draw many to You as _____ reveals Christ and the knowledge of Your glory light (2 Corinthians 4:6). May many come to believe just as the Samaritans did, first by a witness but later in You alone (John 4:42).

One of the last things Jesus told His disciples was to love one another (John 13:34). He assured them how this would best display God's nature (John 13:35). However, teaming issues between Christians are usually the biggest stumbling block on a mission trip. Before participants leave, touch each team member with humility, gentleness, patience, and love (Ephesians 4:2). Grant them diligence to preserve the unity of Your Spirit in the bond of peace, regardless of the offenses that are bound to occur (Ephesians 4:3; Luke 17:1). May their whole team have the attitude of Christ, laying aside their privileges so that Your true nature may be revealed (Philippians 2:5–7, 11). May they go out with joy and be led forth with peace for the glory of Your name (Isaiah 55:12). It is in this holy name that I offer this prayer. Amen.

◆ ◆ ◆

Intercession for Pastor

Holy Father,

Thank You for our pastor's family. It is my joy and delight to pray for (*pastor's name*) and (*spouse's name*). You not only began a good work within them but also promised to be the One who would continue that work throughout their lives (Philippians 1:6). Thank You that You are developing, perfecting, and completing that endeavor inside of them (Philippians 1:6).

As I pray for them, I ask that their love may display itself in a greater depth of acquaintance and more comprehensive discernment (Philippians 1:9). I ask that they learn to sense what is excellent so they can live untainted in Your righteous (Philippians 1:10). Fill them with fruitful service as they allow Christ's life to live through them (Philippians 1:11). Show them how to separate gossip from truth to speak Your Word without fear (Philippians 1:14). May they be a couple about whom it may be said, "To live is Christ, to die is gain."

Unity is not only Your desire but the prayer of every pastoral team (Philippians 2:2). May our church do nothing out of selfishness or conceit but always think about others' interests (Philippians 2:3–4). Reveal Yourself to us that may we mirror the attitude of Your Son to others (Philippians 2:5–8). Thank You, Jesus, for carrying Your obedience to the cross so that we may know Your righteousness (Philippians 2:8).

While (*pastor*) and (*spouse*) stand before You in humility, reverence, and trembling, I ask You to teach them how to "work out" their salvation (Philippians 2:12). They cannot accomplish this in their strength but acknowledge that You are the One who is effectually working to energize and purify their desires (Philippians 2:13). Thank You for being in charge of their spiritual lives.

As they put no confidence or dependence on what they are in the flesh, You will significantly use them (Philippians 3:3). Yes, as they count everything up to this point as loss, give them the insight to see the extraordinary preciousness of knowing You as their boss. May they progressively become more intimately acquainted with You every day (Philippians 3:8). Teach all of us what it means to abide in You (Philippians 3:9).

Their determined purpose is to know You progressively, profoundly, and intimately (Philippians 3:10). May they not have the mere head knowledge but experiential understanding, with Your outflowing power surging through them (Philippians 3:10). Allow them to attain resurrection status, which lifts them out of any deadness they presently feel and into the glory of Christ (Philippians 3:11).

That's a big request. I don't know anyone who has arrived there yet—surely not me (Philippians 3:12)! But I ask Your strength to allow our church to forget what lies behind and press forward to the day of completion (Philippians 3:13–14).

Place rejoicing in our hearts again, Lord. True celebration (Philippians 4:4). Remind us often how very near You are (Philippians 4:5). If we keep Your nearness in mind, we are better enabled to live prayerfully, not anxiously (Philippians 4:6). Teach us how to make specific requests so that we fear nothing from You and are content with our lives (Philippians 4:7). Yes, garrison and guard our hearts in that kind of peace (Philippians 4:7).

Now, we wait for the completion of our salvation. Remind us to bring our thoughts back to truth, reverence, honor, purity, love, grace, and excellence. Whatever is worthy of praise, may we take our ideas to that place and leave them there (Philippians 4:8). Infuse (*pastor*) and (*spouse*) with Your inner strength (Philippians 4:13) and liberally fill their every need to fullness through Your riches in Christ Jesus's glory (Philippians 4:19). In His name, we pray. Amen.

Finding New Church

Holy Father,

Unity is essential to You (Ephesians 4:4–6). The essence of Your godhead is that the Three of You work in tandem to One Another (Matthew 28:19). You designed us in the likeness of the Trinity, causing us to need community (Genesis 1:26). Early on, You said, "It is not good for man to be alone" (Genesis 2:18).

You know we need community yet feel that we are walking among strangers. We don't want to forsake the habit of assembling with other believers but genuinely desire a body with whom we can encourage and who will encourage us (Hebrews 10:25). We need Your guidance to navigate well so that together we will show the world what it means to be Your disciples (John 13:35). Yes, we understand the concept but are finding the fulfillment of it easier said than done.

We are looking for a church home, believing that You have already prepared this place for us. We desperately need to hear You say, "This is the way, walk in it" (Isaiah 30:21). Direct our decisions as we weed through the options. Send us a "cloud by day and a fire by night" to lead us into Your best (Exodus 13:21). May it be a place in which Your eyes are wide open and Your ears attentive to every prayer offered within (2 Chronicles 7:15).

Reveal to us a church that seeks You earnestly and collectively with their whole hearts (2 Chronicles 15:2; Psalm 63:1). Lead us to a people devoted to Your Word, who compare the scriptures with every doctrine that comes along (Acts 17:11). Grant us a body of believers who need our gifts and even now are praying for us. May it be a community that we will hold in high regard while they welcome us with joy (Philippians 2:29). In Jesus's name, amen.

———————— ◆ ◆ ————————

Small Group

Holy Father,

Thank you for _____'s willingness to train those who will "be able to teach others also" (2 Timothy 2:2). You are working not only within her heart but within those in her small group as well. You are always busy at work (John 5:17).

I believe that You have already poured forth your Holy Spirit, but many do not yet receive You (Acts 2:33). Thank You that as many as do receive, You adopt them as Your very own children (John 1:12). Thank you for this small group, which includes several of Your children.

Bind up the deluding influences that would distract them from making You a priority (2 Thessalonians 2:11). May they not give up on getting together, no matter how much stress scheduling creates. May they encourage one another each time they are together (Hebrews 10:24–25). Even though they are few, may they come to know their importance as the body of Christ (1 Corinthians 12:27). Thank You for being with them each time they meet together (Matthew 18:20).

When they are alone, speak to them as individuals, using Your Word to cleanse them from any false ideas about who You are. Be so evident to them that they become increasingly more hungry for Your Word (Matthew 5:6). I pray that each time they open their Bibles, Your Spirit would stir within them, connecting the Written Word in their laps to the Living Word within (Hebrews 4:12). Teach them how to eat Your Word as their joy and delight (Jeremiah 15:16). May this body life be a healthy one, reproducing itself into others. In Jesus's mighty name, I pray. Amen.

Event

Holy Father,

O Lord, God of Israel, there is no god like You in heaven or on earth who keeps covenant and shows lovingkindness to those who seek You with all their heart (2 Chronicles 6:14). Since the highest heaven cannot contain You, Lord, how can we embrace You (1 Kings 8:27)? Thank You for making a way to hear our prayers, keeping Your eye open toward those of us in whom Your Spirit dwells (1 Kings 8:28–29).

You are a God like no other. You see the beginning of time as well as the end, regardless of humankind's or Satan's interference (Isaiah 46:9–10). Thank You for letting us in on Your plan for such a time as this, by instructing us in Your way (Psalm 25:12). As we make final preparations toward *(name of the event)*, we praise You as the God who works wonders (Psalm 66:5–6).

We believe this event is Your idea, so now, as preparations progress, we ask that it continue to be all about You. May every participant and worker come together with an attitude that is God-focused, not people-focused. You have promised that you will orchestrate the details if we continue seeking Your Kingdom and not our own (Matthew 6:33). May each mind be set on things above, not on the things that are on earth (Colossians 3:2).

Grant this day to be one of conviction and repentance. May each heart align with You, confessing Your name and seeking Your heart. Hear from heaven, O Lord, and forgive our passivity and selfishness (1 Kings 8:30). Now, O God, let Your eyes be open, and Your ears attentive to the prayers offered on that day (2 Chronicles 6:19–20). Arise to Your resting place inside us, clothing us with salvation and righteousness (2 Chronicles 6:41).

May each heart be overwhelmed by being "the very dwelling place of God" (1 Corinthians 3:16) and find that as Your temple, everything within us cries, "Glory" (Psalm 29:9). Grant each worshipper unity in praise, filling each temple with Your glory (2 Chronicles 5:13–14). In Jesus's name, I pray. Amen.

Missionaries

Moving Foreign

Holy Father,

Thank You not only for hearing our prayers but also for responding to us (John 11:41; Hebrews 1:2). Your purpose has always been to communicate with us. What a blessed privilege to know that we have the very radiance of God's glory to live within us (Hebrews 1:3; Colossians 1:27).

As (*missionary husband*) and (*missionary wife*) prepare for these last (*weeks*), they find themselves overwhelmed with many things to do. I come to You on their behalf, asking that they might know Your rest (Mark 6:31). Remind them that You are journeying before them, to seek a resting place specifically for them (Numbers 10:33).

Thank You for preparing a place of complete rest for each one of Your children (Hebrews 4:9). Deep down, sourcing from within our spirits, You've placed the fountain of Your Holy Spirit (John 7:38–39). Because Your Holy Spirit is always doing the work of believing, (*missionary husband*) and (*missionary wife*), have within them the ability to believe You in every circumstance (John 8:29; 16:13). After all, believing you is the work that You've called them to do (John 6:29). I ask that they be able to rest in that trust.

Often, our minds and emotions speed into the future, thinking that this will prepare us for what is to come. However, You call us daily to come that we might see You and thus find our souls (mind and emotions) refreshed (Matthew 11:28–29). Your rest comes during the journey (Mark 6:30–34). Reveal how best to rest in Your Presence as life continues around us.

Show (*missionary husband*) and (*missionary wife*) Your face, so as they stare with wide-opened eyes at Your glory, they will find themselves transformed into Your image (2 Corinthians 3:18). May they be at rest and in the stillness find an overwhelming knowledge of Your lordship (Psalm 46:10). When we fix our spiritual eyes upon You, You strengthen and heal us (Hebrews 12:2, 12–13). Do this for these precious ones, O Lord. I ask this with the signature of Your Son upon the request. Amen.

Language Study (Written with Security in Mind)

Dear Dad,

Thank You for continually taking pleasure in Your people (Ps149:4). You delight in the walk of the blameless (Pr11:20). _____ and _____ fit into that category, and I come to You joyful, knowing that You hear me as I discuss their lives with You (Ps116:1).

As You know, they are entering into a significant period of their lives—language learning. There will probably be many days that they won't understand much, but I'm asking that they can continue to hear what You say. You are always the One who speaks peace (Ps85:8). Open their ears to listen for words of truth so that they can repeat them to (*others, their children, etc.*) (Ps78:1, 6).

Regarding their language, I know that You will be the only one on whom they can depend for help (Ps121:2). You don't even take naps (Ps121:3)! As they open their mouths, lavishly fill them, just like You promised to do (Ps81:10). I ask that You accomplish their fluency of language (Ps138:8), setting a daily guard over their mouth so that the stressors of life won't contradict what they have come to do (Ps141:3). When they get exasperated, don't forget to remind them of Your Presence. You're always watching over their paths (Ps142:3). We are very thankful for Your watch care. I'm offering these requests in Your name.

◆ ◆ ◆

General (Written with Security in Mind)

Dad,

Thank You that You chose to dwell *in* mortal flesh (Dan2:11), not just *with* we fleshly ones. You were among us, and now You are inside us (J1:14). What a perfect way to profess Your abundant love by coming to our level.

Your Son began the reconciliation work, and now You commit this work to us (2Co5:19). (*Missionary*) knows this full well, as he is following You into the family business. Thank You that his energy isn't dependent on what his body can produce but on the life in Your Word (J1:4). Reveal to him how to walk without being weary and run without getting tired (Is40:31). I ask You to enlarge within him as he decreases dependence on himself (J3:30).

Show his flesh how to be silent before You, and in turn, watch You stir from Your habitation (Ze2:13). I know You have granted him Your favor, so increase His knowledge of You. Bl-ss him with Your Presence; otherwise, there is no way he can take another step (Ex33:13–14).

Who does he have besides You anyway? Other than You, he has nothing on this earth. I'm sure he has experienced the failure of heart and flesh. Thank You that even in these times, You won't fail him. Be his strength and portion forever (Ps73:25–26).

The enemy works to damage everything within the sanctuary of the soul (Ps74:3). Accomplish deliverance in every place that (*missionary*) goes (Ps74:11). As he seeks the city's welfare, give him protection and peace (Je29:7).

Thank You that Your Word doesn't return to You without accomplishing all that You sent Him out to do (Is55:11). Work out Your purpose in each life that cries out to You. I look earnestly to You because otherwise, there is nowhere else to turn.

As the S-bbath draws near, may (*missionary*) be able to lay down all burdens (Je17:21). Grant him rest (He4:9) and be gl-rified. So be it.

Parenting (Written with Security in Mind)

Dad,

Thank You for delighting in those who understand and know You (Je9:24). When the right ones cry, You hear and deliver out of all their troubles (Ps34:17). What a great promise!

I've been thinking about (*missionary husband*) and (*missionary wife*) recently. I know they have concerns with their children, so I ask that You reestablish their gaze to see only You (Mt17:7). As they parent, may they daily receive their children in Your name and find that in doing so, they are receiving You as well (Mt18:5). Teach them to bind up whatever comes against their family, knowing that You have already bound this in h-aven. Give them the insight to see the abundant gifts You have waiting for them in the h-venlies so that they may loose those things that You have prepared (Mt18:18). Teach them to bend together as a family, claiming that they might see You before them in their very midst (Mt18:20).

Thank You for their sacrifice. They have left houses, brothers, sisters, fathers, and mothers for Your name's sake (Mt19:29). You promise to give them more than they've left, both in this life and in their future one (Mt19:30). Thank You for these promises. I come in agreement with Your character. So be it.

On Stateside 1

Holy Father,

Thank You for the opportunity to pray for (*missionary husband*) and (*missionary wife*) in spirit. Being at home can be difficult, as the demanding schedule can take away from time spent with You. We are very aware that our spirits are willing, but our flesh is weak (Matthew 26:41).

I come to fasten myself to You in intercession for (*missionary husband*) and (*missionary wife*). Lord, You have paid a high price for their freedom by spending Your very own lifeblood (1 Corinthians 6:20). Thank You that they were included not only in Your death but also Your resurrection (Galatians 2:20). Their spiritual address is now in the heavenlies with You (Ephesians 2:6).

Family needs, vision casting, and deputation keep them busy. May their eyes remain open to see Your incredible power poured into their emptiness (Ephesians 1:19). Show them how to take their hands off every responsibility and allow You to work it through them. Grant them greater insight into how to do all things through Christ (Philippians 4:13). Impart Your revelation and wisdom, teaching us all to walk by faith and not by sight (2 Corinthians 5:7). We offer this petition in the mighty name of Jesus Himself. Amen.

On Stateside 2

Holy Father,

Thank You for being the _____ family's shepherd (Psalm 23:1). You have led them back to this place carefully and gently. As they visit family and churches, keep them from falling into the American lifestyle of always wanting more (Psalm 23:1).

Instead, I ask that You allow them to see the comfort of resting in Your Presence, even when there is much that they can eat, drink, and buy (Psalm 23:2). Allow their spirits to continue knowing the quietness of listening to You (Psalm 23:2). Since they have been in a spiritually difficult place, refresh their souls and guide them peacefully into more of Your righteousness (Psalm 23:3).

As they realize America's moral decay since their last visit, may they fear no evil for their family, remembering that You walk with them daily (Psalm 23:4). Comfort them with Your rod and staff, sending the correction needed (Psalm 23:4). Remind them every day of how You provide and refresh with the holy oil of Your Presence (Psalm 23:5).

You prepare goodness and kindness for them not only during furlough but also for the rest of their lives (Psalm 23:6). Continue teaching them how to live amid Your beauty no matter their location (Psalm 23:6). In Jesus's name, amen.

On Stateside 3

Holy Father,

Praise You for sending us Your Son as the exact image of who You are (Colossians 1:15). We not only need Him as our example; we need Him as our very life (Colossians 3:4). Thank You for assuring us that He is before everything that we say or do, as well as everything that we know or experience. Hold us together, Lord, just as You promised (Colossians 1:17).

I come before You today on behalf of the (*missionary family*). I pray that they walk in You in the same way that they received You—by faith (Colossians 2:6). As they progress through this stateside, may they become increasingly more rooted in You, finding their faith established in You (Colossians 2:7). When they fail and ask Your forgiveness, fast-forward their thoughts into the completeness they have in You (Colossians 2:9). As the lure of American commercialism tempts them, remind them that reality belongs to You (Colossians 2:17). Don't allow the evil one to defraud their thinking by chasing every new Christian author that comes along. May they hold fast to You as head, in charge of their growth (Colossians 2:18–19).

Help them walk in the Spirit, even when society wants to give them other rules. Paul also dealt with people submitting to the decrees of humanity (Colossians 2:20). May they not worry about the new "should and should not's" that claim wisdom. These rules are self-made religion that only leads them away from You (Colossians 2:23). May this family keep their minds on You instead (Colossians 3:2). Reveal Yourself to them so that they may become just like You, no matter where they are (1 John 3:3). In Jesus's name, amen.

<hr />

Returning to Field

Holy Father,

How excellent, majestic, and glorious is your name in all the earth (Psalm 8:1). When I consider what You have created and accomplished, I'm baffled at why You care for humanity (Psalm 8:3–4). For some reason, You have made us in Your image, granting us glory and majesty so that we can be a perfected bride (Psalm 8:5; Revelation 21:9). Thank You for being our chosen and assigned portion and for holding our lives in Your hands (Psalm 16:5).

As the _____ family returns to their foreign home, I ask that You make their feet like hinds' feet, able to make progress despite dangerous heights of testing (Psalm 18:33). May the words of their mouths and the meditation of their hearts be acceptable to You each day (Psalm 19:14).

Lead them down the path of right standing with You, not because they have earned it, of course, but because this is Your great promise to them (Psalm 23:3).

Grant them Your unique companionship, revealing the deep inner meaning of keeping covenant with You (Psalm 25:14). Teach them where they should go and continue Your counsel, for I know Your eye sees all (Psalm 32:8). There will be many things confronting them in the coming months, but I claim that You will deliver them out of them all (Psalm 34:19). Thank You that their times are in Your hands (Psalm 31:15). So be it!

◆ ◆ ◆

Return to the States to Stay

Holy Father,

Thank You for being the God of all Comfort and encouragement (1 Corinthians 1:3). After years on the mission field, _____ is now coming home. Years ago, You called them to serve You. They obeyed, not knowing where they were going or what it would be like (Hebrews 11:8). In the beginning, their move was difficult as they adjusted to a new language, a new culture, and new friends. They shared in the sufferings of Your Son by experiencing their share of "loud crying and tears" (Colossians 1:24; Hebrews 5:7). They were afflicted through adjustment and found obedience through heartache (Hebrews 5:8).

Over time, a transformation happened. As _____ began to trade their desires for Yours, they grew in love for their new situation (Philippians 2:4). At first, You commanded them to love, and later, Your love readily spilled from their hearts (John 13:34). Transition expanded their worldview, and obedience enlarged their God-view.

Now, they have yet another transition to make. After pouring their hearts into the people of the world, they must transition into the place they once called home. (*America, Canada, etc.*) has changed, and this transition may prove their most challenging yet. I come to represent their needs before You.

Grant them value, Lord. Despite their difficulties overseas, they knew their ministry counted. Now, returning to their home country, they may not be too sure. The lines of value may be blurred. Show them again who they are in You and how very precious they are in Your sight. Let them hear You say, "You are honored, and I love you" (Isaiah 43:4). They'll need that word for this new transition. Grant them opportunities to use their gifts in this stage of life and know appreciation for who they are.

Grant them friendships. They developed deep friendships overseas that became family, but long-distance relationships are challenging to maintain. Expats living abroad tend to associate freely with those nearby and quickly release those who leave. On the other hand, "home folks" may have already established their relational patterns. _____ may return home to great loneliness—acquainted with many but close to none. Fulfill Your promise and be closer to them than a brother (Proverbs 18:24). Reveal that You are the same, no matter where they live. Send them someone to pray with, cry with, and laugh with. Someone who will allow them to be all that they've become, despite their different worldviews. Grant them friendships that extend into one another's homes (Acts 2:46).

Grant them forgiveness. Offenses are inevitable, and _____ has probably been offended along the way (Luke 17:1). Possibly, this move has involved pain. But, Father, You give us two choices: to send away the hurts or to allow them to feed on our souls (John 20:23). Retaining resentment will eat away at joy and contentment. Only in releasing offenses by forgiveness can _____ move into the future You have prepared. Surge Your power within them to forgive (Luke 23:34). Grant them the strength to be renewed in the spirit of their minds (Ephesians 4:23). Allow them to forget the past and eagerly await the new (Isaiah 43:18–19).

Grant them perspective. _____ may be struggling that they wasted their time overseas—time making relationships, time learning language, time making adjustments. Open their eyes to see how each experience was necessary for this next challenge (Ephesians 1:17). May they see by experience how You are working all things toward their good (Romans 8:28). Allow them to see things from Your vantage point, rather than from an earthly one. Encourage them to keep seeking the things above (Colossians 3:1–2).

Grant them patience. No one can rush grief, but they have lost much and may not yet realize it. A called-out life expects always to know the next step, so grant them forbearance when the future is unclear (Romans 8:25). Grant them peace during the awkwardness and the confusion (2 Corinthians 6:4). Restore their ability to move in obedience to You without understanding (Genesis 22:8). They have done this before. Grant them the strength to do it again.

Grant them wisdom. May they know the mystery of Your will afresh (Ephesians 1:9). Open the eyes of their hearts to understand their calling, even on this side of the world (Ephesians 1:18). Protect them from mistakes.

Thank You that I can bring _____'s need boldly to Your throne (Hebrews 10:19). I realize that there are many requests on this work order. But please note that every single petition has been signed off and paid for by the Lord Jesus Himself. I expectantly wait for You to act. So be it.

New to Faith

Day 1

Holy Father,

Hallelujah! _____ has received Your salvation! Her light has come, for the glory of the Lord has risen upon her (Isaiah 60:1). I join with all of heaven in rejoicing (Luke 15:10). May her path be like a brilliant light that shines more and more intently until the perfect day (Proverbs 4:18).

As she grows, may she receive Your Word with great eagerness, daily searching the scriptures to know truth (Acts 17:11). Sanctify her in truth (John 17:17) to give continued attention to truth (Daniel 6:13). Testify with her spirit that she is now one of Your children and an heir alongside Christ (Romans 8:16–17). Release the Word of God within her to do this work (1 Thessalonians 2:13). Take authority over her flesh (John 17:2), drawing her to submit to You, and find her will transformed into Your image.

May _____'s righteousness flourish like a palm tree (Psalm 92:12), planted firmly in Your dwelling place and thriving in Your Presence (Psalm 92:13). May she prove to be a "forever green" believer, always seeking water from the depths of the Lord. Grant her freedom of anxiety, even in dry seasons, because You bear fruit within her at all times (Jeremiah 17:8). Preserve her new life of faith and don't let her feet slip (Psalm 66:9).

Because there will be days of hardship, bring other Christians alongside _____ to supply what is lacking in her faith (1 Thessalonians 3:10). Grant her teachers who handle the Word of truth accurately (2 Timothy 2:15). Cause her body of believers to increase and abound in love for one another, establishing their hearts without blame in holiness (1 Thessalonians 3:12–13).

Equip _____ to do Your will in everything. May the Holy Spirit work that which pleases You within her (Hebrews 13:20). Open Your heavenly storehouse so widely for her that it seems like the blessings of the Holy Spirit rain down on all she does (Deuteronomy 28:12). Reveal the path You have for her life and fill her with joy as she learns to wait before You (Acts 2:28). In Jesus's name, amen.

Day 2

Holy Father,

It is a blessing to have a God like You that hears our prayers (Psalm 65:2). You never downgrade or despise desperate prayers (Psalm 102:17). What a fantastic privilege it is to come into Your Presence with confidence (Hebrews 10:19).

Teach _____ and me to pray, Father (Luke 11:1). So far, we feel like we do not yet know quite how to do so. But we are so comforted, for the Spirit Himself intercedes for us with groanings too deep for words (Romans 8:26). Hallelujah! Search our hearts, and therein, find Yourself (Psalm 139:23; Deuteronomy 7:21). May the Spirit within us and the Jesus above us be united in power through prayer (Romans 8:26, 34). Squeeze out all in between that is not of You, O Father (Psalm 119:71).

We ask that in increasing measure, we would come to know Your heart (Jeremiah 24:7). How humbled we are to find that as we discover Your heart, we find ourselves therein (Job 7:17). Your trials come only because of Your great concern (Job 7:18). Grant us encouragement alongside endurance (Romans 15:5).

We desire to pray not only with our spirits but with our minds as well (1 Corinthians 14:15). After all, this is one of the reasons You sent Your Son in the first place, to give us understanding so that we might know You (1 John 5:20). Thank You for giving us the mind of Christ (1 Corinthians 2:16). Now teach us to utilize this generous gift by praying without ceasing (1 Thessalonians 5:17). May You be the power that works mightily within us (Colossians 1:29). In Jesus's name, amen.

Day 3

Holy Father,

Thank You that we are not only saved by grace, but we also live by grace (Colossians 2:6). Thank You for (*new believer*), who now houses Your Holy Spirit and is listening each day for Your voice (John 10:3). Thank

You for lifting her burden, just as You promised for all who seek Your face (Jeremiah 29:12).

Now I ask that she embrace the extraordinary work of faith in her life (John 6:29). May she experience in the gift of righteousness, just as she has the gift of grace (1 Corinthians 1:30). May she learn to fully allow You to accomplish all through her (Ephesians 2:10). Increase her faith so that she might live every moment as if she has plunged into the pond of Your Son's life.

Thank You that You not only sent Your Son to die for our sins but that He became sin for us (1 Peter 2:24). When He hung on the cross, the very sin nature that You knew would be within (*new believer*) and me hung there dying as well. Now that we have been relieved from this specific sin, remind us of how You have already crucified those things we may do in the future (Romans 6:6).

How amazing it is that somehow, now (*new believer*) and I embody Your righteousness. Thank You that we are not of those who practice sin deliberately, knowingly, and habitually (1 John 3:4–10). Instead, we are children of God, who have the very sperm of God within our DNA. Work within us that we would look like You. May we act like the partakers of the divine nature You have already made us to be (2 Peter 1:4).

We realize that the only thing that keeps this from happening within us is plain ole unbelief, so increase the Word of Christ within us richly (Colossians 3:16). May we cease from our labor so that You can be about Your business in our lives (Hebrews 4:9–10). We are such active people that You will have to renew our minds here. Otherwise, we can't accept this easily (Romans 12:2). Even in this, stretch our faith muscle to believe, as You have with so many before us. Thank You that it is no longer we who live, but Your life is living with us (Galatians 2:20). Our spiritual lives are Your responsibility, not our own. In Jesus's name, amen.

◆ ◆ ◆

Day 4

Holy Father,

Praise You that You are light, and in You, there is no darkness at all (1 John 1:5). You are not afraid of the dark and go boldly into darkness to shine

(John 1:5). Only as we stand in Your light will we have the ability to see the dark places still residing within us (Psalm 36:9). We ask that You send out Your light and Your truth to lead _____ and me (Psalm 43:3). May the eyes of our hearts be enlightened to know You truly (Ephesians 1:18).

Darkness is where the evil one and his cohorts live, eternally bound by You (Jude 6). Thank You that we are no longer "children of darkness," trapped with no way of escape (Ephesians 5:8). Praise You for delivering us from the kingdom of darkness and placing us into Your Kingdom of light (1 Peter 2:9–10).

Despite Your finished work, the evil one still opposes light (John 3:20), and You have warned us to take heed, lest the light in us become darkness (Luke 11:35). When we tolerate darkness through tolerating our selfishness, we leave the fortress available for the evil one to lurk behind. Could these acts be some of the "speculations and lofty things raised against the knowledge of God" (2 Corinthians 10:5)?

As _____ and I bring our thoughts and emotions to You about our messy lives, I ask that You reveal areas of our thoughts that may align more with darkness than light. May we be people who come to light even though it means exposure (John 3:21). After all, the spotlight isn't supposed to be upon us anyway. If we are in the light as You are in the light, we will have fellowship with those around us and know how to respond in love (1 John 1:7).

Deliver our families and us from the evil one so that they can live a full Kingdom life here on earth (Matthew 6:13). Praise You for hearing our prayer (Acts 10:31), In Jesus's name, amen.

Day 5

Holy Father,

Thank You for being a God who never forsakes us to the teeth of our adversary (Psalm 124:6). The evil one roars about, desirous of sinking the fangs of his deceptive speech into hearts (1 Peter 5:8; Proverbs 12:6).

But thank You for not only encouraging us to pray for deliverance but also promising to liberate us out of the lion's mouth (Matthew 6:13; 2 Timothy 4:17–18). Praise You for bending Your ear to our cries (Psalm 116:1–4).

This hasn't been easy for (*new Christian*). At times, she has probably wondered where You were (Psalm 121:1). Since I know the weight of temptation, I come to You on her behalf. Reveal how I can supplement whatever lack of (*faith, self-control, confidence, etc.*) that she is experiencing. Her help must come from You, even when the particulars aren't immediately visible (Psalm 121:2).

You promised (and put it into writing, I might add) that You are not going to allow her feet to slip (Psalm 121:3). That's a tall order considering the temptations all around her. She needs support and comfort even though her situation may not change quickly. I'm asking that You provide these needs, even while she sleeps (Psalm 121:4).

You also promised to keep her in unbroken continuity. Since You are the same yesterday, today, and forever, Your Presence is the same during this storm as when she walked on the mountaintop (Hebrews 13:5; Psalm 121:5). Shade her from the heat and grant her a big-picture perspective when she feels unprotected (Psalm 121:5; Jonah 4:5–11).

Thank You for guarding her, watching her, preserving her, and protecting her (Psalm 121:6). I appreciate You. Open her eyes to visualize the ways You are doing this, especially in the darkness. Thank You for promising to guard her going out and her coming in from this time forth and forever (Psalm 121:8). Continue to preserve her emotions and thoughts, no matter her circumstances. This must be Your plan, as You repeat it three times in Psalm 121! I will believe on behalf of _____. In Jesus's name, amen.

Not-Yet Believer, Intercession for

Day 1

Holy Father,

How blessed You are, the God and Father of our Lord Jesus Christ (Ephesians 1:3). You, O Lord, made heaven, earth, and everything in between (Acts 4:24). You created the universe as an extension of Your divine Kingdom, creating man in Your image and setting him in charge of upholding Your rule and reign (Genesis 1:26, 28; 2:15).

But man loved knowledge rather than life and lost earth's domain to a dark, pretender prince (Genesis 2:17; 2:6; Luke 4:6). This strong prince of darkness immediately moved to homestead the land (Luke 11:21), asserting his ownership and claiming what You created for man (Psalm 115:16).

When the first man implicated himself with this kingdom of darkness, the rest of humanity was ensnared as well (Romans 5:12). A self-seeking attitude birthed into the nature of every man afterward, smudging our God-image with pride and deceit (Genesis 3:5–6). The consequence destined our entire species for death (1 Corinthians 15:21–22).

Man now owed a debt that only blood could pay. The evil one knew no man could adequately defend himself in heaven's courtroom (Job 10:32–33). Man's destiny looked hopeless.

But Your nature, O God, is salvation. You would not leave Your creation helpless or Your prodigal ones wandering (Romans 8:20; Luke 15:4). You sent Your Son to seek and preserve Your lost ones (Luke 19:10; John 3:17). Paying the top price, You dispatched Your Son, the true Prince, to be born into man's likeness (Philippians 2:6–7; Romans 5:8–9). Your image assumed the likeness of man to buy back our squandered dominion and our wasted lives (1 Corinthians 6:20).

Since our fate was death (Romans 6:23), Jesus had to overcome mortality (Philippians 2:8) by condemning sin in the flesh (Romans 8:3). He paid our debt (Colossians 2:14) and bought our freedom (Galatians 5:1) by spilling His blood (Hebrews 9:11–12).

Therefore, You accepted Jesus as the new perfected Adam (1 Corinthians 15:45) and restored Him as the Sovereign of Your Kingdom (1 Timothy 6:15–16). As King of kings, Jesus abolished the impostor prince's rule and authority and made a public display of him through Christ's royal triumph (1 Corinthians 15:24; Colossians 2:15).

Although You won the conquest, You have not stopped the battle (2 Corinthians 10:3). You rose victorious over the enemy, but love motivated You toward a greater good for Your prodigals. You left the conflict open to woo us through into love (Jeremiah 31:3; John 6:44). You desire our willing affection more than an enforced treaty.

Hallelujah! You, O God, are our Victorious, Loving Deliverer! Your Son, Jesus Christ, now continually mediates for us in Your court (1 Timothy 2:5; Hebrews 7:25). You welcome His intercession, for You desire every one of Your prodigals to know the rescue option (1 Timothy 2:4).

That is why I bring (*unbeliever's name*) before Your throne. You already purchased his deliverance. You do not wish anyone to perish but for all to come into repentance (2 Peter 3:9). Jesus is now in heaven interceding for him, so I stand as earth's envoy entreating with Jesus's same prayer.

Prayer is the key to (*unbeliever's name*) rescue. You have done Your part. Now in prayer, I do my part. You made me an able representative of this new covenant (2 Corinthians 3:6), so I'm here to enforce the liberation You have already secured for (*unbeliever's*) soul.

Jesus, Your work is already completed (John 19:30). You are now seated at the right hand of God, waiting for us to bring these bound enemies to Your feet (Hebrews 10:12–13). Prayer is my part. You are waiting for me to use the authority You've given back to man as I pray (Luke 10:19).

You don't have to draft me into this prayer army. I'm volunteering freely for (*unbeliever's*) salvation (Psalm 110:1, 3). I realize this means that I'm also giving You authority over my life. Only those under authority can command authority (Matthew 8:8–9).

Subdue the enemies of (*unbeliever's*) soul. Knowledge and pride have become hindrances in finding You. He thinks he has the right answers, but he is blind to the truth (2 Timothy 3:7). You deal with cases like this all the time and have given Your recruits spiritual weapons to pull down these kinds of fortresses (2 Corinthians 10:4).

So, in Jesus's name, I bind up the enemies of his soul (*i.e., pornography, stubbornness, past wounds from the church, etc.*—Matthew 18:18). Place spiritual detonators in (*unbeliever's*) life to destroy his previous speculations about You, his current pride against knowing You, and any influences hostile to truth (2 Corinthians 10:5). Align these powerful detonators to discharge at Your perfect timing, removing the blinders so that he may see truth. He is transformed for once he sees You, willingly stepping out of the darkness and into Your marvelous light (1 John 3:2; 1 Peter 2:9).

Thank You that no matter how dismal the situation may look, You are more significant than all doubt within me (1 John 3:20). Increase my allotment of faith by Your goodness and mercy (Romans 12:3; Luke 17:5). Help my unbelief (Mark 9:24). In Jesus's name, I pray. Amen.

◆ ◆ ◆

Day 2

Holy Father,

We thank You for being a God who does not fear the darkness (Psalm 139:12). Sometimes when we look into a world that only exhibits darkness, it causes us to despair. But not You. Darkness never overwhelms you (John 1:5).

As I come before You on behalf of (*unbeliever's name*), I ask You to beam forth the illumination of Jesus into his life (2 Corinthians 4:6). Despite the darkness that would desire to engulf his thinking, may Your light break forth upon him in brilliance. Draw (*unbeliever*) to altogether faith You so that one day he can be the spiritual leader of his home (1 Peter 1:8–9).

Tuck (*name of person witnessing*) tightly within Your righteousness, allowing her to escape all sin so that when (*unbeliever*) sees her, he will know that she is of truth. May she be a pure witness of Your Presence (Psalm 71:2–3). Lean down closely toward her, O Lord, listening to her every prayer. Teach her how to pray for him and open the floodgates of remembrance so that she cannot stop groaning on his behalf.

We also want to stand in the gap for any other Christians who know (*unbeliever*). If there are currently none, move believers into his life. Begin now to purify them, setting their interactions with him on high so that the evil one cannot rise against them and accuse them in his thinking (Psalm 59:1). I ask this by the authority given me by Jesus. Amen.

◆ ◆ ◆

Day 3

O Love that will not let me go,

I stand in awe, knowing that You will never abandon me (Hebrews 13:8). Even if my father and mother desert me, You will not and cannot leave me (Psalm 27:10). You hover over me like a protective mother bird, covering me with Your wings (Philippians 4:5; Psalm 91:4). Thank You for the warmth and safety of Your Presence (Psalm 32:7).

Not everyone knows of Your reassuring love. (*name of unbeliever*) doesn't know Your love's soothing feathers because the (*pain of his past, other*) has left him guarded. Little does he realize that even now, Your Son is lovingly interceding for him in the heavenlies. Your desire, yes, Your will, is that he comes to abide underneath Your wings for comforting warmth (2 Corinthians 1:3). You ache to wrap Your pinions of peace tightly around him, to protect him from the barrage of the world (Luke 13:34).

Jesus, when You returned to the heavenlies, You gave Your children responsibility as Kingdom scouts, eyes and ears here on earth (1 Peter 3:22; 2 Corinthians 5:18–19). I believe (*name's*) heart is in great need of deliverance. He can't see Your desire for him yet, so You send intercessors as Your representatives on the ground. You have opened my heart to see his need and burdened my emotions for him. I am inadequate for this work but cling to Christ's adequacy within me. (*Name of unbeliever*)'s deliverance is complete in You, so I ask You to release Your finished victory within him (Ephesians 1:7; 2 Corinthians 5:20).

Spirit of God, hover over (*name*) with the warmth of Your brooding feathers. By a mere word, You call into being that which does not exist (Romans 4:17). (*Name's*) past has built up a hard shell against knowing You (2 Corinthians 10:5). Underneath that resistant exterior is a life created in Your image (Genesis 1:26). You see him as an offspring of Your divine nature, desiring that he turn and run to You (Acts 17:29–30).

Overshadow him with Your creative mothering instinct. Only Your kindness will stir new life within him so that the constricting shell of his past is cracked open (Luke 1:35). Like a brooding mother hen, You know how to incubate hope and rotate his shell so that the truth seed cannot stagnate and wither away (Luke 8:6). May he hear the soft coo of Your voice coaxing him out of the darkness and into Your glorious light (1 Peter 2:9). In Jesus's name, amen.

Patience

Day 1

Oh, Father,

How I need to practice silencing my mind to focus upon You.

You already know how best to resolve the issues around me. You and Your Son have been discussing this very thing, so why do I spend so much energy trying to figure it out on my own (Romans 8:34)?

As long as my prayers are predominately concerned with "me" and "my," I know they are missing Your depth. Your perspective is always broader and more extensive than the tiny little world into which I confine myself (Psalm 40:5).

I know that Your Spirit has set up residence deep within me, building a temple there for vital connection (1 Corinthians 3:16). My spirit is to be Your house of prayer, with Your heart desires rising in an unceasing flow within me (Isaiah 56:7; John 7:38).

Yet, as long as these source from my head and not my spirit, I'll tap into very little of the vast resource of Your life. When I feel low and dry, it usually is because I have limited my time in Your Presence. Forgive me, Father.

I come before You to wait. I will silence my flesh and wait on Your Word (Psalm 130:5). Yes, my soul will wait, I will resist its sudden movement, and I will be quietened before You (Zechariah 2:13).

You are my Rock, my Salvation, and my Stronghold, so I don't have to worry about the shaking. Thank You that I can pour out my soul before You (Psalm 62:5–8).

Selah. Shhhhh.

Day 2

Holy Father,

I'm so impatient. My soul is like a hummingbird, flitting from flower to flower and truth to truth. I expend most of my spiritual energy skimming over Your Word rather than drinking deeply. Yet You still hold out the daily Sabbath before me, saying, "Today is the day to rest. Today is the day to wait" (Hebrews 4:9, 7).

Because I so rarely stop to drink in the sweet nectar of Your Presence, I assume that You must be hiding from me. I measure Your work by what I feel and am easily discouraged because I don't find an immediate sensation. You must always remind me that You are more stable than my wavering heart (1 John 3:20).

My mind lies at fault. Even my loftiest thoughts cannot perpetuate Your Presence. I think and think, trying to fan a flame of pure intelligence. But new "spiritual" exercises deceive me. I assume that doing stuff for You is the same as waiting before You. I seek goodness within myself rather than within You, my Savior. I'm sorry.

In resting, I'm like a little child, first laid in her bed. I sing, I talk, I toss; then I get up to explain why I didn't need the nap after all. Nevertheless, You know my weak frame and love me anyway. You realize that I'll be incorrigible, crying, and whining at the least provocation without this time of rest. So, You tuck me back in, sometimes quite sternly, seeing ahead to what I truly need.

Resting. Silence. Patience.

I find these to be foreign concepts when it comes to spirituality.

When I do set my will to rest in You, I blame You for purposely dragging Your feet the minute You don't do what I want. Impatience is a telltale sign that actual resting isn't taking place. I must surrender even the timing to You.

Remind me that only You can accomplish what concerns me (Psalm 57:2). Reveal these truths to me in such a way that they permeate my very core. Teach me to allow every spiritual muscle to relax so that my response is faith alone. May I stop working on my confidence and let You take over. Selah.

Day 3

Holy Father,

I exalt You. I give You thanks for all the fantastic things that I have watched You do. In perfect faithfulness, You unfold Your plans ordained long ago. That's astounding to me! (Isaiah 25:1)

As I come before You, I genuinely want to join Isaiah to say, "Behold, this is (my) God for whom (I) have waited!" (Isaiah 25:9). I pray that You will reveal how bumps in my plans are merely waiting practice. How vital patience is to You.

Please teach me how to wait, Lord. Show me how every opportunity to wait on someone else is actually an opportunity to wait on You. Open my eyes to see these situations clearly.

May my life and my family's life be like a strong city. Set up walls to keep us secure, and keep our minds steadfastly trusting in You as our peace (Isaiah 26:1, 3). O Upright One, I ask You to make our path level. Show us exactly where Your light is so that we may walk where You walk (Isaiah 26:7; 1 John 1:7). Thank You that even when our light seems small, we can know this is the very place where we can find even more enlightenment. "In Your Light, we see Light" (Psalm 36:9). In Jesus's name, amen.

Peace

Day 1

Holy Father,

Thank You for being the God of all peace (Romans 15:33). You are never ruffled, rattled, or unsettled. You are never surprised, for You have declared how things will turn out before they even begin (Isaiah 46:10). You are never embarrassed because You work all things according to Your purposes (Ephesians 1:11). Despite all the ways in which the earth looks hopeless, we cannot derail Your plan (Isaiah 14:27). You are amazing.

You are peace and love to speak peace over us (Psalm 85:8). Our world is desperate to hear this voice. You bring us into restful harmony by setting us entirely apart to mature in spirit, soul, and body (1 Thessalonians 5:23). Your Son, Jesus, is the channel through which this peace descends into our hearts (Romans 5:1). Now, teach me to be at peace with myself.

Today, I bring our city into Your Presence. We need Your peace and have difficulty knowing contentment. You promised that when we wait upon You, You will hear our cry and bring us out of the pit of fear (Psalm 40:1–2). I'm asking You to fulfill that promise, setting our emotions and footsteps firm upon You, for I know You can be our rock (Psalm 40:2). Make this place one of praise so that many will see and trust You (Psalm 40:3).

Thank You that Your thoughts toward us are too numerous to count (Psalm 40:5). Allow our churches to hear and dwell upon those tender thoughts rather than discouraging ones. May we listen to You despite all disappointments that surround us (Psalm 40:6).

You have a remnant here who delight to do Your will and have Your law written upon their hearts (Psalm 40:8). Preserve us with Your lovingkindness and Your truth (Psalm 40:11). When our hearts fail to bring peace, overwhelm us afresh with Your peaceful Presence (Psalm 40:12; Ephesians 2:14). Be our Help and our Deliverer. Do not delay, O God, for we need You desperately (Psalm 40:17). In Jesus's name, amen.

Day 2

Holy Father,

Thank You for being the watchful God who never sleeps on the job (Psalm 121:4). You are our keeper, always watching, always guarding, always protecting, and always preserving (Psalm 121:5; Isaiah 27:3). What a good shepherd You are! Thank You for promising to protect our thoughts and emotions from the spirit of fear, who prowls about to devour us with his lies (Psalm 121:7: 1 Peter 5:8). We welcome You to continue the deliverance that You have started within us. You have delivered, are delivering, and will continue to do so (2 Corinthians 1:10).

Despite all of this, I still struggle to remain at peace. Clothe me afresh in Your restfulness and let me experience tranquility (Matthew 11:28). Sometimes, when I am weary, I can't find my way into Your lap. Release the drawing power of Your serenity to enable my soul to relax into You (Matthew 11:29). Remove all of my random and distracting thoughts and replace them with the largeness of who You are (1 John 3:20).

May my worship be steadfast and singularly focused upon You, for therein is peace and rest (Isaiah 26:3). Thank You for Your rushing and gushing love, which flows freely through my heart (Romans 5:5). May I become overwhelmingly aware of Your peace. In Jesus's name, amen.

◆ ◆ ◆

Day 3

Holy Father,

Thank You for being the God who is near (Philippians 4:5). Your nearness is not just something to talk about but a living Presence within me (Romans 10:8). I need a reminder of Your Presence by a glimpse daily of Your face. Honestly, if Your Presence doesn't go with me, then there is no reason to move forward. Lead me to know Your Presence and rest there (Exodus 33:14–15).

Lord, I am very familiar with surging emotions. Often, my feelings overflow me like a tempestuous sea spills into the bow of a ship. Yet I believe that You can calm the sea with Your Word (Mark 5:39). You said, "Hush and be still," and it was accomplished.

I am awestruck, realizing that You literally commanded the winds to "mute and muzzle." Both of these actions are involuntarily enacted upon the wind, regardless of the storm's purpose. So, please stand before my emotions, commanding them to be muted and muzzled. Silence them by cutting off the flow of their negative speech, not for my glory but the glory of Your name (Ezekiel 36:32).

Don't forget, Father, that You gave Your Son authority over all flesh (John 17:2). Surely this includes the fleshliness of my emotions. As the exact representation of God's nature, I ask You to enact heaven's rule upon my feelings (Hebrews 1:3). Bring them under the authority of heaven, where Your Word is forever settled (Matthew 18:18; Psalm 119:89). Begin now making that eternal reality true in my life.

Give me the strength to deal with daily stresses without wavering in unbelief (Romans 5:20). I confess I have a fluctuating experience: sometimes obeying Your law and sometimes obeying the law of sin, all in the same day (Romans 7:25). May I not focus on guilt but on returning to You.

Thank You that you don't condemn me despite my tendency to waffle between spirit and flesh (Romans 8:1). I am Your child and stumble in many ways (James 3:2). Help me to fix my eyes on Jesus instead of the situation (Hebrews 12:2). I need You, Lord, so please grant this request that bears the signature of Jesus. Amen.

Day 4

Holy Father, thank You for giving Your children the very mind of Your Son (1 Corinthians 2:16). Yet when I am busy, I can get into a task mode that precludes Your eternal mind-set. Even my time with You becomes a checklist for chapters and prayers.

You are Spirit and the very essence of life (John 6:63). You have life within Yourself and have sealed Yourself within us to keep us focused (John 5:26, 6:57; 2 Corinthians 1:22). But honestly, it's sometimes simpler to tick things off a list than to wait and rest in You. Forgive me when I treat Your relationship like an encumbrance rather than a priceless pearl.

I think _____ is going through some of the same struggles. As I bring her to Your throne today, I remind You that You are a God who gives life to the dead and calls into being that which doesn't even exist (Romans 4:17). Stir a spiritual hunger within her that restores her to life-filled actions rather than drudgery. You promised to give rest to the weary and heavy-laden, and I know she qualifies (Matthew 11:28). Reveal Your gentleness and humility as You open her eyes to see the place wherein she can find real rest (Matthew 11:29).

Refresh her love for Your Word, just like a newborn baby seeks her mother's milk (1 Peter 2:2). Fill her with a taste of Your goodness (Psalm 86:10; 34:8). May her spirit, emotion, and thoughts be so satisfied that she overflows with praise (Psalm 63:5). Be the first one she thinks of every morning as she awakens to Your largeness (Psalm 17:15). Keep her thoughts fixed on You and her activity anchored on hope (Hebrews 12:2; 1 Timothy 4:10). Thank You for hearing my prayer (Psalm 65:2). In Jesus's name, amen.

Pregnancy

Healthy Pregnancy

Father, You are all about life. As we look at the names of Your Son, we find so many along this vein: Author of Life (Acts 3:15); Bread of Life (John 6:35); Eternal Life (1 John 5:11); Light of Life (John 8:12); the Living One (Revelation 1:18); the Living Stone (1 Peter 2:4); Word of Life (1 John 1:1); Spirit of Life (Romans 8:2); The Life (John 14:6); My Life (Colossians 3:4). Wow! And now You have granted a portion of Your life to grow within (*name of mom*). This pregnancy is just another way to allow us a living example of how You feel about us.

As this little one is (*mom's name*), but also (*dad's name*), You show us how You can be human yet divine. As he will reflect his mom and dad's personalities, You will emphasize how You are an exact representation of Your Father's nature (Hebrews 1:3). As they will love him even before he is born, You will teach us a little more about how you loved us first (1 John 4:19). And as this little one will one day disappoint them, You allow them to share in Your true nature that only desires what is best for Your children (Psalm 81:13).

Be this couple's patience as they wait through the years of growth. Be their consistency to enforce whatever ground rules they establish. Be their grace to ask forgiveness when they've made a mistake. Be their love on that day when they are out of their own.

Establish this family as a strong example of day-by-day Spirit walkers. In Jesus's name, I pray. Amen.

Pregnancy Complications

Holy Father,

Thank You for granting us Your magnificent promises (2 Peter 1:4). Thank You that we can share Your divine nature through these promises, although we continue to be fragile vessels (2 Peter 1:4). Because we are Your children, we have bold confidence to enter into the holy place to present our prayers to You (Hebrews 10:19). Thank You for being faithful to Your promises (Hebrews 10:23).

As we come to You on behalf of _____, we claim that You are the way, the truth, and the life—the way of healing, the truth of comfort, and the life that will strengthen their little one to grow (John 14:6). I pray that You will increase their faith, just as the disciples prayed that their faith would enlarge (Luke 17:5).

I ask that they have the confidence to contemplate their weakness without doubting Your strength (Romans 4:19). May they not lose heart, Father. Give them a heavenly viewpoint rather than a physical one (2 Corinthians 4:16–18). Grant them faith to see Your grace as sufficient during this time. Show them that when they are weak, You become very, very strong (2 Corinthians 12:9–10).

Allow the baby to grow within _____ until able to live outside the womb. Place Your hand upon _____, restoring her to health and enabling her to complete this pregnancy. Reveal Yourself to them, even as they sleep, and grant that they find Your Word to be the joy and the delight of their hearts (Jeremiah 15:16). In Jesus's name, amen.

Baby's Birth

Holy Father,

What great joy to thank You for the delivery of new birth. Just as all those who see (*baby's name*) are joyful about (*his*) birth, we remember that in the face of Your Presence, there is fulness of joy (Psalms 16:11). As (*family members' names*) look into (*baby's*) face, I ask that they seek Your face. Each day, may they find the time to stop all activity and rest in Your Presence, for only as we look at You are we transformed (1 John 3:2).

As we think of (*baby*), we ask that Your will would be done in (*him*), just as You see it already being played out in heaven (Matthew 6:10). We know that Your Word is already settled in heaven without question (Psalm 119:89). Grant this same type of faith to (*baby*). May (*he*) be a (*man*) who takes Your Word for face value, receiving and never doubting.

Thank You that Your storehouse already has a magnificent treasure waiting for (*baby*) to access (Luke 12:33). Thank You too for giving (*him*) (*his*) very own representative (*a Christian parent or grandparent*) to pray before You on (*his*) behalf (Matthew 18:10). Strengthen this representative to pick up all that You have available in the heavenlies (Matthew 16:19). Give (*baby*) eyes to see (*his*) inheritance early and an eagerness to seek after You with all (*his*) heart.

If we look at world events, we can be fearful for (*baby*), trembling at what lies ahead. But thank You for preparing for the future of this child by stockpiling hope (Colossians 1:5). Adjust (*his*) eyes early to see Your reality more clearly than what (*he*) can touch and feel (2 Corinthians 4:16–18). Grant (*him*) the heart of a faith walker, not merely a sight walker (2 Corinthians 5:7).

The evil one's job is to stand before You night and day, accusing this family (Revelation 12:10). You raise many to pray for them so that their faith will never fail (Luke 22:32). Place obedience in their hearts so that the evil one will be mightily ejected from Your Presence each time he stands to mention their names (Luke 10:18). We ask all of this with Your Son's name as the signature on this request. So be it.

◆ ◆ ◆

Miscarriage

Holy Father

Thank You that even in the day of our distresses, You remain our Refuge and our Stronghold (Psalm 59:16). (*Wife*) and (*husband*) are at the end of their strength, but we are comforted knowing that You are reliable even in the depth of our weakness (2 Corinthians 12:10). We can depend on Your strength, even when we have absolutely none of our own (Psalm 59:16).

You are a God of Deliverance (Psalm 68:20). You have already delivered (*wife*) and (*husband*) from the kingdom of darkness, but right now, it is difficult to focus on this fact (1 Peter 2:9). Quietly and gently, I ask You to continue Your process of delivering them from their grief (2 Corinthians 1:10).

The apostle Paul believed that You would deliver him "from every evil deed" (2 Timothy 4:18). We know that didn't mean deliverance from heartache, as he experienced plenty (2 Corinthians 11:23–33). After it was all said and done, Paul used those trials as a starting point to boast in You (1 Corinthians 2:2). I know that (*wife*) and (*husband*) can relate—feeling that indeed You, their treasure, are in a very earthen vessel (2 Corinthians 4:7). They, too, feel afflicted, perplexed, and maybe even persecuted with the question of "Why me?" (2 Corinthians 4:8–9).

I ask that despite all, they not feel crushed, despairing, or forsaken. Miraculously renew their faith little by little, day by day (2 Corinthians 4:16). Open their eyes to see things with Your eyes—eternal eyes—and be comforted as they glimpse the heavenlies where You hold their precious one (2 Corinthians 4:18). Thank You that the realm she now lives in is already the Kingdom of our Lord and Christ (Revelation 11:15)!

May we hold tightly to final reality, O Father. Do Your work and flood the heavenlies onto earth through our prayers (Matthew 6:10). May it be even now, Lord. May it be. In Jesus's name, amen.

Purpose

Day 1

Holy Father,

Thank You that You are the source of all help, the One who made both heaven and earth (Psalm 121:2). You are also the source of my salvation (Jeremiah 3:23) and the keeper of my spiritual walk (Psalm 121:5, Isaiah 27:3). Hallelujah!

As I come before Your throne, You know that I am walking through many challenges. Some days, I find myself saying with the psalmist, "My foot has slipped!" but even when I stumble, I can know You grip my hand (Psalm 94:18; 37:24). You never sleep but watch over my every step (Psalm 121:3). Grant me wisdom and discretion so that I can walk securely and sleep soundly (Proverbs 3:21–23).

Grant me rest, Father, allowing me to sleep without worry or fear (Proverbs 3:24). Reveal Yourself as my stronghold in need, my shelter in the tempest, and my shade when I'm sunburned with burning words (Isaiah 25:4). Keep me protected from evil by reminding me that I am tucked inside Your life (Psalm 121:7).

As I walk through the coming months, remind me not to rely upon my wisdom or direction (Jeremiah 10:23). You are the Lord of Hosts, the One who knows my heart and feels all that I experience (Jeremiah 11:20). Give me faith to cling to You so that I am set apart for Your renown, praise, and glory (Jeremiah 13:11).

Despite all of these changes, set me free for purposes of good (Jeremiah 15:11). May I diligently ingest Your Word every day as my guide, joy, and delight (Jeremiah 15:16). Grant me wisdom to separate the precious from the worthless when I speak for You (Jeremiah 15:19). Keep me safe from the power of my selfishness and reveal the blessedness of trusting in You (Jeremiah 17:5, 7). In Jesus's name, amen.

Day 2

Holy Father,

Thank You for Your Word, not only in printed form but especially in the form of Your Son (John 1:17). I remain astounded that the Word spoke the heavens into existence and now resides within me (John 1:3; Luke 17:21). From this vantage point, You are faithful to remain until all Your purpose is accomplished (Genesis 28:15). May Your Word be implanted, spread rapidly, and be glorified within me (James 1:21; 2 Thessalonians 3:1).

You desire that I am sanctified entirely, body, soul, and spirit (1 Thessalonians 5:23). Use Your Word as a separation between my soulish and spiritual man (Hebrews 4:12). May my soul be under the authority of Your Spirit daily, not under my flesh (Romans 8:6). I desire to worship You in spirit and truth (John 4:24).

Grant me a thirst and longing for the pure milk of Your Word (1 Peter 2:2). Sprout this desire deep within me, transforming my emotions and thoughts and influencing my actions (Luke 11:28). May I bear fruit with perseverance (Luke 8:15).

Thank You that when I stand in a little bit of Your light, I can rest assured that is the place where I will find even more light (Psalm 36:9). When my spiritual eye is clear, then my whole body will be full of light (Matthew 6:22). Grant me great discernment so that I can recognize the difference between good and best in my schedule. I know this will take much practice (Hebrews 5:14). May I learn how to distance myself from pleasing people and get closer to fully pleasing You (1 Peter 2:11).

I need a shepherd to provide for my needs and guard my soul (Psalm 23:1; 1 Peter 2:25). May I experience a contented heart by trusting You fully as my Great Shepherd. May I learn what it means to do all things *through* Your strength, not on my own (Philippians 4:13).

Show me when to lie down, even though there may be something to do nearby, and show me when to keep going, even when I'd like to stop (Psalm 23:2). Restore my soul to be Your tender, obedient servant (Psalm 23:3). In Jesus's name, amen.

Day 3

Holy Father,

Thank You that You not only wait for me but also actively call out to me through Your Spirit (Isaiah 55:1). Thank You that Your offer is at a price that every single person can afford—the price of obedience (Isaiah 55:1). Praise You that Your spiritual food is both life-giving as well as delightful (Isaiah 55:2).

I've had a setback, Lord. According to Your great mercy, I'm asking that You revive my soul (Isaiah 55:3). Renew my desire to seek and call upon You while You are near (Isaiah 55:6). I desire to submit in such a way that convicts others of Your compassion, but I need a fresh touch of Your Spirit to do so (Isaiah 55:7). Grant me the vision to see Your abundant pardon poured out in this disappointment so that my reaction may influence others with Your love and mercy (Isaiah 55:7).

Thank You that Your thoughts are higher than mine and Your ways higher than mine (Isaiah 55:8–9). Remind me of this often when things don't go as planned. I purpose to praise You, knowing that Your promised Word will come to completion in every situation because You are steadfast (Isaiah 55:10). What a delightful character quality.

Continue to speak Your Word to me so that I may know what You are about to do through this sequence of events. Lead me forth in joy and peace, Lord, so that I may live a life that exalts Your name (Isaiah 55:12–13). In Jesus's name, amen.

◆ ◆ ◆

Day 4

Father,

Thank You for not only establishing my steps but for catching me when I stumble along the pathway (Psalm 37:23–24). You promised to instruct and teach, meaning You always have to keep Your eye on me (Psalm 32:8). I need that! I make plans, but You are the One who gives me strength for the journey (Proverbs 16:9).

My life has taken several unexpected turns in the last several (*years, months, days*). As I pray through Isaiah 40, I ask that You begin by comforting me with Your kindness (Isaiah 40:1). Grant me eyes to see the future when the tree of these perplexing difficulties will be resolved (v. 2).

Because I earnestly desire You to enter into this wilderness, teach me how to clear the way for You (v. 3). May I make smooth roads for Your Presence, no matter how dry and desertlike the setbacks. Grant me the strength to lift every valley and bring low every obstacle by focusing on You rather than my circumstances (v. 4). Reveal Your glory and speak so I can hear (v. 5). Despite my weakness, may Your Word prove more enduring than ever before (v. 6–8).

May my personal life be one that exalts what You can do with surrendered life (v. 9). Be my Shepherd, gathering me into Your arms as I tend to the lambs under my influence (v. 11).

You are great beyond comparison. Lead me into the pathway You choose and encourage me when the going is difficult (v. 12–26). Thank You for never becoming weary or tired. Oh, how I need You whose understanding is inscrutable (v. 28).

Give me strength when I am weary and might when I lack power (v. 29). May I wait upon You, even as I wait on a stoplight or in a postal line. Grant me experiences both to wait and to watch You renew my strength and purpose. May I find I can soar like an eagle, run like a cheetah, and walk like a camel (v. 31). In Jesus's name, amen.

Relationships

Dating

Father,

Thank You that You are _____'s keeper (Isaiah 27:3). Every single moment, You water her with Your life and give her all that she needs for godliness (2 Peter 1:3). Thank You that You placed her inside of Christ by Your doing, not by her works (1 Corinthians 1:30). Remind her that as she lives day by day, it is Your doing that keeps her there, not her own (Jude 1).

As she looks into the future, there are many things that she doesn't know. But You say that as she makes her ear attentive to wisdom, her heart inclined to understand, and her desire alert for discernment, she can discover Your best for her (Proverbs 2:2–5). You not only can give wisdom, but You also want to do so (Proverbs 2:6). You have knowledge stored up for her and a shield prepared for her as she walks toward it (Proverbs 2:7).

Continue to be the place where she puts her burden (Psalm 55:22). May she see herself as You do: "a crown of beauty in the hand of the Lord." May she know experientially and intimately Your delight of her and what it means for You to be her husbandman as she waits for You (Isaiah 62:3–4). May she capture a vision of Your desire and reciprocate it with her love (Song of Solomon 7:10). As she waits for Your best, I ask that You woo and draw her with Your lovingkindness (Jeremiah 31:3).

As she begins to date, may her eyes be attracted only to what looks just like You. May she not settle for any less but daily set her mind where You are (Colossians 3:1–2). Teach her how to use her spiritual eyes, not the flesh, to detect attraction (2 Corinthians 5:16). Bring her out of bondage to relationships for her self-worth and into Your freedom (Deuteronomy 7:8; Galatians 5:1). In Jesus's name, amen.

Wisdom Regarding Continuing

Father,

Thank You for promising that You will not break a bruised reed or extinguish a wick that is faintly hanging onto the fire (Isaiah 42:3). Thank You for being the One who called us into Your righteousness and that it is dependent upon Your action, not upon our own (Isaiah 42:6; 2 Corinthians 5:21).

I come to You today on behalf of _____. You have placed her in my heart (Philippians 1:7). I join with the many who genuinely want the very best for her. She has indeed been in the furnace of affliction, and we trust that it has been for Your very own purposes (Isaiah 48:10). We believe that You are in control of all the twists and turns of our lives. You will establish Your objective for her, for You accomplish all that pleases You (Isaiah 46:10).

I ask that You do something new in this relationship—something so refreshing it would be like a road through a wilderness or a river in a desert (Isaiah 43:19). Only You know the outcome of this friendship, yet I ask that You grant them both a time of refreshing as they wait for You to reveal Your Presence (Acts 3:19). Open the heavenlies as they talk, and allow them to see You better as they speak to one another. May they come away from the time full of gladness because You showered them with the brilliance of Your Presence (Acts 2:28). I ask this with the very name of Jesus, Your Son, upon the request. Amen.

————————◆◆◆————————

Singleness

Holy Father,

Praise You for a reason to rejoice and exult in Your name (Isaiah 61:10). Thank You for sending Your Son to wrap us in righteousness that we do not deserve (Isaiah 61:10). I pray that through our lives, _____ and I will be the soil in which righteousness and praise springs to life. Allow us to grow in Your grace so that the nations will see and glorify Your name (Isaiah 61:11).

As I come before You today on _____'s behalf, I ask that You reveal to her the new name that You have given her, as designated by Your heart (Isaiah 62:2; Revelation 3:12). Thank You that as she follows You, she can hold to the promise that she is neither forsaken nor desolate, but Your delight is in her (Isaiah 62:4). Pull back the veil of her desire for a mate and grant her deep contentment in Your Presence first.

I ask that as she waits upon Your next steps, snuggle her close so that she genuinely knows that she is a woman "already taken" (Isaiah 62:4). Open her spiritual eyes to see how You daily rejoice over her and sing her love songs (Isaiah 62:5; Zephaniah 3:17). And, Father, since You have yet to take away her desire for physical marriage, would You either take away that longing or bring her the one You have chosen? How blessed is the one You choose and bring near. May we await Your answer patiently, well satisfied in Your Presence (Psalm 65:4). In Jesus's name, amen.

◆ ◆ ◆

Reconciliation

Holy Father,

Thank You for Your promises. I appreciate knowing You promised to remain with Your people (Psalm 94:14). I claim this promise on behalf of _____ and _____ this morning.

Things in their relationship are messy right now. Feelings they once shared toward each other are now cold and dead. Nothing they say or do helps repair their connection. Yet You are the God who heals (Exodus 15:26). You are the One who gives life to the dead and calls into being that which doesn't exist (Romans 4:17). You are resurrection power (John 11:25). So, out of the deadness of their situation, I ask that You restore the time that the locust has eaten and awaken new hope into their hearts (Joel 2:25; 1 Peter 1:3).

Father, their strength has weakened, and their hearts and flesh have failed (Psalm 102:23; Psalm 73:26). They've cried out to You with loud tears, angry tears, and hurt tears. Please show them the bottle into which You have saved every drop (Psalm 56:8). Set them free of the offenses, letting them relax and quieten to see who is genuinely in charge (Psalm 46:10). You are the God who rules all and have the power to strength and exalt (1 Chronicles 29:12). You made _____ and _____ and have their spiritual journey in the palm of Your hand (Psalm 100:3). Lead them onto paths of righteousness for the sake of Your name (Psalm 23:3). And don't forget the green pastures. They need to lie down and rest (Psalm 23:2).

You have promised that we will become like You when we see You, full of grace and truth (1 John 3:2). _____ and _____ need to fix their eyes on You and find themselves transformed from the inside out. May Your Word become their life, not just something they read on a page (John 1:17, 18; Colossians 3:4). For it is Your four-dimensional Spirit who gives life, not their two-dimensional words (John 6:63). Surge rivers of living water from within their innermost being (John 7:38) because if You don't lead them out of this place, then they won't be able to move at all (Exodus 33:14). Reclaim their souls into peace from the battle that is against them (Psalm 55:18). Show us all the hidden values of who You are. Yes, Lord, show us Your glory (Exodus 33:18). In Jesus's name, amen.

Revival

Day 1

Holy Father,

The evil one seems to be coming out of the woodwork. All around me, I hear stories of his conquests against life: shootings, bombings, tornados, suicide, and cancer. All point to telltale signs of a destroyer in the neighborhood (John 10:10).

Watching a funny movie or diverting my thoughts with social media isn't the plan of action You have for Your people. You have asked us to be vigilant in prayer. We are to be on the alert—not for suspicious-looking characters but for an adversary on the prowl (1 Peter 5:8). Open my eyes to see his hand and resist this strong man by believing in You, the One who is always stronger (Luke 11:21–22).

We are in a war, and yet sometimes I'm too afraid to suit up for the battle (Ephesians 6:11). I struggle to balance vigilance with evil and gentleness with others. Then I remember that the war is fought in the spiritual realm, not the fleshly one (2 Corinthians 10:3).

Lead me daily to Your inner closet (Matthew 6:6). Destruction of violence and chaos happens in prayer, not reading more articles or watching more news footage (2 Corinthians 10:4). Start eliminating deceit in my thoughts by captivating them with truth (2 Corinthians 10:5). Standing in Your light is the place where I come to know more light (Psalm 36:9).

Give many the desire to honestly know You by preparing the soil of their hearts to receive Your implanted Word (James 1:21). Open their eyes with increasing love for truth, for that's what leads to salvation (2 Thessalonians 2:10).

Send out bold laborers to speak truth with gentleness and peace (Matthew 9:38; Zechariah 9:10; 2 Timothy 2:25). Prepare my heart for speaking truth. Reveal Yourself to me that I may speak from love rather than religion. Knowledge puffs up, but love makes a difference (1 Corinthians 8:1).

Open my eyes to see You often because that is the only way to hope (1 Timothy 4:10). Indeed, You are my hope (1 Timothy 1:1), for seeing You increases my expectation (1 John 3:2–3). Praise You for holding all things together (Colossians 1:17). Because You have promised and cannot lie, I have strong encouragement (Hebrews 6:18). I have a hope cable anchored firmly within my thoughts and emotions that holds the anchor secure within the heavenlies (Hebrews 6:19). Hallelujah to my Deliverer, the One who will bring me safely into His Kingdom. To You be the glory forever and ever. In Jesus's name, amen (2 Timothy 4:18).

◆ ◆ ◆

Day 2

Holy Father,

You amaze us. Although You are the Creator of all things, You still do nothing unless You first reveal Your secret counsel to Your servants (Amos 3:7). This is quite mind-boggling.

As we ponder on Your brilliance, we see a stark contrast with our country and our world. We know that You desire everyone to drink the water of life You have provided without cost (Revelation 22:17). Thank You for loving every single person with extravagance (John 3:16–17).

When we come to the throne room, we find that You and the Son are already busy discussing our world (Romans 8:34). We are surprised to see that You have already prepared gifts of life and godliness for all people. You are just awaiting someone to come pick them up for delivery onto the earth (1 Peter 1:3). You are expecting us, the intercessors, to collect and distribute that which You've already prepared (Psalm 2:8).

And so, right now, I join my prayers with the groanings of other saints on behalf of our country. Although our prayers seem relatively small individually yet joined together with others and added to Your prayers, they become "much incense" (Revelation 8:3–4). They billow and smoke before You like a sweet fragrance, which is pleasing to Your nostrils.

I don't feel adequate to be doing this. But what if my attempt is all You expect? Yes, even though I often feel inadequate, You have made me righteous so that I can pray effectively (2 Corinthians 3:5; 5:21; James 5:16). Keep me focused in prayer.

Heal our land, O Lord. Raise intercessors who will desire You with their whole hearts and seek You earnestly and fervently (2 Chronicles 15:15). Stir up within me, as well as all intercessors, the ability to preserve in prayer, realizing that there is a reward for our work (2 Chronicles 15:7). Send us revival, Father. And may it begin in me. In Jesus's name, amen.

<hr />

Day 3

God of all Peace, Comfort, and Encouragement,

Oh, how we need You. Our world seems upside down in its understanding of truth. As long as we listen to humanity's report, the swirl of fear clouds our eyes, and we stumble from one anxious thought to another. We desperately need divine intervention to break this cycle, for only a fresh outpouring of Your reviving Spirit will clear the fog.

In Joel 2:28, You promised to pour out Your Spirit on all humankind. Your flood of life was not only fulfilled through the first-century church, but You've sent revival in nearly every century since. In the Great Awakening of the American colonies, the Welsh revival of 1905, and the 2006 revival in India, individuals thirsty for You asked You to "pour out water on the thirsty" (Isaiah 44:3). Thirst is always the prerequisite for the deluge of Your power.

Thank You for the unsettling that the worldwide panic has caused. The church needed something to shake us from our comfortable religion and place us before You, the ever-stable God (Hebrews 12:27–28). Our anxiety regarding the future is stirring thirst within us. May our dehydration for truth drive us toward a prayer of humility. When we recognize our utter dependence upon You, we can't help but pray it through. What a blessing!

Increase this thirst, Lord. The larger our emptiness, the greater Your filling. May our hearts be like the empty containers at the wedding in Cana—just waiting to be abundantly filled and transformed (John 2:6–10). Jesus, You are the living water, awaiting the thirsty one to come and drink (Revelation 22:17). Stir thirst within Your church like a parched land thirsts for rain (Psalm 143:6 NLT). Stir me individually to desire You passionately, so that You may come to me like the spring rain that waters the earth (Hosea 6:3).

Our world is thirsty, Father. "The afflicted and needy are seeking water, but there is none. Their tongue is parched with thirst" (Isaiah 44:17a). This global crisis has revealed our desperate need. But Your heart can't leave Your prodigal people like this: "I, the Lord, will answer them Myself, as the God of Israel I will not forsake them" (Isaiah 41:17b). You already have an abundance of water waiting to satisfy all spiritual desires (John 4:14).

Your purpose is to take the wilderness lives of pornography, addiction, abuse, and neglect and transform them into a flowing pool of living water (Isaiah 41:18). You love to "split the rocks in the wilderness and (to) give them abundant drink like the ocean depths" (Psalm 78:15). You desire to "come down like rain upon the mown grass, like showers that water the earth" to see fruitfulness and life unfold (Psalm 72:6).

So, we ask that You open up the heavens and rain down buckets of Your goodness (Isaiah 45:8 MSG). Break up the rocky soil and turn over the heavily trodden so that they may bloom salvation and spout right living (Hosea 10:12). Until that day, we will seek You diligently for the spirit of grace and of supplication (Zechariah 12:10).

Revive us again, Father. Revive us again.

———————————◆◆◆———————————

Day 4

Holy Father,

We praise You that Your reign has no geographic boundaries or cultural limits (Psalm 22:28). You form mountains, create wind, and walk on the earth's high places (Amos 4:13). You also sit on the ultimate throne, ruling and directing all nations, despite their own elevated perspective of their wisdom (Psalm 47:8). Thank You that indeed one day the earth will exalt You and truth will return to preeminence (Psalm 46:10).

Lord, I waver between worrying about our country and ignoring our problems altogether. On the issues that I think I can change, I spout my opinion and gripe loudly about the leaders who aren't pleasing me. In other instances, I intentionally disregard them, feeling that there is nothing I can do about it anyway.

Forgive me for both attitudes, Father. I know that cursing our rulers is akin to cursing You (Exodus 22:28). You are the One who both removes our governmental leaders and sets them up (Daniel 2:21). You have power over all worldly kingdoms and bestows authority according to Your will (Daniel 4:17).

When I focus on my worldview, I seldom ask for a glimpse of Yours. Reveal what You have stored up in the heavenlies for our nation so that my prayers may mirror Yours. Show me how to bind on earth what You've already secured in the heavenlies (Matthew 18:18).

I lay my motives bare before You. You know my weaknesses, hidden desires, willingness, and stubbornness (Romans 4:15 CEV; 1 Kings 8:39). Although I claim to be praying the "if My people" verse, I admit that I often don't want to turn from my selfishness to fulfill my portion of the promise (2 Chronicles 7:14).

Make me willing to be willing, Lord. Fulfill Your purpose within me so that I can pray with authority for our country (Matthew 6:10). Focus me on Your Spirit so that light can marginalize the darkness (Romans 8:6). Be my light (John 1:4) and scatter the night (Psalm 18:14).

Think Your thoughts through me (John 14:26). Make me a holy satellite hub that finds my desires met in You. In this way, I know that my every wish for our country will be granted (Psalm 37:4–5). Radiate Your brilliant glory from the depths of all I am (Zechariah 2:5). In Jesus's name, amen.

Day 5

Father,

Thank You that we do not wage spiritual warfare with our emotions, thoughts, or actions but with Your powerful weapons (2 Corinthians 10:3). Despite the devil's intent to devour, we have You for our protection (1 Peter 5:8). Hallelujah!

As I come before You on behalf of (*name*), I am immediately aware that this situation is more significant than my ability to pray. Yet she has asked me to pray, so I come with the boldness that You grant Your children (Hebrews 10:19). I ask that You destroy speculations and every lofty thing raised against knowing You. As You bring specifics to mind, I reach out in spirit to grab hold of those thoughts and deliver them to Your feet (2 Corinthians 10:4–5).

Grant wisdom to both (*name*) and me so that we may scale the walls and bring down the strongholds of tradition and law influencing this situation (Proverbs 21:22). You desire unity among Your people, yet there is a decisive spirit prevalent. Reach out and put this lofty stronghold to shame (Psalm 44:7). Shatter it to pieces (Jeremiah 48:1). I pray that knowledge of You will flow in such a way that You spill over from them into the community, city, state, and even the world (Isaiah 11:9).

True, right now, the fortifications of bitterness and strife seem unassailable (Isaiah 26:5). Yet we bring them to You, asking that You lay them low—so low that when this is over, we won't be able to tell it was ever within their midst (Isaiah 25:12). Distract the disunity in such a way that it dissolves while (*name*) silently awaits You (Isaiah 25:9; Exodus 14:14).

We ask this because our globe needs to see more of You. Deliver (*name*) that the earth may know that You alone are God (Isaiah 37:20). In Jesus's name, amen.

Day 6

Holy Father,

In the wake of (*school, city, national*) violence, I've heard it said that prayer is insufficient to stop the harm to (*our school children, our city's residents, our citizens*). Thank You, Father, that this is not true. You absolutely hear prayer (Psalm 65:2).

Granted, in and of ourselves, we are powerless to stop the spew of violence erupting against (*our children, our residents, our citizens*). No amount of regulated control can prevent the overflow of bitterness pouring from a wounded heart. Indeed, it is "out of the heart (that) evil thoughts, murders ... false witness and slanders come" (Matthew 15:19). But we are reminded that You are more significant than our hearts (1 John 3:20). So, we turn our eyes toward You and ask for Your intervention (2 Chronicles 20:12).

You promised to heal our land when we humble ourselves, pray, seek Your face, and turn from our disobedience (2 Chronicles 7:14). So, I begin here, Father—doing my part so that You can do Yours. What is within me, O Lord, that harbors offense and violence against my fellow man? To whom am I angry? What gossip and slander have I propagated? From whom have I withdrawn my patience and kindness? Who do I need to forgive? What methods of violence and malice do I entertain within my own heart?

O Father, forgive me for taking offense. Forgive me for breeding a doubt of character in the one who has hurt me. Forgive me for amusing myself with aggressive or gruesome entertainment. I recognize that each of these is the seed within my heart that, when played out to their logical conclusion, leads to the very violence I speak against so vehemently. May I be quick to hear, slow to speak, and slow to anger; after all, my passion can never achieve Your righteousness (James 1:19–20).

As each of Your children individually allow Your Kingdom to rule within us, Your peace will expand within our sphere of influence. Your Kingdom will come on earth, just as it has already begun in heaven (Matthew 6:10). May Your light shine so brightly within each of us that You alone are glorified (Matthew 5:16). Overtake the darkness as Your light shines out of me (John 1:5). Praise You for being the King who dwells in unapproachable light—to You be honor and eternal dominion, amen (1 Timothy 6:15–16).

Scriptural bullet points for revival prayer:

- Convict me personally in any area that conceals hidden sin (Psalm 24:3–4).
- Expose the deeds of darkness to the light (John 3:20–21).
- Send Jesus to attack and overpower the strong man (Luke 11:21–22).
- Strip evil of his armor and distribute it back to those he aims to destroy (Luke 11:22).
- Rescue the prey of the tyrant and let them know that God is on their side (Isaiah 49:25).
- Disarm the evil rulers and authorities. Make a public display of them (Colossians 2:15).
- Send God's breath to wither the influence of evil (Isaiah 40:24).
- Subdue the uproar of evil. Silence their song (Isaiah 25:5).

Self-Esteem

Day 1

Holy Father,

Thank You for actively seeking me out for Your Kingdom. Without any "umph" on my own, You reached down to make way for me to come out of darkness (Colossians 1:13).

Amazingly enough, this emancipation didn't just include moving from a dark place into a light one. You also rescued me from the domination of the evil one's choices. No longer does he get the first choice with what happens to me. I am no longer under his jurisdiction. Now my entire body, emotion, thought, and spirit are under the rule of the Kingdom of light! Hallelujah! This indeed is Good News.

Now, I ask You to grant this same insight and deliverance to (*friend in need of liberation*). In You, there is a releasing effect (Colossians 1:14). Enter into her emotions and thoughts and reveal that You have erased the handwritten note of requirements that Satan had against her (Colossians 2:14). Jesus took care of all Satan can accuse her of, allegations for yesterday, today, and even tomorrow (Isaiah 43:25; Acts 3:19; Hebrews 13:8).

There are still times when we find ourselves serving You on the one hand and acting on a fleshly impulse the next (Romans 7:25). But hallelujah, You don't condemn us for those mistakes because now we are in Christ (Romans 8:1)! Reveal this blessed truth to (*friend in need of deliverance*) as well. Jesus's life sets us free from the "ought to's" of our old way of life (Romans 8:2). Praise You for forgiving us of *all* our transgressions (Colossians 2:13). That is truly mind-boggling.

Reveal to (*friend in need of deliverance*) how to live and walk in this Kingdom of light (1 Peter 2:9; Galatians 5:25). Disclose Your Son clearly that she may see You, the invisible God (Colossians 1:15). You hid all the treasures of wisdom and knowledge in Your Presence (Colossians 2:2–3). Open her eyes to be riveted upon You, the Holy One, who is her ultimate reality (Hebrews 12:2). Bring her into Your light because it is from this perspective that she can see more light (Psalm 36:9). In Jesus's name and His light, I pray. Amen.

Day 2

Holy Father,

Thank You for desiring our good and sending Jesus as our hope (1 Timothy 1:1). Your Son came to deliver the promise of life (2 Timothy 1:1). How amazing! You, the Giver of that life, said we are to lift those without strength, and I'm here to do so on _____'s behalf (Romans 15:1).

Thank You that Your divine power granted us everything we need for abundant, godly life (John 10:10; 2 Peter 1:3). Your promises are packaged and waiting for _____ at heaven's door, so I've come to pick up that abundance for her (Matthew 16:19). As I pray, I ask that You deliver these promises directly to her heart and soul as I speak Your powerful Word into her life.

The accusation has left _____ broken. But You promise to be near the brokenhearted and save the crushed in spirit (Psalm 34:18). The afflictions of the righteous are many, but You promised to deliver us from all of them. Work within her in a way she can recognize mightily (Psalm 34:19).

_____ feels wrongly criticized. Yet You promise to save those who are afflicted (Psalm 18:27). You have gone beyond just an act of saving; You promise to relight her lamp so that her darkness will be illuminated (Psalm 18:28). Since her body's lamp is her eye, allow her to see what You are doing with this situation (Matthew 6:22; Psalm 32:8).

_____'s future seems like a large, impregnable wall. But by Your strength, she can leap over that wall (Psalm 18:29). Dread may seem inevitable, but I ask You to be the defense of her life, removing all anxiety (Psalm 27:1). _____'s times are in the palm of Your hand (Psalm 31:15), so please extend a flow of strength and peace from Your nearness (Psalm 29:11). May the deep recesses of her spirit continually overflow with an awareness of Your power and glory (Psalm 29:9).

_____ felt attacked by (*situation*). Yet, You promise to protect her mind and emotions from all evil (Psalm 121:7). May she know Your nearness from the moment she awakes each day (Philippians 4:5).

(*If the individual is a Christian*)

_____'s desire is to delight in Your Word (Psalm 1:1–2). Therefore, I claim that You have already planted her roots by streams of water to access necessary life flow (Psalm 1:3).

(*If the individual isn't a believer*) Make known to her the life-exchange path, for therein lies the fullness of joy (Psalm 16:11).

Father, hide _____ away from the negative voices and place her in the secret place of Your Presence where Your strength can shelter her (Psalm 31:20). Show her the truth, for, in You (the Truth), she can be free (John 8:32). In Jesus's name, amen.

◆ ◆ ◆

Day 3

Holy Father,

You have been my Deliverer in the past and continue to seek ways to liberate me (2 Corinthians 1:10). Not only do You untangle what is entangled, You are a God who breaks the trap altogether (Psalm 25:15; 124:7). Hallelujah! Emancipation must be one of Your superpowers. Thank You for being the Rock I can run to whenever I am overwhelmed (2 Samuel 22:2). You are worthy of praise (2 Samuel 22:4).

My commission on earth represents Your Kingdom. I am a watchman for enemy activity (Ezekiel 33:7). On this reconnaissance mission, I've become aware of a hostage situation of my friend _____. (*Negative self-talk, depression, low-esteem, gluttony, and lack of joy*) have ensnared her thinking. Not only is she chained to these thoughts, but the enemy is also bombarding her with torrents of terror and hopelessness (2 Samuel 22:5–6). She feels trapped.

So, in authority and with the armor of Jesus, I willingly represent the advance unit in Your campaign to establish peace in _____'s heart (Luke

10:19; 1 John 5:4–5). As I defend the line in prayer, I ask that You send in reinforcements on her behalf. Dispatch Your angel specialists, a holy SWAT team, to break through and rescue her from this hostage situation (Hebrews 1:14).

I'm not only asking for ministering angels but for You, the Commander in Chief, to come. Hear these cries and deliver her from disturbing thoughts (2 Samuel 22:7). I know You are ready and willing to rescue. May Your anger stir toward these enemies, not of flesh and blood but forces of darkness (2 Samuel 22:8; Ephesians 6:12). Stimulate hope within _____ as her fear of the destroyer turns into anger against the assassin. May she be angry yet sin not (Ephesians 4:26).

Command the darkness to obey You as You radically change her thought patterns (2 Samuel 22:12–14). Overturn the evil one's strategy and deliver her from her strong enemies (2 Samuel 22:17–18). No matter how mighty the fear, You remain greater (2 Samuel 22:18). Your plan is not just in defeating her foes but in showering her with Your delight (2 Samuel 22:20). Hallelujah! May _____ cling to this truth every moment of the rescue.

Reveal Your uprightness and blamelessness in a tangible way (2 Samuel 22:26). You are her lamp, O Lord. Light her way in every dark path (2 Samuel 22:29). Grant me faith to envision her storming enemy soldiers herself one day and leaping over all walls built up against knowing You (2 Samuel 22:30; 2 Corinthians 10:5). Begin now to set up full emotional health for her because Your way of deliverance is a perfect one, and Your Word is tried and trustworthy (2 Samuel 22:31). I commit her case into Your competent hands. I sign this military battle request with Jesus's name. Amen.

Stress

Day 1

Holy Father,

Thank You that You placed Your Life within me, not because of what I do but because of Your mercy (Titus 3:5). Your brilliance beams into my heart, but it's evident that Your light is within a very earthen vessel (2 Corinthians 4:6–7). I am very aware that I am a cracked pot.

Your grace is contagious and spreads like wildfire when given any freedom to work (2 Corinthians 4:15). Despite this fantastic reality, discouragement and stress are never far away from my mind. So, even when my attitude and action fall apart, remind me again that inside of me, You are the new life that sprouts up fresh daily (2 Corinthians 4:16).

Give me a renewed perspective to see how my experience is useful for returning my thoughts and emotions to focus on Your perpetual life (Romans 5:3–4). You could say these pressures are relatively light, considering the fantastic value of who You are within me (1 Peter 1:7–8). Your hidden life is more weighty, more costly, more valuable than can even be described with words. Better than the best, higher than the heights, deeper than the depths (Job 11:7–9); I honestly can't explain You. This reality is not just for today but continual, stretching out of this time into the next (Ecclesiastes 3:11). What a fantastic thought: I have already started eternity. Please help me to live like it (2 Corinthians 4:17).

To see the real value of perpetual life, I must stop emphasizing my situation. That isn't easy to do. Train my eyes to see into the heavenlies and pinpoint my gaze upon You, the invisible One (Hebrews 11:27). Take my eyes off my present situation to see with a heavenly perspective (2 Corinthians 4:18; Ephesians 2:6). May it be, Lord, please. May it be.

Day 2

O Lord of Hosts,

You alone are the pre-existing One (Nehemiah 9:6). You made the visible universe with its prairies, mountains, streams, and oceans. Everything beneath my feet and above my vision came into being by Your spoken Word (John 1:1).

When I consider the galaxies You affixed into place, I grapple to understand how each star may represent an angel, created for Your praise and our service (Psalm 148:2; Hebrews 1:14). "To you, O God, belong the greatness and the might, the glory, the victory, the majesty, the splendor; Yes! Everything in heaven, everything on earth; the kingdom all yours! You've raised yourself high over all" (1 Chronicles 29:11 The Message).

My mind struggles to comprehend all that You are, yet I can easily fall back into small thinking. I whine and fret for things to "get back to normal," for I confess I was well-contented with my previous life of little growth. Yes, Father, I radically needed a change.

So, once again, You spoke, and this time shook my world to the core of my being (Hebrews 12:26). My life of frenzy and agitation, amusement and entertainment, distraction and diversion, rocked violently and crumbled underneath me. As I stood stripped of their facade, I remembered what matters amid the silence.

Thank You, Father, for the upheaval. I needed this minuscule dose of affliction, for it's given me a pixel-sized share of the sufferings currently served up across the world (Psalm 119:71). This stress tested my confidence and disciplined my reactions (James 1:2-3; Hebrews 12:7). You reveal that only heat can purify faith (1 Peter 1:6-7).

No matter how much I react, thank You for counting me worthy for this exercise of endurance. Even Your first-born Son learned lessons of obedience through suffering (Hebrews 5:8). Grant me strength and steadfastness so that I may become mature and complete, lacking in nothing (James 1:4).

I don't want to go back to my former life. Doing so would squander the sifting's value with a wishful, backward glance (Exodus 14:10-12). I've taken Your advice and considered Lot's wife (Genesis 19; Luke 17:32). Thank You for being a forward-thinking God, Who always puts the goal in front of me, never behind (Hebrews 12:1). Give me eyes to see the life-seed of reconciliation, renewal, and revival amid this rubble. You are truly doing something brand new (Isaiah 43:18-19). Grant me the patience to see it come forth.

Stress may have rocked my righteousness, peace, and joy, yet it was only my consciousness of those things that fluctuated. Qualities hidden within Your Spirit cannot crumble (Romans 14:17; Hebrews 12:27). "The mountains may be removed, and the hills may shake, but (Your) lovingkindness will not be removed from (me) and (Your) covenant of Peace will not be shaken" (Isaiah 54:10). Thank You for being the solid Rock on which I may build my life (Psalm 62:2).

Don't return me into the clouds of shallowness, selfishness, and distraction. These only serve to veil the sun and canopy Your brilliance. Draw me upward, to live above the turbulence in the calm light of Your Presence. In that realm, I see You more clearly and remember Who is in charge of light and darkness, well-being, and calamity (Isaiah 45:6-7). I desire You and no other, so lead me on, Gentle Shepherd.

Suffering

Personal

Holy Father,

I've noticed something about the stony spiritual path. The proper trail may lead to an intensive trial.

You led Abram onto a bridleway of blessing (Genesis 12:1–2). Yet, upon arrival, a famine occurred, and he had to escape into Egypt. There was a trial along the trail (Genesis 12:10).

You chose Moses to walk in the direction of a deliverer (Exodus 3:4, 10). But along the way, Moses stumbled into years of complaining and rebellion from the very people he had freed. A trial along the trail (Exodus 14:11; 15:24, 16:2; 17:2; 32:6; Numbers 11:4–6; 12:1–2; 14:1–4; 16:41).

You led David in the paths of righteousness, but as he followed boldly on, Your walkway dumped him into the valley of shadows. A trial along the trail (Psalm 23:3–4).

Are you trying to tell me something?

Your calling, choosing, and leading are not into an avenue without anxiety but into an alleyway of greater dependence. The further we follow You, the more we depend upon Your Presence.

Just because I scrape my knee climbing over a boulder on the footpath doesn't mean I've taken the wrong road. The beaten-down grass before me signals Your Presence, and I'm drawn along by Your magnetism—my weakness attracted by Your strength.

When Your track leads me to famine and dryness, I find it's easier to seek earnestly for You, the Living Water (John 4:14).

When Your course leads me amidst complaining and unrighteousness, I'm more eager to hear the way, the truth, and the life (John 14:6).

When Your direction finds me in a deep depression, I must believe through the fog. You are somewhere close by, and my prayer for increased faith is granted (Psalm 23:4; Philippians 4:5).

You lead inwardly more than outwardly, as my footwear of peace is more important to you than my hiking boots. May I accept Your order—for Your Spirit to shepherd my inner man and guide my outer man.

After all, when I've put away my map, I'm better able to accompany You (Mark 8:34). Selah.

◆ ◆ ◆

Intercession for Friend

Holy Father,

I come to You on _____'s behalf. You've promised that all who are weary can come to find a place to pause (Matthew 11:28). As she lifts Your yoke onto her neck, give her insight to see that You are wearing the same collar.

As she comes, she finds You to be the load bearer in the relationship. Allow her to see that in yoking herself to You, the humble yet Strongest One, she has shared her burden with the One who once carried it alone. You know what this feels like and now regard her as more important than Yourself (Philippians 2:3–4). You promised her an intermission within her spirit, so I come to release that strength to her (Matthew 11:29). Send her Your Presence so that _____ may cool off with Your refreshing second wind (Acts 3:19).

You promised that mountains melt like wax in Your Presence (Psalm 97:5). I pray that you will melt away whatever mountains have arisen within _____'s life as You surge within her. Armed with the sword of the Spirit and girded with Your righteousness, I wage war with any thought raised against knowing You (2 Corinthians 10:4–5).

Pull down the shadow casting fortresses so that the evil one will flee from her. He hates the light, so shine Your radiant brilliance and accustom her eyes to Your luminescence (Ezekiel 1:27–28). In this light, allow her to see Your hidden, mighty hand extending toward her (Habakkuk 3:4). Encourage her, Lord, with a fresh glimpse of Your holiness.

Together, she and I come before You in dire need. If You do not go before us, we cannot move (Exodus 33:15). We are in this not for the sake of religion, not for the sake of a denomination, but to give You glory. Reveal Yourself unto us that we may truly live. May our lives be an exact representation of Your glory, just as You represented Your Father (Hebrews 1:3).

May we be spirit walkers who find our spirit so strengthened that our bodies (both mind and emotion) must follow after Your leading. Clarify how to exist in the living law of the Spirit rather than the death law of sin (Romans 8:2). Indeed, live through us (Galatians 2:20). In Jesus's name, amen.

◆ ◆ ◆

Intercession for Chronic Pain

Holy Father,

As I come to You today, I'm reminded of the words of Oswald Sanders, "To Him, all difficulties are the same size—less than Himself." Praise You that whether the difficulty before us is the size of a tree or the size of a mountain, either can be removed as we faith You (Luke 17:6; Matthew 17:20).

_____'s pain issues seem mountainous in size. It is chronic and ongoing. But as we fix our eyes upon You on her behalf, we ask You to untangle this mess (Psalm 26:15). Sort out the web of (*damaged nerves, arthritic joints, bulging discs*), restoring them to Your divine factory settings. She has been waiting faithfully for the moving of the waters (John 5:3). Deliver her from the oppressive bondage of the enemy (Luke 13:16).

Encourage _____ to flush her body with ample water, reminding her that You are the Living Water that satisfies and hydrates (John 4:14). Send Your Spirit to hydrate (*her joints, hip, shoulder*) and every individual nerve ending. You call into being that which does not exist, so we ask that You grow healthy joints and new nerving endings in place of the damaged ones (Romans 4:17). As You restore _____ to health, we praise You that she remains in the joy of her salvation (Psalm 41:3; 51:12).

We bring this work request to Your throne, signed by the name of Jesus. Amen.

Temptation

Day 1

Holy Father,

How blessed I am to be able to come boldly to Your throne, even when I feel I shouldn't have the right. You knew of my desperation before I was born, so You demonstrated Your love long ago (Romans 5:8). You even knew this day of shame would come. Despite all my repeated failings and this sin so easily entangling me, You still sent Your Son to die for me (Hebrews 12:1; Romans 5:6). This boggles my mind.

I bow before You, for I can't look You in the face. I promised I wouldn't allow myself to be tripped up like this again, but it seems "the good that I wish, I do not do, but I practice the very evil that I do not wish" (Romans 7:19). Evidently, "Nothing good dwells in me, that is, in my flesh" (Romans 7:18). I want to disappear.

It is at this point that I must come before You and look into Your face. Like King David, I ask You to be gracious to me according to Your lovingkindness (Psalm 51:1). But unlike David, I don't have to fear that You might "cast me away from Your Presence" or "take Your Holy Spirit away from me" (Psalm 51:11). You have tabernacled within me and sealed Your Spirit within my heart (2 Corinthians 1:22). The Holy Spirit won't leave me because You have made it spiritually impossible!

As my eyes meet Yours, I find that You do not condemn me (Romans 8:1). You see my pathetic state far better than I see myself, and yet You care (1 Peter 5:7). You pity me, favoring me just as a tender mother would her disabled child (Psalm 103:13–14). "Go your way and sin no more," You say (John 8:11). Indeed, You are a God who sees (Genesis 16:13) and loves anyway.

Since my initial salvation was not deed-based, my salvation continues in the same vein, by faith (Titus 3:5; Galatians 3:2). You called me according to Your purpose, not according to my works (2 Timothy 1:9). Your desire for me is that I believe in You (John 6:29). Thank You that what I do (or neglect to do) doesn't affect my standing with You because works do not justify a person, but faith in Christ (Galatians 2:16). How utterly amazing that my spiritual life does not depend on me at all but on Your life, You the God of mercy (Romans 9:16)!

I'm not sure why this is so hard for me to understand. I suppose that all those verses about being diligent and obedient make me think it's my responsibility to "be good." The evil one deceives me on this precise point. He tells me that I am not as perfect as I hoped, and then he deceives me by saying that You won't accept my attempts at pleasing You. Indeed, he is the father of all lies (John 8:44).

Praise You that my righteousness sources out of You, based on faith (Philippians 3:9). All my deeds, good or bad, have been traded in for Your Son's righteousness (Philippians 3:7). You look at my desire, not my fulfillment of that desire. Like a divine foreign exchange agent, You slid Your righteousness toward me and took my rubbish in exchange (Philippians 3:8; 2 Corinthians 5:21). My old person died when Your Son did, and now I stand with His life resident within me (Romans 6:6; 2 Corinthians 5:17; Colossians 3:3)!

I confess my sin to You—not because You demand it for my forgiveness but because I need to talk it over with You, my Dearest Friend (Isaiah 1:18). In Your opinion, You already separated sin from me, as far as the east is from the west (Psalm 103:12). You have already perfected and sanctified me, my past, present, and future by Your once-for-all obedience (Hebrews 10:10, 14). When I confessed my sins the first time, You forgave me and cleansed me from all unrighteousness (1 John 1:9). It is finished, and once You have forgiven me, then neither You nor I can make any offering that will further absolve my sin (John 19:30; Hebrews 10:18). Hallelujah!

Looking deeply into Your eyes, I see that this isn't about me at all. I stand here in Your light and find that the only actions that matter to You are those You produce (John 3:21). You are Spirit, and Your worshippers must relate to You spiritually, something I obviously cannot do alone (John 4:24). Thank You for already preparing those spiritual works for me to accomplish. Reveal how I can walk in them (Ephesians 2:10).

Take my eyes off my tendency to waver and rivet them onto Your brilliance (Hebrews 12:2). Capture my heart with Your beauty and allow me to see

You so clearly that my heart beats faster at a mere glance (Song of Songs 4:9). Remove whatever veil is between You and me, for seeing You purifies me (1 John 3:2–3). Keep my eyes open widely that I may I behold Your glory as You absorb and transform me into Your image (2 Corinthians 3:18). Grant me as much patience with myself as You have. In Jesus's name, amen.

* * *

Day 2

O Lord,

You have set up Your temple within me, yet I still manage to defile it as Your dwelling place (Ezekiel 8). From the outer court to the inner court, I can make an idol to worship rather than You, my One True God. I am often no better than the Israelites who made high places under every green tree.

Everywhere I find a place of ease or comfort, I tend to rest there in selfishness and pleasure, playing the harlot with things that bring me happiness (Ezekiel 6:13). Although I know that friendship with the world is enmity with You, I gloss over my love for fleshly things like it is no problem at all.

I am a temple of Your Holy Spirit (1 Corinthians 3:19). But I confess I have allowed detestable things to take up space in my outer court. Lusts of the flesh (*gossip, lies, judgmental thoughts, religiosity, any sinful form of sexuality*), desires of the eyes (*shopping, how I look, secretly delighting when someone who has offended me falls*), and the boastful pride of life (*what I do, where I go, what my future holds, and who knows about it*) have caused a den of activity (1 John 2:15–16). None of this pleases You (Jeremiah 7:30–31), yet I excuse myself saying, "Oh, that's just me," "It's my personality," and "I've always been like that."

You are in authority over all flesh, even mine (John 17:2). But I've short-circuited the power of transformation by justifying my fleshliness (Jeremiah 32:33–34). How can Your house be a "house of prayer for all nations" when

I am so filled with myself (Mark 11:17)? Don't let me continue to turn a stubborn ear to this ruckus (Zechariah 7:11–12).

Instead, O Lord, I consecrate everything to You, beginning with that of most value to me (1 Chronicles 29:3). (*Be specific here.*) Bring to mind what I talk about and what I think about, which reveals what I treasure (Matthew 12:34–35). I offer these unto You as a personal living sacrifice (Romans 12:1). I will not make a sacrifice that costs me nothing (2 Samuel 24:24).

Come into the hidden parts of my heart and make me know wisdom (Psalm 51:6). Restore to me the joy of Your salvation and sustain me with a willing spirit (Psalm 51:2). May I be a spiritual house that offers spiritual sacrifices that You accept through Your Son, Jesus (1 Peter 2:5). I pray all of these things in His name. Amen.

———————— ◆ ◆ ◆ ————————

Day 3

Holy Father,

Thank You for being my Lamp in the darkness. As I look back, I can see Your shining light in every dark situation (Psalm 18:28). I have to admit that there have been times when I felt quite blinded, but thank You that Your light is an inner one. You lead me out of the depths, despite what I think or feel (Psalm 18:16–17). With You as my hope, I know that You will not only keep guiding me but also be my place of refuge when I can't see clearly (Psalm 18:1; 119:105). I'm glad to know that no matter what the future holds, I carry within my frail heart the brilliant power of God (2 Corinthians 4:7).

The future looks scary, Father. If I let my emotions take over, I'll slip and slide, falling and failing at every turn. But when I remember that I can always run to You, I am comforted knowing that You are my hiding place—one that I can ever run into and find shelter (2 Samuel 22:33). You have given me hinds' feet—perfect for stepping through precarious situations and scaling the high things of the Kingdom (Psalm 18:33). Keep me moving toward glory, not merely toward being dulled with entertainment, sin, or knowledge (2 Corinthians 3:18; 2 Timothy 3:7).

Teach me to pray. Train my spiritual hands to use Your weapons deftly for both offensive and defensive battles in the heavenlies (Psalm 18:34). Reveal Your heart to me. I desire that my every prayer press forward on behalf of the world, always shielded by Your faithful salvation (Psalm 18:35).

As You know, I'm quite a mess, Lord. Enlarge my steps underneath me, so my feet won't slip back into sin and selfishness but walk firmly in Your Spirit (Psalm 18:36; Galatians 5:16). Gird me with daily strength for the war room while You align my thoughts and emotions with Yours (Psalm 18:39; 2 Corinthians 10:5). Deliver me from the contentions and complaints that the enemy shouts in my ear (Psalm 18:43).

You are alive and active, O Lord (Hebrews 4:12). Remind me to exalt You as my strength and the rock of my salvation (Psalm 18:46). Draw me after You so that together we may run forward (Song of Solomon 1:4). In Jesus's name, amen.

Thanksgiving

Day 1

Holy Father,

Over and again, You remind me of the importance of a grateful heart. Yet I confess to You thankfulness is not my strength. I am always an enterprising woman on an assignment. Unfortunately, all of these actions often takes my eyes off who You are.

So now, I pause to say thank You. Thank You for being my strength and my shield. You have sheltered me and offer me a place of refuge at all times (Psalm 91:2). How easy You make it to trust You (Psalm 28:7). Because of the history of Your steadfast love, I know that You are a good Father that I can trust (Psalm 107:1). Thank You for being the best Abba ever. Remind me when life gets hard to look back and recall Your ways (Psalm 23:4, 6).

Because I am rooted and built up in Christ, my spirit overflows with thankfulness. Father, may it flood on those around me (Colossians 2:7). May my family be the first beneficiary of my thanksgiving. Thank You for drawing them to Yourself and for the many ways they love me. Remind me to speak out my gratefulness in their hearing and to do it often.

You are my God, and I thank You for that gift (Psalm 118:28). In Jesus's name, amen.

Day 2

Holy Father,

Where do I begin to say thank You? Waiting for this answer made the answering even more significant. I was not only desperate but now I can see You were enlarging my capacity for joy (Nehemiah 12:42). I join the apostle Paul to say, "What thanks can we render to God for you, in return for all the joy with which we rejoice before our God on your account?" (1 Thessalonians 3:9) I am one of many who are rejoicing because of (*specific situation*).

Once again, You proved to be our Refuge and Strength, a very present Help in trouble (Psalm 46:1). We want to look back on this situation and say that we didn't fear the what-ifs, but honestly, our faith was pretty shaky on the hard days. I'm sure that (*individuals involved*) have felt at times that this was just a bad dream. But thank You that we have beheld Your face in righteousness and Your likeness when we awakened (Psalm 17:15). Praise Your Son, Jesus, for always standing like a ladder to bridge heaven and earth for us (Genesis 28:12; John 1:51).

You, precious Jesus, could see past the limitations of time and space into what was truly best for this (*situation, family*) (Ecclesiastes 3:15). You could see how the proof of faith, which is more precious to You than any gold, would be found to result in Your praise, glory, and honor (1 Peter 1:7). As You kept Your eyes wide open, never slumbering and never sleeping (Psalm 121:4), we held our feet on the ground, firmly planted in faith against the evil one (1 Peter 5:8–9). And somehow, through this miraculous activity called prayer, the angels of God ascended Your body into heaven with our requests and then descended Your body with this perfect answer (Genesis 28:12). We look back and realize that all the while, those ministering spirits were doing their work, rendering service for the sake of (*situation, family*), for whom You were planning great salvation (Hebrews 1:14).

Most of the time, we honestly didn't know how to pray. We searched for words and grappled with limited understanding. But hallelujah, You were interceding Yourself with groanings too deep for words (Romans 8:26). Thank You that our lack didn't detract from Your abundance. We prayed as we could, not as we couldn't (2 Corinthians 8:12). Once again, You have caused all things—even (*list situations: i.e., lack of work, cancer, etc.*)—to work together for good (Romans 8:28). What the evil one meant for harm, You meant for good (Genesis 50:20).

Now unto the King eternal, immortal, invisible, the only God, be honor and glory forever and ever. Amen (1 Timothy 1:17). Hallelujah.

Day 3

Holy Father,

How majestic is Your name in all the earth (Psalm 8:1). When I think about the heavens, the stars, and galaxies that You have made with Your own hands, I can't grasp why You would care for us. Yet You have given us a place in Your Kingdom government just a little lower than Your own. You indeed are magnificent beyond our understanding (Psalm 8:3–5, 9).

Today, _____ and I remember the importance of a grateful heart (Ephesians 5:20). Yet, we recognize this isn't our strength. We are women on a mission, full of activity, movement, and purpose. Unfortunately, all of this busyness often takes our eyes off of Your quiet Presence in our midst.

So now, _____ and I pause to say thank You. We come before You with joyful singing, remembering that You are our God (Psalm 100:2-3). We are Your people, who you created, and now are Your sheep, who You tend (Psalm 100:3). No wonder we can enter into a time of thankfulness and bless Your name. You are good, not only to us but also to those we love (Psalm 100:4-5).

Amazingly, we aren't only grateful during the good days, but we can look back and see Your hand in our difficulties. When we sought You, You delivered us from our fears and stationed Your mighty angel army around us (Psalm 34:4, 7). As we look into the past, we notice You watching and listening to our cries (Psalm 34:15). Thank You that even within our current brokenness, we can know You are near (Psalm 34:17). Hallelujah. Teach us to remember so that we may grow in gratitude daily. In Jesus's name, amen.

Thoughts

Day 1

Dear Father,

Thank You for speaking to us through Your Son, Jesus (Hebrews 1:2). You knew that we would need an identical image of Your nature to live truly (Hebrews 1:3; John 14:6). Indeed, my only hope is to allow Christ to become my life (Colossians 3:4).

As I struggle with my thought life, reveal to me how to set my mind on You so that I can know life and peace (Romans 8:6). I know those who are according to the Spirit set their minds on the things of the Spirit (Romans 8:5). But my mind is so often distracted that I need supernatural help to affix my thoughts on You.

Grant me wisdom and insight into daily focusing on You as my determined purpose (1 Corinthians 2:2). Since You, O Lord, are the One who gives understanding, please make this a reality within me (Proverbs 2:6). You want my thoughts to feed on the tree of Your life, not upon the tree of whether something is merely right or wrong (Genesis 2:9). Focusing only on good and evil isn't life-giving (Genesis 2:17). Thank You that my thought life doesn't depend upon my works but upon You, the One who calls (Romans 9:11).

Thank You for giving me the mind of Christ (1 Corinthians 2:16). May I know experientially all that You have already freely given me (1 Corinthians 2:12). Grant me the diligence to keep You in priority focus daily so I may follow as You lead (Hebrews 12:2; Hebrews 4:10; Romans 8:14). In Jesus's name, amen.

Day 2

Holy Father,

Preparing a heart to receive truth is a lot of work, isn't it?

Just like working the ground before planting, a heart's soil must be softened by the water of Your Word (Psalm 65:10). You know just how to moisten the hardest heart through situations and experiences designed individually for each heart-soil. Indeed, it often takes the storm of a crisis to ready a life for You. Today, I'm asking You to water my heart-soil so that Your truth has a chance to grow.

Once moistened by the tenderness of Your showers, You must till our soil for planting. No matter who we are, we rarely welcome the blades of the tiller. Yet, overturning our hardened hearts is the only way we can grasp the One we will never understand.

Sometimes I feel trampled down and dried out. I wonder if this is the reason I often have a hard time seeing You. Problems easily root in a history of pain. I welcome You as my Gracious Tiller, knowing You will be as gentle as possible when preparing my soil.

As You prepare, remove anything that would contend with the seeds of Your Spirit. Unearth any stones of jealousy, roots of bitterness, pebbles of people-pleasing, or thorns of worry. Pull them out and get rid of them. Knowing their loss in my life will remind me to watch my words when I see others struggling with their soul excavation.

Begin even now to grant me the desire to receive Your implanted Word (James 1:21). I realize that to sprout, Your seed must go into the depths of my motivation. Grant me the insight to see what is holding the reins of my heart (Psalm 51:6) so that I may pray specifically. You are the One who should be holding my reins (Psalm 139:13 KJV).

Growth takes a while, doesn't it? You don't prepare heart-soil overnight. I want to be patient soil, with the perseverance to continue asking my requests until I see the sprouts of truth coming to life. You won't give up on me, and I appreciate that. Praying in the persistent name of Jesus, amen.

Day 3

Holy Father,

Thank You that you hear both our weeping and our supplication (Psalm 6:9). You even promise to respond to the prayer of the destitute (Psalm 103:17). Surely I meet one of those qualifications as I come before You today, seeking to know what You are saying to the Son about me (Hebrews 7:25). Open my ears to hear what You would say about my past (Psalm 40:6).

You desire to give Your children every place on which the sole of their feet tread (Joshua 1:3). Granted, the world and the devil want to throw heartache, distress, ill-treatment, and uncertainty our way (Romans 8:35). But no matter what our experiences, Your purpose is that we overwhelmingly conquer our past through Christ who loves us (Romans 8:37). You promise to be with us, never failing or forsaking us (Joshua 1:5). So, I ask that You open my eyes to see the strength and courage You provide as I seek to walk in Your ways (Joshua 1:6–7).

The prayers that Your Son prayed on earth were words initiated from Your very heart (John 14:10). As I listen for You, bring to pass my healing as I faithe You (John 14:12). As I see Your holiness, others will also know that You are the Lord (Ezekiel 36:23).

Despite my desire to please You, my history often condemns me. Since You can heal the blind and the lame, I believe You can heal the wounds from my past as well. I ask that You fill me so entirely with knowledge of Your will that the pain of my memories is displaced wholly by Your love (Colossians 1:9).

Purify me by sprinkling Your cleansing water that dissolves all of my baggage of mistreatment (Ezekiel 36:25). Remind me that You chose me to obey Christ, not because You thought I could, but because You would accomplish it Yourself (1 Peter 1:1–2). I need to see this clearly. Continue renewing my heart and spirit so that I can relax into a manner that pleases You (Ezekiel 36:26–27).

Show me how to forget the past and focus instead on my faith's Author and Editor (Isaiah 43:18; Hebrews 12:2). As I redirect my thoughts, I ask that You continue to renew my life. Do this new thing in me by making my wilderness experiences into paths straight to Your heart (Isaiah 43:19). I'm believing in You because I can't do this any other way. In Jesus's name, amen.

◆ ◆ ◆

Day 4

Holy Father,

Thank You for loving me with an everlasting love and drawing me to Yourself (Jeremiah 31:3). How precious it is that even before I call out, You are answering, and before I speak, You are listening (Isaiah 65:24). I know You are listening even now.

As I come before You, I think about all the turmoil (*new job, homeschool, moving, etc.*) has caused. Indeed, the evil one has asked permission to sift me, and he has been busy shaking me violently (Luke 22:31). But I am joining my prayer to Yours that my faith will not fail (Luke 22:32). Although this situation seems baffling, You are not a God of confusion but peace (1 Corinthians 14:33). May I live protected and guarded by Your peace, brightly shining as I receive daily insight from Your Word (John 16:33; Daniel 12:3).

Since all of the treasures of wisdom are hidden in You, please release them within my thoughts (Colossians 2:3; Matthew 18;18). You have a storage of hope built up, and I could use a large delivery of that as well (Colossians 1:5).

As You well know, I must have the necessary supplies to keep faithful. I can't bear fruit when confused and discouraged. You've promised to hold all things together, so I'm asking that You use this situation as a prime example to the world of Your divine authority (Colossians 1:17). Allow me to hear You sing over me with shouts of joy in the morning and notice Your quiet display of love in the evening (Zephaniah 3:17).

Thank You that nothing is too complicated with You (Jeremiah 33:27). As I call to You daily, I know that You will answer because You've promised to do so (Jeremiah 33:3). You are a God of Your Word (Isaiah 46:10). Reveal the profound things despite the apparent darkness of the moment (Daniel 2:22). Reveal Your secret counsel by declaring Your thoughts specifically as I wait (Amos 3:7; 4:13). Tuck me away from the strife of doubt so that I may live each day in the shadow of Your wings (Psalm 32:20; Psalm 17:8). I'm putting Your signature at the bottom of this request, not mine. So be it.

Day 5

Father,

Thank You for being available to listen to me by sending Your Son as the mediator (Luke 11:9). Since Jesus is Your replica (Hebrews 1:3), the more I know Him, the more I know You. Even so, Your ways are higher than mine, and there is still much I don't understand (Psalm 92:5). Send Your Spirit to pray through me.

As I come before You on behalf of _____, I thank You that I may use Your name as the signature on my requests. You promised that anything we ask according to Your desire would be granted (1 John 5:14–15). So, I want to claim the promises that You have already stored up for her.

Grant her the desire to know You (Psalm 63:1). Often, because of distractions, we crave other things before longing for You. Yet I ask that You make _____ willing to be willing. Change her desire so that she will hunger and thirst intensely for Your righteousness (Matthew 5:6).

In Your name, protect her from the evil one, binding and loosing her experience to match how Your will is currently taking place in heaven (Matthew 18:18). Your Word is forever settled in the heavenlies (Psalm 119:89), so establish it in her heart as well. May what You say be enough for her. Stir faith to grow within her heart every time she hears Your voice.

The evil one has a habit of accusing _____. This should be no surprise because accusation is the very meaning of Satan's name (Zechariah 3:1). In Your name, I ask that You rebuke all these accusations, covering her mind with clean thoughts because of what You have done (Zechariah 3:5).

Remind her of the turban You created for her to wear. It has an engraved tag that says, "Holy to the Lord" (Exodus 28.36).

Thank You for being her high priest, seated in the heavenlies to cleanse her conscience from the "ought to's" (Hebrews 8:1; 9:13–14). You are her warrant against all accusations so that she can be guiltless, both today and on the day of Christ's return (1 Corinthians 1:8 AMP). May she live daily by pleasing You, not by obeying humanity's rules.

As I pray in Your name, may _____'s accuser be so violently refused that he plummets from Your Presence with lightening force anytime he mentions her name (Luke 10:18). Instead of allowing him to point his finger at her, please point Your finger of disregard at him. May we watch Your powerful Kingdom fill _____ (Luke 11:20). Grant her the obedience necessary to hear Your Word and do it (Luke 11:28). I offer all these things in Your name. So be it.

Warfare

Day 1

Holy Father,

I praise You that I can come boldly in prayer to Your throne today (Hebrews 10:19). You have provided me with every spiritual blessing through Christ and have granted me everything for life and godliness (Ephesians 1:3; 2 Peter 1:3). You have given me the keys to the kingdom of heaven, and You have already loosed Your love, approval, and completeness into my life through Your life (Matthew 16:19; Ephesians 4:7; Colossians 2:10). Teach me how to use these keys to access all that You have in store for me and the world around me. How blessed I am that the Almighty King of kings is also my Abba, Father (Galatians 4:6).

Thank You for forgiving all my sins (Hebrews 10:12, 17). My past sins, my present sins, and my future sins are all forgiven—not because I have done something right but because You have (Titus 3:5). Because of Christ's once-for-all obedience (Romans 5:19 Darby Translation; Hebrews 9:11–12). You choose to keep me forgiven not because I'm "doing better" but because the blood of Christ satisfies You (Romans 9:16; Exodus 12:13; 1 Peter 1:18–19). My entire Christian experience is now lived out within Christ, not within me (Galatians 2:20). Because of Christ's death and resurrection, Satan is my defeated foe (Revelation 12:10). Remind me often of that fact.

Granted, Satan continues to condemn me of faults. He is a lying accuser at his core (John 8:44; Zechariah 3:1). Father, remind me not to look at my works for justification (Galatians 2:16). Satan was rendered powerless in my life because of Your doing, not mine (Hebrews 2:14–15). You, O God, have acquitted and absolved me (Romans 8:33; Isaiah 50:9). What right does anything or anyone have to condemn me (Romans 8:34)? Christ's blood cleanses me, even when my conscience criticizes me (Hebrews 9:14). Praise You, Father, for being greater than all, including my oversensitive heart (1 John 3:19–20).

Thank You not only for forgiving all my transgressions but for canceling every bit of the debt I owed You (Colossians 2:13–14). What my religion could not do, You did, by fulfilling Your own requirements for me (Romans 8:3–4). Hallelujah! You nailed me on the cross with Christ so that my old Adam-like nature is dead and gone (Romans 6:6, 8). Christ's blood dealt with my past actions, and Christ's cross separates me from a daily bent toward disobedience (Romans 7:4). I came into this world as a living soul. I've been born again into Your Kingdom by Your life-giving spirit (1 Corinthians 15:45). Grant me a spirit of wisdom and revelation to know all that I have in You (Ephesians 1:17).

Although You have freely given me every Kingdom provision, I still war against the forces of darkness and wickedness (Romans 8:32; Ephesians 6:12). The evil one prowls about, trying to devour me and mine at every turn (1 Peter 5:8). Thank You that because I am in You and You are in me, I do not have to fear Satan (Colossians 3:3; 1:27; Hebrews 2:15). You are more significant in me than the power of the evil one around me (1 John 4:4). Help me when my belief in this fact wavers (Mark 9:24).

I will not cower in fear because, in You, I have an overcoming power, an overwhelming love, and a perfect, sound mind (2 Timothy 1:7). I have the very mind of Christ Himself (1 Corinthians 2:16). I will resist the evil one, firm in my faith, and watch Satan fall (1 Peter 5:9; Luke 10:18). Thank You for Your faithfulness. In Jesus's name, amen.

◆ ◆ ◆

Day 2

Holy Father,

Thank You for providing me with full spiritual armor against the schemes of the devil (Ephesians 6:11). I agree with my status as a victor by wearing my armor proudly (2 Corinthians 2:14). Every piece is Christ Himself.

I cinch my emotions with Your truth, my heart with Your righteousness, my mind with Your salvation, and my direction with Your peaceful preparation

(Ephesians 6:14–15, 17). I vigorously lift the action of faith, knowing that trusting You is the only way to extinguish Satan's fiery doubts effectively (Ephesians 6:16). Faith is my triumph and Satan's defeat (1 John 5:4). I will walk by substantiating what You say, not by reliance on what I can see (Hebrews 11:1 Darby Translation; 2 Corinthians 5:7). Lord, increase my faith (Luke 17:5).

Now, Father, I take up my only offensive weapon, the blessed Word of God (Ephesians 6:17). Alive and active, Your Word is specifically suited to destroy Satan's strongholds (2 Corinthians 10:4). All around our culture and even within my mind, the devil has constructed lies, twisted truth, and cast insinuations against Your Word (2 Corinthians 10:5). Layer upon layer, Satan's deceptive darkness raises distractions, doubts, and distrust against Your truth (Genesis 3:13).

Yet today, I stand against this work and bring every thought captive to Your feet. Reveal any area of my thoughts or emotions that side with the enemy (Philippians 3:15). May both the words of my mouth and the meditations of my heart be acceptable to You, O Lord (Psalm 19:14). I invite Your razor-sharp Word to pierce through my emotions and thoughts so that springs of Your Spirit already living in my inner person can overflow through my outer actions (Hebrews 4:12; John 7:38). May I handle the sword of the Spirit accurately so that Your Word may spread rapidly and be glorified (2 Timothy 2:15; 2 Thessalonians 3:1).

As I look around me, I see evidence of a strong man, fully armed, guarding his homestead (Luke 11:21–22). Father, You know that the spirit of deceit and despair (*materialism, greed, pleasure, pornography, lust, promiscuity, lewd sexuality, homosexuality, abortion, fear, inferiority, intimidation, negative self-talk, addiction, unforgiveness, philosophy, dementia, manipulation, self-love, pride, etc.)* vigilantly attack me and those I love.

But You, O Lord, are the Stronger Man—exceeding all these others in power (Psalm 68:34). You ride upon the highest heavens and speak forth against these spirits with a great and mighty voice (Psalm 68:33). Your Son accomplished death for the very purpose of destroying spirits like these (1 John 3:8).

Jesus has now finished His work and is sitting down at Your side, awaiting me to bring these enemies to Him as bound captives (Hebrews 10:11–13).

In obedience to Jesus, my holy Joshua, I bring these enemies out of darkness (Joshua 10:22). I put my foot down upon their necks to prove their total subjugation to Your Kingdom (Joshua 10:24). In the name of our Lord Jesus, I tread upon this lion of fear and this cobra of deceit (Psalm 91:13). Using Your name, I trample them underfoot (Psalm 44:4–5). Come, God of peace, and crush them underneath my feet (Joshua 10:26; Romans 16:20; Psalm 60:12).

I join with You in telling them, "No!" especially as they whisper deception into my life and into those I love (Titus 2:11–12 NIV). (*You may want to mention specific situations or individuals here.*) No matter where darkness has shadowed my thinking, I step out boldly into the light (John 3:21). Expose these dark spirits with Your light (Ephesians 5:13). Remove the influence they have held over me and restore the places in my life of defeat (Joel 2:25–26). I ask that You use for good all that Satan meant for evil (Genesis 50:20). Take all that he once stole from me and redistribute it back into Kingdom use (1 Chronicles 26:27). I also ask this for others I know who have fallen under the deceit and destruction of the strong man (1 Samuel 17:54).

Thank You for giving me complete authority over all the power of the enemy (Luke 10:19). Regardless of my feelings, You have given my prayers authority to put to flight a thousand of these spirits (Joshua 23:10). Just think about what I can do when united in prayer with other intercessors (Matthew 18:19–20)! How thankful I am that You are my best prayer partner (Hebrews 7:25; Romans 8:34; Revelation 8:3–4).

Continue to give me a hunger and thirst for Your Word so that I can discern between good and evil (Matthew 5:6; Hebrews 5:14). Even though Satan can sometimes disguise himself as an angel of light, I will not allow him to take advantage of me because I will not remain ignorant of his schemes (2 Corinthians 11:14; 2:11). I will set my mind on things above, not on the earth's counterfeit things (Colossians 3:2). I will daily take refuge in Christ, who is truth, and my firm anchor of hope (John 14:6; Hebrews 6:19–20). In the name of the Lord Jesus Christ, I pray. Amen.

Day 3

O Father,

Thank You for revealing Yourself to us as God Almighty (Genesis 17:1). You are more powerful than any other being ever was or will be (Revelation 11:17). This is good news, especially when I feel overwhelmed.

The evil one is always on the prowl to destroy Your creation (1 Peter 5:8). Sometimes he uses individuals or groups to do his bidding, and we are offended. Yes, offenses are inevitable, but we recognize that flesh and blood aren't to blame (Luke 17:1). This is a spiritual war, and our wrestlings are with spiritual opponents of darkness, not against humankind (Ephesians 6:12). Thank You for giving us weapons suited explicitly for this kind of warfare (2 Corinthians 10:3).

As I come before You in prayer, I'm aware that this situation is far more extensive than my ability to pray. Yet with the boldness that You have given me, I enter into the fray (Hebrews 10:19). Destroy the speculations and every lofty thing refusing to know You. As You bring to mind specifics, give me the clarity to reach out in spirit, grab hold of these thoughts, and lay them at Your feet (2 Corinthians 10:4–5).

Grant wisdom, Lord, so that in Your strength, I can scale the walls and bring down the strongholds of oppression *(like tradition, law, pornography, sinful expressions of sexuality, hatred, etc.*—Proverbs 21:22). You desire unity among Your people, yet a divisive spirit remains prevalent. Put to shame this lofty stronghold by the power of Your Word. Shatter it into pieces (Jeremiah 48:1). I pray that *(the meeting, the confrontation, the phone call, etc.)* won't result in hurt but that Your knowledge will spill over into my circle of influence in my city, state, and even world (Isaiah 11:9).

Right now, the fortifications of *(bitterness, strife, chaos, fraud, etc.)* seem unassailable. Yet I bring them to You, asking that You lay them low (Isaiah 26:5). I pray that when this is all over, I won't be able to tell that it was ever in my midst (Isaiah 25:12). May Your power fight for me as I silently await You (Isaiah 25:9; Exodus 14:14).

I ask this because our globe needs to see more of You. Deliver me from the evil one, that the earth may know that You alone are God (Isaiah 37:20). In Jesus's name, amen.

———————————◆ ◆ ◆———————————

Day 4

Holy Father,

As I come to You, I can thank You abundantly. I call upon Your name and remember Your wonderful deeds that You have already done in my life. (*List out some incidents in which you can sincerely thank Him.*) Yes, Father, the wonders and glory of Your holy name are everlasting (1 Chronicles 16:8–12).

Because You are great and greatly to be praised, because splendor and majesty are before You, because strength and joy are in Your place, I come boldly to Your throne (1 Chronicles 16:25, 27). Listen to my prayer and let Your face shine (Daniel 9:17).

Look down from heaven and see every fear, attitude, and difficulty that surrounds me (Psalm 33:13). You have fashioned my heart from conception and understand how I work (Psalm 139:13, 16; 33:15). My situation is no surprise to You because Your eyes are continually upon me and my family (Psalm 33:18).

You don't just look; You care (1 Peter 5:7). Whether I feel like it or not, You are near to my broken heart, and You promise to save when I am crushed in spirit (Psalm 34:18). My afflictions are many—emotional, mental, physical, attitudinal—but, You have gone out on a limb and promise to deliver me out of *all* of these (Psalm 34:19).

Your kindness always directs toward repentance (Romans 2:4). I know that for any change to come about, I must first do my part. I must humble myself, pray, seek Your face, and turn from my selfishness (2 Chronicles 7:14).

So, Father, I ask You to reveal any disobedient selfishness to which I still cling.

Is there something You have told me to do that I am not yet doing, or something that You have told me not to do that I've continued?

Is there an unforgiving heart within me?

Am I harboring an offense, allowing it to grow into bitterness?

Is there any area of fear that I have allowed to be bigger than You?

I come to Your light, asking that You expose the secret places of my heart so that I will align with what You want to do (John 3:20–21). Selah.

Thank You, Father, that when You shine the light of conviction upon a heart, it is not for shame but the sake of truth. Hallelujah! Thank You for being greater than my heart and for knowing all things (1 John 3:20). So, as "seeing Him Who is unseen," I have the confidence to enter the holy place by the blood of Jesus—drawing near to my Great Intercessor with a sincere heart in full assurance of faith (Hebrews 11:27). Thank You for sprinkling evil consciences clean with the sanctifying work of Your blood and for doing so continually (Hebrews 10:19, 22, 14; 1 Peter 1:2).

As I stand before You, I recognize the adversary prowling about like a lion, seeking a comprised place to strike (Job 1:7; 1 Peter 5:8). Father, I'm so very tired of living out in the savannah with these wild beasts. You have promised to be my Refuge and Strength, present whenever there is trouble (Psalm 46:1). Now would be a good time. You have promised to give Your angels charge concerning me, to guard me in all my ways (Psalm 91:11). I need insight into the entrance for this divine refuge of peace (Psalm 91:1, 4).

Like Elisha's servant, I ask that You open my eyes to see the mighty angels of strength and provision surrounding me that are greater than this enormous problem (2 Kings 6:15–17). Since the heavenlies are warring on my behalf, and since Your Spirit is stronger than the jaws of the evil one, then indeed, who can be against me (1 John 4:4; Romans 8:31)?

Please, Father, open my eyes to see You in Your glory. Adjust my eyesight to focus not on the situation but only on what faith sees (2 Corinthians 4:16–18). Yes, Lord, increase my faith and help me where I am doubtful (Luke 17:5: Mark 9:24).

There is a lion of (*depression, disobedience, anger, fear, hatred, etc.*) and a cougar of (*defiance, disunity, promiscuity, deceit, disease, etc.*) attacking. I ask that Your Spirit mightily come as I invite others to join me in prayer. May our prayers connect with Your prayers to go directly for the jaws of these beasts. Shatter the teeth in their mouths and break out their fangs (Psalm 58:6).

In the authority of the name of Your Son, I ask that the spirits of (*deceit, hopelessness, defiance, disunity disobedience*) be torn apart (Judges 14:5–6). Come, Father, strike his evil head, laying him open from thigh to neck. Take the weapons that (*deceit, hopelessness, defiance, disunity, disobedience*) are using against me and destroy evil with their own weapons (Habakkuk 3:13–14).

I ask that in months to come, I will be able to circle back to this place and find that these carcasses have produced sweetness. Something to eat will come out of the eater, and something sweet will come out of the strong (Judges 14:8–9, 14). Take these very things (*name the difficult situations*) that Satan meant for evil and reveal how You will work it for good "to preserve many people alive" (Genesis 50:20; Romans 8:28).

Open my eyes to see how truly large, mighty, and all-encompassing You are. Then it won't matter what kind of host encamps against me; my heart will not fear! I will remain confident (Psalm 27:3). Heal souls as You heal these situations (3 John 2).

Despite the situation, may my emotions and thoughts dwell in the house of the Lord (Psalm 27:4). Teach me how to see Your beauty and meditate on Your indwelling Spirit who fills my temple every moment (Psalm 27:4). Lift my head above these enemies so that I can offer sacrifices with shouts of joy from the midst of Your indwelling (Psalm 27:6). May this promise be my reality! In Jesus's name, amen.

Day 5

Holy Father,

Thank You for desiring that all obtain salvation rather than wrath (1 Thessalonians 5:9). Indeed, You intend that all are saved and come to the knowledge of the truth (1 Timothy 2:4). So, You sent Jesus to manifest glory within us and we in Him (2 Thessalonians 1:12). You have called us out of the darkness and into Your light, but it is a choice we must make (1 Peter 2:9).

As I bring _____ before You today, I am aware that the evil one wants to kill, steal, and destroy Your purpose (John 10:10). This is no surprise, for the devil's intention is always against Yours (1 John 3:8). Sometimes the evil one looks like a roaring lion (1 Peter 5:8) and sometimes like an angel (2 Corinthians 11:14), but his dark essence never changes. He is always evil and anti-good. Thank You for being more potent than he is (1 John 4:4; Luke 11:22).

As I pray for _____, I claim the work of Christ over his fear. Although the evil one seeks to curse his life, You have paid the fee by taking the loathing upon Yourself (Romans 5:19). You became the curse for him (Galatians 3:13)! Break any curses spoken over him in the past.

Wherever Your Spirit is, there is great freedom (2 Corinthians 3:17), so I ask that You fill _____ with Yourself. Wherever he is spiritually, I ask that Your light will come as a lightning bolt through the darkness. I stand to reject all effects of fear or deceit.

(If this individual is already a Christian)

You have given him the mind of Christ (1 Corinthians 2:16). You have already rendered the devil powerless by conquering fear and death (Hebrews 2:14–15). You have promised to rescue him from temptation, even the temptation to doubt and fear (2 Peter 2:9). You have promised to deliver him from every evil deed and to bring him safely into Your Kingdom (2 Timothy 4:18). You have guaranteed to be the Stronghold he can run into (Psalm 94:22). You have promised that You will encamp around him (as Your temple) so that no oppressor will trample over him anymore (Zechariah 9:8). I pray that right now, even if he is too afraid to move, You will seize his hands and yank him into safety (Genesis 19:16).

(If the individual is not yet a Christian)

You came to seek and to save those who are lost (Luke 19:10). No matter what he has done or what mistakes he has made, You died for _____ while he was yet a sinner (Romans 5:8). I believe that You do not want any to perish but all to come to repentance (2 Peter 3:9). So following what You already want to happen, I am claiming this life for Your Kingdom. You said that if I pray according to Your will, You hear, and if You hear, I'm granted the requests that I ask (1 John 5:14–15). Draw a sanctifying circle around him and put the Spirit's influence within this boundary (2 Thessalonians 2:13). Set up spiritual detonation devices in _____'s pride, especially in his darkened thoughts about You and his environment. Destroy everything in his life built up against knowing You (2 Corinthians 10:4–5). Grant me the perseverance to pray this through, no matter what kind of obstacle Satan throws my way (Daniel 10:12–13). Teach me how to pray without losing heart (Luke 18:1).

I speak these things aloud in Your Presence because that's the example You have given. When You speak, the Word from Your mouth boomerangs with fulfillment (Isaiah 55:11). For me to use the sword of the Spirit (the Word of God), I must take You out of the sheath (Ephesians 6:17). I do this not only for _____'s situation but for others in his family who are under discouragement and fear. Break the cycle, Lord. Stop the effects of the evil one over his family members. Satan is a defeated foe. Crush him underneath our feet as we agree with Your Word (Romans 16:20). In Jesus's name, amen.

Wisdom

Day 1

Holy Father,

Thank You for being God, our Father, and the Father of Jesus Christ (Colossians 1:3). No matter where we are and what we are doing, You care (1 Peter 5:7). Thank You for sending the Word of Truth into our lives that spreads and grows wherever You enter (Acts 13:49).

How amazing that the seed of the Word is "constantly bearing fruit and increasing" even within me as well (Colossians 1:6). May I be filled with the knowledge of Your will in all spiritual wisdom and understanding, even during a busy week (Colossians 1:9). I desire to walk worthy of Your name and bear fruit no matter what I do or where You send me (Colossians 1:10).

Teach me to pause each day to seek You and to set aside time for Your Word (Psalm 119:10). As I meditate on You, teach me to delight in Your Word (Psalm 119:15–16). Show me how to value Your Word in today's dark world and turn my eyes away from anything worthless or useless (Psalm 119:34, 37).

Focus me on the eternal, rather than the temporal, with plenty of practice in discernment (2 Corinthians 4:18; Hebrews 5:14). Urge me to seek visits with You, the only use of my time that will result in freely walking in liberty (Psalm 119:45). Your Word is the source for proper discernment and all knowledge (Psalm 119:66).

When situations pressurize or depress me, send Your Word quickly to revive me again (Psalm 119:50). Open my eyes to see how these afflictions are good for me, granting me better insight into Your precepts (Psalm 119:71). I want to know by experience that Your truth is better than silver or gold, so hold me near (Psalm 119:72).

Increase my ability to recognize You while strengthening me with Your power (Colossians 1:10). Grant me patience and steadfastness despite the deficiency of these characteristics in today's world (Colossians 1:11). Thank

You for holding me together with Your hand (Colossians 1:17). I need that desperately. In Jesus's name, amen.

◆ ◆ ◆

Day 2

Holy Father,

Oh, the depths and riches of Your wisdom and knowledge (Romans 11:33). Your insight and understanding are like a boundless vein of gold, ready to be mined without measure. You have already granted me Your mind through Christ Jesus and encourage me to grow in the wisdom You desire to release (1 Corinthians 2:16: Proverbs 1:20–23). Teach me to explore Your understanding, digging the depths for the treasure found in Your Son (1 Corinthians 1:30).

You promise riches over and again to me. Untapped treasures are available through Your grace and inheritance (Ephesians 1:7, 18). I can mine these "unfathomable riches of Christ" through "the surpassing riches of His grace in kindness" (Ephesians 3:8; 2:7).

There is no end to Your bounty as You desire to supply all my need according to those riches of wisdom (Philippians 4:19). This abundant value increases my hope and grants me assurance and comfort (Colossians 1:27; 2:2). What more could I ask?

Thank You that Your ever-watching care is enough for all my needs (1 Peter 5:7). Keep my eyes open to notice my ample supply and watch daily for fresh resources (Philippians 4:18: Proverbs 8:34). In Jesus' wise name, I pray. Amen.

◆ ◆ ◆

Day 3

Father,

Thanks for favoring (*name*) through Your love (1 Corinthians 1:4). During these days, they need to remember that. You have enriched them in everything they say and think (1 Corinthians 1:5). Right now, they are eagerly awaiting the revelation of Your Son so that they can know how best to proceed (1 Corinthians 1:7).

These swirling decisions have them burdened beyond their strength (2 Corinthians 1:8). I ask that You intervene. How comforting to know that a great cloud of witnesses surrounds them (Hebrews 12:1). Give (*name*) insight to see those who have gone before them, helping them to realize they, too, possess the very same inner strength and wisdom.

Making life decisions is full of hardships. When we focus on all that surrounds us, it seems that it will be impossible to gain clarity. I ask that they be able to fast-forward a bit and see the scene as You see it. Reveal to them the state of being in which all becomes clear. Remove the veil so that they can visualize Your very apparent glory stationed securely within their own heart (2 Corinthians 3:18). Allow them to see this so clearly, that it decreases the amount of emotional energy they spend on this decision. May they live in the secret place, looking past the now and living in their glorious future (Romans 8:18).

Work out all of the details, including plans for (*the children, finances, the move, etc.*), regarding Your best (Romans 8.28). We know that none of this depends upon what (*name*) can do but totally on You (Romans 9.16). In Jesus's name, amen.

* * *

Day 4

Holy Father,

Thank You for taking the time to create and form us (Isaiah 43:1). We were not something that You just threw together but a project that You took time to pre-think every small detail. You planned us and did the math to decide just how our environment would best fit our needs. Down to each minute detail, You formed each portion of our body. You didn't stop with creation but saw our sin and stretched out to redeem us. You have even given us a name and taken us as Your own (Isaiah 43:1). Thank You.

Now, as _____ passes through the rough waters regarding (*her move, her change, her decision*), I know that You are with her, not that You *will* be but that You *already* are (Isaiah 43:2). Although these decisions seem like a raft, swirling her amidst river rapids, You promised that it would not capsize her (Isaiah 43:2). Thank You for that great news. I realize the outcome; she may get wet but won't catapult from the raft! That is reassuring. May she hold onto that promise.

As she thinks through her last (*decision, investment, job move, etc.*), she feels burned. But You have promised that when she walks through this fire, it will not scorch her (Isaiah 43:2). No flame will even lick her clothing (Daniel 3:27). Although this is a big decision, she can know that having given the choice to You, You will allow the fire of this trial to have no power over her (Daniel 3:27). I claim that she will come out of this, not even smelling like smoke!

Thank You that You are not only the God who made _____ but the God who is still wielding His craft knife to smooth her edges. Even so, she is not a project to You but a precious, treasured child. Because she is valuable, honored, and loved, she can rest assured that You will be arranging (*housing, jobs, schooling, etc.*) so that she might have Your planned result (Isaiah 43:4).

Strengthen her faith so that she can have no fear since You are in charge (Isaiah 43:5). Thank You that You are her Savior (Isaiah 43:11). May she be able to put aside the learning lesson of (*a disheartening incident*), knowing that this is just a thing of the past (Isaiah 43:18). Thank You for promising to do something new. I ask that it begin even now to spring forth (Isaiah 43:19). I pray that _____ will be able to perceive what it is that You are doing and give heed (Isaiah 43:19). In Jesus's name, amen.

PART II

THIRTY–DAY GUIDED DEVOTIONAL

Day 1

A standard package—taped, addressed, and covered with postal stickers. An everyday journey—traveling by railcar 229 miles from New York City to Washington, DC. An ordinary postal worker—carrying the package in his satchel, the one from which he had delivered so many others.

Almost everything about this package was conventional for the USPS, everything except the contents. Within the plain brown wrapping lay one of the most valuable shipments in United States history: the Hope Diamond.

Even in 1958, this 45–carat, dark blue diamond had a value of $1 million US dollars. Today, the cost is closer to $250 million. Yet, for a while, this massive diamond was enveloped in ordinary brown paper.

What a beautiful picture of the children of God, humbly packaged, but we are glorious in content. "We have this treasure in earthen vessels, that the surpassing greatness of the power may be of God and not from ourselves" (2 Corinthians 4:7). As His children, we house the very brilliance of God "for behold, the kingdom of God is within you" (Luke 17:21).

Our God planned His move into us for a long time. Both Zechariah and Ezekiel prophesied of His indwelling Spirit. "I will be the glory in her midst" (Zechariah 2:5). "I will give you a new heart and put a new spirit within you … and I will put My Spirit within you" (Ezekiel 36:26–27).

Now, because of Jesus's life, death, and resurrection, you are that "temple of God," built solely to house His Spirit (1 Corinthians 3:16). You may not feel like you are much now because you are still in the process, "being built up as a spiritual house" (1 Peter 2:5). But, this dwelling place, this residence within you "shall be called a house of prayer" (Matthew 21:13). When we pray, "the glory of the Lord (fills) the house of the Lord" (1 Kings 8:11). Because of the outpouring of His Spirit within your temple, everything within you is automatically crying, "Glory!" (Psalm 29:9).

Our minds and emotions get in the way of listening clearly to the holy worship within our inner self. Information from our physical senses muffles a clear signal from the heavenlies. But when we quieten ourselves long enough to "look not at the things which are seen, but at the things which are not seen," we find ourselves "with unveiled face beholding as in a mirror the glory of the Lord" (2 Corinthians 4:18; 3:18). His Spirit always flows from higher to lower.

May we purpose our mind and emotions to the reality within. Let's "keep seeking the things above, where Christ is" (Colossians 3:1), setting our minds "on the things above, not of the things that are on the earth" (Colossians 3:2). "Fixing our eyes on Jesus" is the only way (Hebrews 12:2; John 14:6).

"His divine power has granted to us everything pertaining to life and godliness" (2 Peter 1:3). He "has blessed us with every spiritual blessing in the heavenly places in Christ" (Ephesians 1:3). Let's forget "what lies behind and reach forward to what lies ahead" by letting our minds dwell on those things that are honorable, right, pure, lovely, reputable, excellent, and praiseworthy (Philippians 3:13; 4:8). That way, when we arrive in the heavenlies one day, we will already feel at home. Dressed in humble packaging, we have the Hope within (1 Peter 3:15).

◆ ◆ ◆

Day 2

I stood at the edge of the ballroom, overwhelmed with the grandeur. I'd received the invitation but questioned the privilege.

As my eyes scanned the magnificent space, it became apparent that royalty presided here. Lofty arches, splendid tapestries, and fresco paintings lined the walls. Gilded sconces bordered the edges, reflecting light from the carefully placed mirrors of ornate gold leaf. I shielded my eyes from the brilliance as I looked upward to the stately ceiling. Opulent chandeliers hung heavily laden with brilliant diamonds and carefully cut crystal. All spoke of untold wealth and unlimited resources.

Lined along the marble walls were heavily carved but unused chairs crafted long ago from some exotic wood. As I marveled, I noticed that dozens of attendants stood in hushed tones around the perimeter. Only two individuals sat on the palatial thrones, presiding in regal majesty and shining glory from their exalted platform. Above them, a single crown suspended overhead, a perfect replica of those worn by the aristocracy below. Jewels without number studded their crowns, blazing with flashes of rubies, sapphires, emeralds, and topaz, each ignited with a living inner fire.

My pupils widened as I grappled to take in the opulence of the scene. Despite the extravagance of their surroundings, the royalty themselves were what riveted my attention. Both King and Prince wore snowy robes, glittering and radiant from beautiful, unknown fabric resembling pure gold. Although resplendent in appearance, the two were somehow personable as well, obviously enjoying each other's company. Intent together, they discussed matters of state, pausing to ponder and nod before resuming their colloquy.

There must be truth in the power of a gaze, for although I remained tucked into the background, I caught the Prince's eye, and he shifted to look directly at me. The whispers around me silenced as all attention turned my way. Inadequate, my knees went limp, and I dropped trembling to the ground, prostrate and abject. I shouldn't have come.

For the most prolonged moment of my life, I lay quivering, trying to pray. Then a hand touched my shoulder and gave me the strength somehow to stand. Assuming ejection, I kept my head down, unwilling to incur further humiliation.

Yet instead of a rough jerk, a gentle hand cupped my chin, raising my face to eye level. There before me was the Prince himself with eyes burning from a flame of love. "Come, My sister," He said and gripped my shaking hand with His firm, steady one. As in a dream, we moved together toward His throne while He motioned for me to sit beside Him. Confused and keenly aware of my glaring imperfections, I looked into the King's face, searching for the expected disapproval.

"Relax, My child." The King smiled, nodding His approval. "Bring her a regal robe of wisdom, righteousness, and holiness." Within minutes, I too was clothed like nobility. As I marveled at my new position between the two of them, they leaned forward to continue their dialogue. "We were just talking about your world," the King said directly to me. "Would you like to join us?"

"God … seated us with Him in the heavenly places, in Christ Jesus … who is at the Right Hand of God, interceding for us" (Ephesians 2:6; Romans 8:34). How can we not take our place of honor? May we boldly draw near with a sincere heart in full assurance of faith to hear His thoughts and join His desire (Hebrews 10:19, 22; Amos 4:13). He promises to grant all of these requests (1 John 5:14–15; John 15:16).

◆ ◆ ◆

Day 3

"God, I feel hopeless. How do I even begin to pray?"

Then, as softly and gently as a whisper, I heard His voice, "May the God of hope fill you."

Shocked, I asked, "Could I expect an infusion of hope? Was this a promise to which I could cling?" With an eager search, I found this fragment nestled within Paul's epistle to the Romans. "Now may the God of hope (Greek: *elpis*) fill you with all joy and peace in believing, so that you will abound in hope (*elpis*) by the power of the Holy Spirit" (Romans 15:13).

Elpis. Hope. Expectation. Anticipation. Thayer's Greek Lexicon says all New Testament usage of this word is an expectation of positive good. "To anticipate, usually with pleasure."

Hope. This is just what my weary soul needed. "Thank You, Father, for sending Your timely Voice," I responded. "But, how may I best access Your hope?"

My eyes fell again on the open chapter in Romans, and He answered my meager question as quickly as I'd asked it. "Through perseverance and the encouragement of the Scriptures we might have hope" (Romans 15:4). Two actions are necessary on my part. First, rather than hoping in a situation or person to change, I must have a steadfast, constant, targeted endurance that hopes in His consistency. Secondly, that hope expands as I cling to His comforting, ever-present Voice in God's Word.

Too often, my prayers are scratching and beggarly, demanding that I gain the desired result. My emotions hinge on the outcome, happy when answers go my way and upset when they do not. I tend to measure the success of prayer by how nearly the solution aligned with the way I wanted.

I think of the importunate widow in Luke 18. Wasn't her tenacity and intensity encouraged by Jesus Himself? But, on closer inspection, I see that her hope was not in the result but the man (the judge — Luke 18:2-3). When she laid her case at his feet, she also gave him the burden of resolution. Her expectation lay totally on him.

Do I hope in my heavenly Father like this?

The aged apostle writes, "If we ask anything according to His will, He hears us" (1 John 5:14). As he looked back over years of answered prayer, this beloved disciple knew the value of having His Father's ear. John emphasizes the words, "He hears us," by repeating them twice in this magnificent promise.

Too often, I race to the second portion of this promise, knowing that if He hears, then I get (1 John 5:15). But in rushing to answer, how often I've missed the significance of an Almighty Ear. The success of my prayer isn't first in the answer. My triumph is that He "bends down to listen" (Psalm 116:2 NLT). The rambling words of my incomplete understanding touch the Heart of majestic splendor.

Herein is hope. Not that I see every individual healed or every relationship mended. Not that every enemy surrenders in my lifetime or every sorrow subsides. The answer for hope is so near that I've been looking straight past Him as He stares me in the face. The nearness of God is the very best answer in every situation, and He has promised to show up every single time I call (Psalm 73:28; 34:17).

◆ ◆ ◆

Day 4

The fly slipped inside quickly as the cold air poured past him onto the covered patio. The grandsons were visiting, and the back door was left ajar—again.

They'd been reminded, gently at first and then more sternly as the afternoon passed, yet to no avail. The door separating the kitchen and their badminton game suited them better when left wide open. As I closed the door behind them, the Father reminded me that His Son left a door open too.

Our first glimpse of the divine door is through the Gospel writers' eyes at Jesus's baptism. "And immediately coming up out of the water, He saw the heavens opening, and the Spirit like a dove descending upon Him" (Mark 1:10). The Greek original in Mark's version is most expressive, depicting a violent ripping open of the heavens. Mark uses this same word (*schizo*) at the end of his Gospel when he describes the temple's veil torn in two from top to bottom (Mark 15:38).

Hundreds of years earlier, Isaiah had beseeched God to "rend the heavens and come down" (Isaiah 64:1). Now, just after Jesus's baptism, God answered this prayer. The heavens were not only opened but left standing open from that day forward.

Just before his death, Stephen saw "the heavens opened up" (Acts 7:56). In the Joppa vision, Peter also saw the "sky opened up" (Acts 10:11). On the Isle of Patmos, the apostle John mentions this phenomenon twice (Revelation 4:1;19:11). All four verb references are in the perfect passive tense, meaning "to be or stand open."

The door to the heavenlies is standing open for you and me! Rather than letting out cool air, this opens God to us. The abundant riches of the heavenlies are awaiting our access.

But how do we access such wealth? Jesus revealed the answer just months after His baptism. "You shall see the heavens opened, and the angels of God ascending and descending on the Son of Man" (John 1:51). Christ is the ladder in between our realm and God's.

The One who became flesh and tabernacled among us (John 1:14), the One who appeared as a man (Philippians 2:7), the One who was seen and heard and handled (1 John 1:1). He is our bridge, granting us access to the Father by being our Jacob's ladder to God (Ephesians 2:18).

Every tear we shed in private, every prayer we groan in secret, every desire we cry in unison rises through His name into the open throne room of

God. Our requests ascend the ladder to plead with God, and the answers descend on that same ladder. He is the way, both of presenting our requests and receiving them.

The foot of the Ladder stands firmly within us. The top of our Ladder pierces through the heavenlies. Our Living Ladder continuously makes intercession for us, mediating between heaven and earth for the right of our inheritance (Hebrews 7:25). He is the channel processing all requests and the way dispensing all supplies.

Will you reach out today to grasp the bottom rung? The power of the open door lies within you.

◆ ◆ ◆

Day 5

Troubled, the artist stepped back from the canvas and critically scanned his masterpiece. From the look on his face, something was not quite right, and I craned my neck to see what it might be.

Catching my first glimpse of the landscape, I stared wide-eyed as the vibrant colors pulsed from an inner glow. This painting was indeed a pièce de résistance. Created from the light of a million hues, this masterstroke exhibited pure genius. Captivated by the realistic beauty, I held my breath as if expecting the canvas to come to life at any moment.

For several moments, I stood spellbound, frozen with the splendor of the showpiece. Gradually, from the corner of my eye, I noticed the artist had turned from his work and was now intent upon me. Taken aback, I shifted away to give him creative space. He smiled and moved toward me, pointing to my right hand.

Knowing my hand empty, I raised it toward him, proving it held nothing he needed.

As our eyes met, his gaze shifted again to my outstretched palm, causing me to reexamine it more carefully. In the crevice of my lifeline was a speck, no more significant than the head of a pin. "It's the pixel I need for completion," he said. "May I use it?"

I stood baffled as his hand moved gently toward mine. Taking both my palms in his, we reached together for a wet paintbrush, still ladened with shiny scarlet oil. Dreamlike, the minute flake transferred from my palm to His brush then onto the canvas, with a swiftness I have yet to comprehend.

In the blink of an eye, the masterpiece surged to life. The brook splashed my face while a distant eagle squawked to her young. Sunlight caused the glistening snow to sparkle as I deeply inhaled crisp mountain air.

Then I awoke.

Questioning the dream, I moved to God's Word. As my eyes fell on a familiar passage, a particular word pricked my interest. Searching the Greek lexicon through BlueLetterBible.org, I found the translation for *synantilambanomai* buried within Romans 8:26. "In the same way, the Spirit helps our weakness when we don't know how to pray as we ought."

Helps. *Synantilambanomai.* This compound word was formed from at least three root words, pointing to no half-hearted, disinterested assistance. When all meanings merged, this help meant "to take hold of opposite together," an exact hands-on type of support. Like the masculine marksman who envelopes his trembling tutor, the Spirit stands directly behind the intercessor, enveloping His arms around us to steady and lift every burden.

I stopped to reflect excitedly upon my dream. Could it be? The Spirit's purpose in joining us in prayer is to actively reach forth His mighty, skilled hands to direct our weak and inadequate ones? With all the heavenlies at His fingertips, does He wait to release resources through our tiny pixel of prayer? Then shouldn't our concern be less with particular words and more with the utterance of them?

Astounding. God awaits us to invite His will into our situations before releasing His Kingdom to come upon the earth as it is in heaven. His mighty arms envelop ours, so the kingdom of this world can truly become the Kingdom of our Lord and Christ (Revelation 11:15)! We must enforce through prayer all that He has already readied to action.

"May the Lord give you increase, you and your children. May you be blessed of the Lord, Maker of heaven and earth. The heavens are the heavens of the Lord; but the earth He has given to the sons of men" (Psalm 115:14–16).

"Come take hold of us as we pray, O Lord. Envelope and gather us into Your purposes while teaching us how to intercede for our world."

Day 6

"The ills that shake the very foundation of our civilization have their roots in the spiritual and not in the material." (Duncan Campbell)

Over seventy years ago, the Scottish evangelist Duncan Campbell watched God perform one of the most remarkable divine renewals of the twentieth century. Occurring among the outlying islands of Scotland called the Hebrides, the Holy Spirit descended supernaturally into parishes that were long devoid of His Presence. From 1949 to 1953, spiritual awareness of God seemed to fall from the heavens, gripping people with their need of Him even as they tended their fields, walked the roads, or drank in the pubs.

The spiritual climate of their day was not unlike our own. The desire for comfort and prosperity had replaced the love of truth, and selfishness reigned supreme. Churches found themselves at a loss to keep their youth in attendance after high school graduation. The Presbytery of the Isle of Lewis grappled with their low state by publishing a declaration of concern "to take a serious view…not only of the chaotic conditions of international politics and domestic economics and morality but also…to realize that… the Most High has a controversy with the nation."

This declaration impressed two older women in the parish of Barvas to pray for the young people in their community. In their eighties, Peggy and Christine Smith decided to commit six hours twice a week in prayer to God. Requesting their minister to visit, they challenged him and the "office-bearers" of their church to join them. "You've tried special evangelists, Mr. Mackay," they told their pastor. "But have you tried God?"

So it began. In two locations, the two elderly sisters within their cottage and the men in a barn, this handful of faithful began to pray every Tuesday and Friday evenings from 10:00 p.m. to 4:00 a.m. Over the next six weeks, they claimed the verse God had given through the Smith sisters: "I will pour water on him that is thirsty and floods upon the dry ground" (Isaiah 44:3). Mercy drops may have fallen around them, but it was for the showers they pled.

One night in the barn, a deacon read Psalm 24: "Who shall ascend the hill of God? Who shall stand in His Holy place? He that has clean hands and a pure heart." Then speaking directly back to the God of this Word, the young man asked, "God, are my hands clean? Is my heart pure?" Even as he spoke, the Holy One fell upon the barn and soon throughout the parishes and neighboring islands.

Evangelist Duncan Campbell would later testify that hunger and thirst gripped the people. Altar calls were unnecessary for God's Presence and were experienced in the pub as well as in the church. Hundreds of people would simultaneously show up together, sometimes at 11:00 at night and sometimes 4:00, magnetically drawn together by a spiritual hunger they could not explain. Publicity and planning were not needed, for God directed the schedule.

Oh, that the Lord would rend the heavens and come down upon us during these days (Isaiah 64:1). Do we not sense the urgent necessity of His divine intervention? Let us learn from the Hebrides Revival that the outpouring of His righteousness is in direct correspondence with His people's faithful prayers.

"Wilt Thou, not Thyself revive us again, that Thy people may rejoice in Thee? Show us Thy lovingkindness, O Lord and grant us Thy salvation" (Psalm 85:6-7).

Day 7

The room fell quiet as the Spirit simultaneously hushed our verbal prayers.

Months ago, Tara and I prioritized intercession in our times together. Opening our Bibles in prayer, we eagerly await His direction for our friends, our church, and our world by allowing His Word to direct ours. His guidance has gifted us with many blessings of ah-ha moments as we seek His wisdom and insight.

But this day proved different. Words escaped us as we sat in silence, waiting for what we thought would be His direction and prompting.

Waiting often reminds us of the psalms where David stirs himself toward patient watching. But on this day, our waiting made us keenly aware of His nearness. Our emphasis changed from wanting to know something to wanting to know someone. As we sought Him, I sensed our hearts expand and tilt upward, leaning toward a glimpse of His glory.

While we stretched toward His Presence, my mind's eye suddenly saw an image of two gentle hands reaching for my heart. When His fingertips met my soul, I realized the form of my heart was like that of a stringed instrument. Unexpectedly, but quite naturally, He began to tune my heart like a master musician adjusting His instrument for proper pitch.

Although I was aware of strings, neck, fingerboard, and tuning pegs, these were not what riveted my attention. My sight fixed toward the Master's hands, not my stationary instrument. I trembled as He deftly tightened or loosed the strings one by one, tweaking them to resonate with His Spirit's frequency.

Within moments, the dissonance faded, and His fingers gently coaxed a singular melody from my trembling heart. Low and weighty, the resonant sound wasn't a song I recognized yet was full of peace and pleasure. Like a cello in the hands of a virtuoso, I rested on the tailpin while He played. His touch coaxed the desired refrain as I anticipated the next note.

Within a few measures, the music enriched and enlarged. The separate yet harmonious sound of a violin began to blend with the original tune. Lustrous and bright, resonant and lyrical, this higher strain added pleasure not only to the Musician but also to me, His instrument.

He had tuned Tara's instrument as well.

I want to say that we sat in silence for hours while He coaxed His melody from our hearts. The truth is that I was so excited, I broke the silence to hear what Tara was sensing. Her eyes were large as she testified, "I didn't see what you saw, but I did feel it."

I'm sure our experience that day isn't singular but has been shared over the years by many eager seekers. After all, if we are clay in the hands of our master potter (Jeremiah 18:6), could we not be other mediums in His hand?

An instrument in the hand of the Musician.
A canvas under the hand of the Artist.
A raw mineral in the hand of the Gem Cutter.
A loom in the hand of the Weaver.
Marble in the hand of the Sculptor.

May His hand freely draw His best from each of us. Even so, Lord Jesus, come.

◆ ◆ ◆

Day 8

"What? Could you not watch with Me one hour?" (Matthew 26:40 NKJV)

I quickly recognize the scenario. In His most trying hour, our Lord found His closest friends asleep. While He poured out His soul in agony, their eyes closed with exhaustion. I shudder to think of their complacency but then wonder, *Does my life exhibit any difference?*

"Child, could you not watch with Me one hour?"

I rise in the morning to begin my busy day. Work, family, and finances fill my thoughts as I look past His Word and into my crowded schedule.

"Child, could you not watch with Me one hour?" He calls.

I join others at weekly worship and find my thoughts wandering. I close my Bible, content to return home without realizing I've not seen the One I came to glorify.

"Child, could you not watch with Me one hour?" He repeats.

I gather in a small group, but there is little of the Word and only brief prayer. Instead, we tell our stories, check our phones, answer our calls, and consider how each needs to slip out early.

"Child, could you not watch with Me one hour?" He rejoins. "Are you still passively prayerless? Get up. It's time to act."

His urgency jolts me awake, and I stare wide-eyed at the noise of the impending enemy. Lawlessness has increased, and all around me, love grows cold (Matthew 24:12). Will the chill touch me? Have I waited too long to begin to watch and pray? My spirit is willing, but my flesh is altogether weak (Matthew 26:41).

I will listen to these lies no longer. I rouse to join the One who lives to make a stand between kingdoms on behalf of humankind (Hebrews 7:25). He stands in the very Presence of God on my behalf, illumining my darkness (Hebrews 9:24). Will I be light in my dark portion of the world?

What about you? Will you watch with Him faithfully? Even now, He is nudging you to join Him in prayer.

Oh Father, may our prayer "be counted as incense" before You (Psalm 144:1). Gather our prayer together with the saints around the globe that the golden bowls may be "full of incense" (Revelation 5:8) and tipping with power. Search our hearts and minds (Revelation 2:23) to find us faithful. In Jesus's name, amen.

◆ ◆ ◆

Day 9

Two o'clock in the morning. Most nights, I habitually wake within minutes of this hour. I'm not a night owl or an early riser. Yet, I've been awake in night's blackness for at least thirty minutes for almost a year now.

I feel the need to pray, but as night images meld with inky darkness, my mind swirls unsettled and unfocused. I desire to use this time wisely but find it difficult. However, with the clarity of daytime prayers, I've stumbled upon initiating these hours into an activated faith.

My secret? The psalms.

Every night, before retiring, I open a Bible app on my phone that allows for audio listening. Finding the psalms, I ready my phone as well as my earbuds by my bedside. Then, when my night waking occurs, I put in one of the earbuds and press play. Without disturbing my husband, I can begin to agree with the prayers of David, Solomon, and other Old Testament poets.

I'm discovering what the church father Athanasius spoke of in the fourth century. "To me, it seems," he explains, "that the Psalms are to him who sings them as a mirror, wherein he may see himself and the motions of his soul, and with like feelings utter them. So also one who hears a psalm read takes it as if it were spoken concerning himself." Listening to these prayers, praises, and hymns in silence, I resonate with the words of the psalmist, allowing these ancient words to pray through me.

Since this revelation some months ago, I have cycled through the psalter's entirety several times. I have no goal per night, nor do I bother if I fall asleep midchapter. One night, having dozed through David's psalmic prayers, I dreamed through all of the proverbs to awake somewhere in the middle of Ecclesiastes.

Most nights, I pick up where I stopped the audio the night before, joining my heart with the writer, whether in joy, weeping, or resentment. I've discovered myself praying for the following:

- My husband—"Who is the man that fears the Lord? He will instruct him in the way he should choose. His soul will abide in prosperity, and his descendants will inherit the land" (Psalm 25:12–13).
- My children—"Let our sons in their youth be as grown-up plants, and our daughters as corner pillars fashioned as for a palace" (Psalm 144:12).
- My anxiety—"When my anxious thoughts multiply within me, Thy consolations delight my soul" (Psalm 94:19).
- A sick friend—"The Lord will protect him, and keep him alive, and he shall be called blessed upon the earth; and do not give him over to the desire of his enemies. The Lord will sustain him upon his sickbed; in his illness, Thou dost restore him to health" (Psalm 41:2–3).
- A struggling friend—"Do not deliver the soul of Thy turtledove to the wild beast; Do not forget the life of Thine afflicted forever" (Psalm 74:19).

- Fake media—"O God, shatter their teeth in their mouth; Break out the fangs of the young lions, O Lord" (Psalm 58:6).
- Our country—"Had it not been the Lord who was on our side, when men rose up against us; then they would have swallowed us alive when their anger was kindled against us; then the waters would have engulfed us, the stream would have swept over our soul; then the raging water would have swept over our soul. Blessed be the Lord, who has not given us to be torn by their teeth" (Psalm 124:2–6).

Need I go on?

Whatever the sentiment of our soul, the psalms well express every detail. These divine words allow us to cry, rage, and express our disappointments. But rather than spiraling us into the hopelessness of introspection, praying the Psalter always lifts hearts into praise. Let's journey together to "be satisfied with (His) likeness when (we) awake" (Psalm 17:15).

◆ ◆ ◆

Day 10

My hands gripped the steering wheel as the initial shock of the impact subsided. A small crowd of curious bystanders gathered on the sidewalk, and I heard a faint hissing sound underneath my car. I was in a foreign country, and another vehicle just T-boned me.

I'd maneuvered down this narrow lane hundreds of times. In a city of more than two million residents, I had routinely chosen this road, barely wide enough to accommodate my compact car. Because it was one-way, this street remained less congested than others, an essential factor considering the myriads of cars tangled in knots at other intersections.

At least I wasn't the one who had run the stop sign. I had the right of way and had been driving the speed limit. It wasn't my fault.

Or so I assumed.

A week or so later, we received the call: although both drivers had insurance, I would be responsible for my repairs. The reasoning? It was 50 percent my fault. Why? "If the foreigner had been in her home country where she belonged, this wouldn't have happened."

Incensed, I expended weeks of emotional energy-demanding privileges that I discovered weren't mine by law. After I reluctantly paid the damages and my anger subsided, I realized that my home country's expectations weren't a given in this adopted country. Foreigners living abroad did not always have the same rights as residents.

In the twenty years since this incident, I've discovered there is only one passport whose legalities transcend all nationalities. Regardless of locale, holders of this citizenship have standardized legal sanctions. Although I am a "stranger and alien" of this world, God has given His children unshakeable rights (Hebrews 11:13; John 1:12; Hebrews 12:28).

When I lived abroad, I wanted to exercise privileges I did not possess. Sometimes today, I feel incensed about my violated rights. If my American rights are so important to me, why not take advantage of the heavenly benefits afforded to me now? Why do I spend so little time familiarizing myself with my Kingdom rights?

The feisty widow in Jesus's prayer parable knew her rights. "Give me legal protection from my opponent," she demanded (Luke 18:3). She was only asking for what she knew she deserved.

Are we as well versed in our Kingdom rights as children of the Most High? We have the following:

- the right to draw near to the Head of the Supreme Court, who is also our Father (Hebrews 10:22; Ephesians 3:12–14)
- the right to ask our Father anything according to His will and be assured delivery (1 John 5:14–15)
- the right to command even our most grievous sin to leave us alone (Romans 6:14)
- the right to live without anxiety and fear (Luke 1:74–75)
- the right to live in peace despite our circumstances (we have peace with God, why not with ourselves? Romans 5:1; Ephesians 2:14)

These and many more rights are ours as we assume heavenly citizenship. As we read through our Kingdom's constitution, we find "as many as may be the promises of God, in Him, they are yes" (2 Corinthians 1:20)! Why would we squander so high a prerogative?

Appear before the Court of courts today and begin to talk to your Father Judge about the rights He has already promised. The law of the Spirit of life in Christ Jesus is on your side (Romans 8:2).

◆ ◆ ◆

Day 11

As we grapple with how best to pray, we often feel prayer a mystery. Praying regularly with a select group has been a valuable experience for me, confirming the adage that prayer is better caught than taught. So, let's gather around Abraham, a seasoned veteran of petitioning, to find a few of his prayer principles.

Principle Number 1:

God desires to show us what He is about to do (Genesis 18:17).

The God of the angel armies wants to reveal His plan to us. He says it repeatedly in His Word:

"And the Lord said, 'Shall I hide from Abraham what I am about to do? ... For I have chosen him ... in order that (I) may bring upon Abraham what (I have) spoken about him" (Genesis 18:17–19).

"Surely the Lord God does nothing unless He reveals His secret counsel to His servants" (Amos 3:7).

"The secret of the Lord is for those who fear Him, and He will make them know His covenant" (Psalm 25:14).

God desires to speak clearly to us, but we must be in communion with Him to hear. He is a Spirit being; our connection with Him is through the spiritual method called prayer. Nineteenth-century author E. M. Bounds defines this clearly: "God's secrets, councils, and cause have never been committed to prayerless men."

Principle Number 2:

Even righteous people need intercessors.

Abraham's nephew Lot was considered a righteous man (2 Peter 2:7) and one of prayer. When he asked the angel to allow him to escape to a smaller city, the angel responded, "I will grant you this request also" (Genesis 19:21). Lot had experience in prayer, and God granted more than one of his requests.

Nevertheless, Lot needed the prayers of Abraham. As we read through the narrative, we see it was Abraham's prayers that clinched Lot's deliverance. "God remembered Abraham and sent Lot out of the midst of the overthrow" (Genesis 19:29).

How many times have we been embarrassed to ask someone to pray for us? We earnestly seek the Lord privately but are hesitant to ask for reinforcements. God dramatically values corporate prayer, and sometimes, the power of agreement is needed to overthrow the adversary's plan. Don't delay. Request intercessors!

Principle Number 3:

Sometimes, it appears the Father has not answered our prayer. Usually, however, perseverance proves differently (Genesis 19:27–29).

When Abraham appealed to God's love of the righteous, he reasoned that surely God wouldn't wipe out a city with fifty right living residents. When Abraham remembered the morality of the place, he adjusted his requirements. "How about forty-five righteous? Wait. Forty? Thirty? Twenty?" Abraham did the math: Lot, his wife, his two daughters, their fiancés, Lot's sons (Genesis 19:12). "How about ten?" he compromised. I wonder if he slept at all that night.

Finally, when the dawn neared, Abraham "arose early in the morning and went to the place where he had stood before the Lord; and he looked down toward Sodom and Gomorrah." All he could see was lots of smoke (Genesis 19:27–28). It seemed that his answer had been a resounding "No!"

Abraham didn't know that somewhere in a nearby cave, Lot and his two daughters were safe (Genesis 19:30). God remembered Abraham and extended compassion to Lot. The request wasn't precisely what Abraham asked for, but God rewarded this earnest prayer, despite Lot's reluctant stubbornness (Genesis 19:15–17).

Prayer releases the heavenlies into the earthly, even when the person we are praying for is unwilling to do God's will. If He rescued Lot, He surely knows how to save our loved ones from temptation (2 Peter 2:7, 9). God desires to reveal His plans and deliver from evil (Amos 3:7; John 17:15). Sometimes, we must call other warriors to pray with us for the breakthrough as Daniel did ("we are not presenting our supplications before You on account of any merits of our own" Daniel 9:18). But may we persevere so that our prayers reinforce the strength of our angelic warriors (Daniel 10:12–13). Let's not allow the deceit of the evil one to keep us from persevering together to initiate God's purposes into our situations.

Day 12

I always enjoy the story of Samuel. I love Hannah's sincere prayer and God's gracious answer (1 Samuel 1:9–18). I enjoy rereading about little boy Samuel who hears the Lord and learns to respond, "Speak, Lord, for your servant is listening" (1 Samuel 3:1–10).

But on this particular day, my heart stopped as I read a passage sandwiched between these two accounts. Before God spoke to young Samuel, He had already talked to the priest Eli.

God didn't mince any words with Eli or me. His words went straight to both of our hearts. "Why do you … honor your sons (or daughters) above Me?" (1 Samuel 2:29) In trying to be the perfect parent, both of us had placed our children's importance above God.

While I didn't know Eli personally, I knew it was true in my life. My actions bore it out. When God called, I put Him off. But when my daughters whined, I jumped up readily. I liked their dependence on me because it made me feel important. When God desired my time, I sighed and gave Him the least amount possible.

Is there someone (or something) in your life that you have exalted above God? If so, know that this attitude is weakening your prayers. Even though you may be religiously praying for your children, prayer has no real power if you desire to glorify someone else other than God.

Will you allow the Lord to reveal areas in your life that rank above Him? Do you genuinely want power in prayer? Then hear His secret: "Those who honor Me, I will honor, and those who despise Me will be lightly esteemed" (1 Samuel 2:30). Efforts to exalt your importance, even to your own children, never come to a rightful end (1 Samuel 4:11–18).

Father, grant me wisdom to see when I am honoring someone or something besides You. I desire to have power in prayer and see the world changed. Uncover anything within me that is ranked above You. Open my eyes to see my motives as You do. I trust You. Amen.

◆ ◆ ◆

Day 13

As Creator and Owner of heaven and earth (Psalm 89:11), God has ultimate authority. As Senior Commander, He chose man to be His delegate on earth by deputizing man to rule over every living thing (Genesis 1:28). God intended man to establish heaven on our planet through Kingdom fruitfulness.

But man desired self-knowledge more than fulfilling God's purpose. Adam squandered away his right to the Kingdom and gave away his God-given dominion to the evil one (Genesis 3:1–6). From that moment, man lived in a two-kingdom system—the Kingdom of light and the kingdom of darkness (Luke 17:20; John 18:36).

Jesus came to restore man into his Kingdom rulership by opening his eyes to see the difference between Satan's dominion and the dominion of God (Colossians 1:13; Acts 26:18). Jesus didn't deliver with overt aggression but by placing the Kingdom of God within all who believe in Him (Luke 17:21).

Today, when we pray, "Thy Kingdom come," we are rejoining the purpose of God's original plan. This enlistment means we declare war against any thoughts within that are "raised up against the knowledge of God" (2 Corinthians 10:5). Because the battle still rages. Any notion that doesn't align itself with God's Word sources from the "prince of the power of the air" (Ephesians 2:2), not the Prince of Peace.

No matter how long our past has held us captive to unworthiness and shame, we take a stand against these lies. We focus our holy anger onto the kingdom of darkness to put a stop to the devil's deceitful thoughts (Ephesians 4:26–27). "You were formerly darkness, but now you are light in the Lord; walk as children of light" (Ephesians 5:8). We remind ourselves daily: "Stop channeling the thoughts of the other kingdom. Transmit light instead."

Next, we wage war with the darkness we can see. "Thy Kingdom come into the situations surrounding me." Jesus was the light of the world for a short time (John 9:5), and now it's our turn to enlighten and push back the darkness (Matthew 5:14; John 1:5). Granted, we live in the "midst of a crooked and perverse generation," yet our call is to appear as a beam in the night (Philippians 2:15).

Christ has finished His work by disarming rulers of darkness and rendering the devil powerless (John 19:30; Colossians 2:15; 1 Peter 3:22; Hebrews 2:11). Now, Jesus sits at the right hand of God, "waiting until His enemies to be made a footstool for His Feet" (Hebrews 10:12–13). But for what is He waiting?

He is waiting for us to sound the battle cry: "Thy Kingdom come. Thy will be done." The way the heavenlies come to earth is through our thoughts and our influence. No wonder this prayer is vital.

We are already in the midst of a war. "Your adversary, the devil, prowls about like a roaring lion, seeking someone to devour" (1 Peter 5:8). Cowering in fear will not protect us from attack. But before we can ask Jesus to deliver us from evil, we must boldly ask His Kingdom to come (Matthew 6:13). "Do not be afraid, little flock, for the Father has chosen gladly to give you the Kingdom" (Luke 12:32).

One day, the kingdom of this world will totally and ultimately become the Kingdom of our Lord and Christ (Revelation 11:15). Until then, "be strong in the Lord, and in the strength of His might" (Ephesians 5:10). Suit up to "contend earnestly for the faith" (Jude 1:3) and be one "who knows their

God (and can) display strength and take action" (Daniel 11:32). After all, "He has made us to be a Kingdom" (Revelation 1:6).

Yes, Lord. I welcome Your Kingdom.

———————————◆ ◆ ◆———————————

Day 14

"(Jacob) sent across whatever he had. Then he was left alone, and a man wrestled with him until daybreak. And when he saw that he had not prevailed against him, (the angel) touched the socket of his thigh; so the socket of Jacob's thigh was dislocated while he wrestled with him" (Genesis 32:23b-25).

God revealed Himself to Jacob several times during the lifetime of this supplanter. The first proved quite memorable to Jacob. After he dreamed of a tall ladder reaching into the heavens, Jacob awoke and exclaimed, "Surely the Lord is in this place, and I did not know it … How awesome is this place!" (Genesis 28:16–17).

The second was another God-revealing dream, this time directing him to return home (Genesis 31:13). God then sent angels to meet Jacob as he neared the inevitable encounter with his twin brother, Esau. Did these angels give Jacob direction to appease the tension between the two men (Genesis 32:1–2)?

In this defining moment of Jacob's life, he doesn't merely dream about God or encounter His messengers. This time, Jacob lays hold of God and won't let Him go (Genesis 32:28). Despite being desperate and afraid, Jacob was spiritually aggressive. What made the difference?

First, Jacob was alone. Solitude often gives the best opportunity to ponder our lives and discover God. He'd been alone during the other times that he had God encounters. Maybe we should begin seeing loneliness as an opportunity rather than a disadvantage.

Secondly, Jacob emptied himself of all he had. Even his location on the bank of the Jabbok grants insight. In Hebrew, the translation of this river is "an emptying." He had left his home of twenty years and now sent away both his family and his livelihood. How often am I willing to empty myself to encounter God?

Lastly, Jacob prayed an anguished petition. The Scripture says that he was "greatly afraid and distressed" of possible attack (Genesis 32:7, 11). Possibly Jacob had cried out to God desperately before, but now he did so with humility. "I am unworthy of all the lovingkindness and of all the faithfulness with Thou hast shown to Thy servant" (Genesis 32:10).

Jacob's hardships with Laban in Paddan-Aram worked insight and endurance into his life. The very conniving behavior Jacob used on his brother was now returned upon him (Genesis 29:21–30). Jacob, "the supplanter" (literally, "the layer of snares"), was ready to become Israel, "the one who strives with God" (Genesis 32:28). He had always possessed passion. Now, desperation and endurance drove him to use that intensity in prevailing prayer. Jacob would never walk the same again (Genesis 32:31).

How often has Jesus approached me, and I have indifferently allowed Him to pass? Arthur Matthews says, "We have confined our living and interest to earth and have ignored our responsibilities in the heavens." Grappling with God must be an exercise of my whole body, soul, and spirit. Jesus said we "ought to pray at all times and not lose heart" (Luke 18:1–8). Am I whining passively about my situation or praying aggressively over it? Could it be that the adversity in my life was allowed purposefully to strengthen my resolve and drive me to prayer?

May it not be, O Lord. Make us bold with strength in our souls (Psalm 138:3). Give us the wrestling spirit of Jacob that takes hold of You and won't let go, even if it takes emptiness, desperation, and weakness. May Your strength be evident (2 Corinthians 12:9). In Jesus's name, amen.

◆ ◆ ◆

Day 15

The leather gave only slightly to the blow as the weighted bag bobbled under her best uppercut. Pummeling with all her might, she drove her glove into the bag, groaning a little with each jab. Stabbing and striking, ducking and dodging—every move exhausted her but also strengthened her for the next fight.

Every morning, she met her trainer. Every morning, she honed her skill. Sometimes, her instructor stood nearby, and sometimes he coached while steadying the bag. He challenged her, pushed her, and angered her—while always encouraging her.

She learned to pour her passion into every punch. Every disappointment, frustration, and humiliation propelled her glove deeper and farther into the Everlast bag. When her anger drained and her head cleared, she stepped into the shower, ready once again to face her world.

I'd seen this movie before, but this time, my mind raced with the similarities. "This is a depiction of that Greek word I just discovered," I mused aloud. "This is *hypōpiazō*—'to disable an antagonist as a boxer. To beat black and blue.'" Yes, I could see it now—a boxer standing firm and hard against her opponent.

I turned back to Luke 18. There in the scripture reference, the fighter was surprisingly a wiry, little widow lady. She had no money, no prestige, and no prominence. But. She. Was. Feisty. She knew her legal rights and demanded them.

Unfortunately, her deciding judge couldn't care less. He was wealthy, arrogant, and unethical. Nevertheless, morning by morning, she kept knocking, standing persistently with her constant and continual demand. She wouldn't take no for an answer.

So, in time, the big bully caved into the spirited little boxer. "Good grief!" he said. "I'll give her protection before she beats me black and blue (hypōpiazō)" (Luke 18:5).

And then Jesus spoke directly to me: "Hear what the unrighteous judge said?" (Luke 18:6).

But had I heard? Had I caught the significance?

He wants me a pugilist in prayer. Despite the sweat, determination, and perseverance, I'm called to get into the ring. My Great Trainer awaits, desiring to build my confidence and guide me through the next round.

But how often do I show up for the fight? How often do I pelt the enemy of passivity, pushing forward despite exhaustion and fatigue? How often do I endure the training when desperation passes and the mundane takes over? Do I target my passion onto my dark opponent, or do I angrily punch those around me?

"Lord, make me a pugilist in prayer. Strengthen me with Your power in my inner man that I may be able to fight the good fight of faith (Ephesians 3:16; 1 Timothy 6:12). Make me alert to see my true enemy, the one trying to devour both the ones I love and me (1 Peter 5:8). May I spend my passionate energy knocking down the works of the evil one to build up Your family. In Jesus's name, amen."

———————————————— ◆ ◆ ————————————————

Day 16

Why do breakthroughs in prayer still surprise me?

I'd prayed over this request specifically for over two years, but God's affirmative answer still shocked me. Maybe desperation holds more sway with God than I realized. In this journey, I learned three powerful lessons regarding desperate prayer that will forever shape my critical intercession.

1) Just because prayer is a battle doesn't mean we have to accept defeat.

When God gave the Israelites instructions for warfare, He said, "When you go out to battle against your enemies and see … people more numerous than you, do not be afraid of them; for the Lord, your God … is with you. Do not be afraid, or panic, or tremble before them. For the Lord Your God is the One Who goes with you—to fight for you against your enemies, to save you" (Deuteronomy 20:1, 3–4).

Fear and anxiety often describe my dread of the unknown. But God knows that. It is like He says, "Stop it! Don't even let your mind go there. Look here at Me. I'm not only Your Commander in Chief. I'm also Your Father. I've got this!"

2) His Word is more powerful than all opposition.

We don't have to understand how His Word works (Mark 4:27), but the fact of the matter is He does work. When we pray His Word, power explodes. His Word is:

- sharp enough to slice away the competition (Hebrews 4:12)
- surging with inner life (Hebrews 4:12)
- far-reaching in effectiveness (Acts 6:7)
- forward advancing (Acts 12:24)
- forceful, potent, and dominant (Acts 19:20)
- continuously strengthened with fresh reinforcements (Colossians 1:6)
- activated to move quickly (2 Thessalonians 3:1)

Our prayers command power in direct proportion to our knowledge of His truth.

3) When His Word has authority over our lives, our lives have power over the enemy.

Under the old covenant, God promised to conquer the enemy of those who fully obeyed the written law (Joshua 23:6, 9). But when Christ came, He repealed that law (Hebrews 7:12). He set aside all the complicated conditions for victory and gave us only one: faith (John 6:29). Our faith has success because we believe (not in our own conduct but) in His indestructible life (Hebrews 7:18, 16). "Through the obedience of One, the many will be made righteous" (Romans 5:19). Not through mine!

Under the new covenant, God promises to conquer the enemy of those who faith Him (1 John 5:4). When we hold up the shield of faith and move offensively with the sword of His Word, our prayers pack a punch. "One of your men puts to flight a thousand, for the Lord your God is He who fights for you, just as He promised you" (Joshua 23:10). "A thousand may fall at your side, and ten thousand at your right hand, but it shall not approach you" (Psalms 91:7).

But what about the crafty serpent—the devil, who prowls about like a roaring lion (Genesis 3:1; 1 Peter 5:8)?

"The battle is not yours, but God's" (2 Chronicles 20:15). "You will tread upon the lion and cobra, the young lion and the serpent you will trample down" (Psalm 91:13). "Behold," says Jesus, "I have given you authority to tread upon serpents and scorpions, and over all the power of the enemy, and nothing shall injure you" (Luke 10:19).

Let's go into the war room together this week, shall we?

◆ ◆ ◆

Day 17

God desires to answer your prayer. He yearns for it as much as you do.

How can I be sure? Because answered prayer glorifies Him, the very thing that He desires. When prayer is answered, praise automatically springs to life in our hearts.

Think of an example in your life. When was a time that a supernatural answer came in a way that you could not have orchestrated on your own? The expression in your soul was not obligatory gratitude but pure rejoicing in what He accomplished. Thanksgiving bubbled up from the fountain of your heart as a natural overflow.

Of course, God's Word repeatedly encourages us to praise and thank Him. Why, then, would we assume that He is reluctant to do the very thing that produces praise and thanksgiving within us? God loves to answer prayer.

So, what is the difficulty? Why must we feel so frustrated with so many unanswered prayers? In my case, one of the problems is because I give up too quickly. I get discouraged and stop asking. My doubt plays directly into the hand of the enemy.

The real enemy of prayer is the adversary, who works steadily against all of God's purposes on earth (Job 2:2). This same enemy tried to thwart Jesus's answers to prayer and desires to do so with us as well (Luke 4:1–13). Jesus knows this and encourages us to "keep praying until the answer comes" (Luke 18:1 TLB).

Honestly, facing a supernatural enemy raises my anxiety level. I visualize myself standing alone, besieged by an entire battalion of enemy soldiers. My only weapon is a single-loaded pellet gun, and I don't know how to shoot!

Yet the Father reveals that our weapons are "divinely powerful" (2 Corinthians 10:4). Commentator H.M. Spence says that "divinely powerful" translates to mean "powerful in His estimate." God has entrusted us with a secret weapon that is dangerously destructive to a divine degree. This is powerful even in God's evaluation.

A far cry from the plastic BB gun of my imagination, our Chief Commander has given us power like a ballistic nuclear missile produced specifically in His divine factory. God describes this warhead as *dynatos*, the Greek word from which we derive the word *dynamite*. Just like the most advanced stealth bombers with pinpoint target ability and heat guidance systems, our warfare weapon of prayer must not be handled carelessly.

God gives every one of His children this explosive power, even the youngest babe in Christ. Our wise training Sergeant begins our basic training with the fundamentals of prayer. As we progress, He instructs us to utilize His more sophisticated techniques. It is no wonder that our coaching in prayer is lifelong.

Although we hold such exceptional potential in our hearts, our Chief Commander is also a God of mercy and love. He knows every heart, desiring that none perish but that all join His royal family (2 Peter 3:9). He is a God who seeks to build up rather than tear down (2 Corinthians 13:10).

And He grants this power to children, who often just want to blow something up. So, we remain in training.

Although His explosive power works forcefully within us, we must maintain a student's attitude, ever on our knees, with His patient voice whispering in our ear to guide the accuracy of our prayers (Colossians 1:29; Isaiah 30:21). God desires to answer prayer with efficiency so there will be as little destruction and as much praise as possible.

◆ ◆ ◆

Day 18

Where is your enemy? I didn't say who, but maybe that needs to be clarified first. I'm not talking about the love-your-enemy-type enemy.

I'm talking of the enemy of your soul. The one who whispers, "You aren't enough," in your head. The one who entices you to "take one more bite" or "say what you feel." The one who degrades your children, demeans your family, and demoralizes your relationships. Yeah, I'm talking about that enemy.

Just where is he right now? Any ideas?

Well, I will tell you where he is supposed to be. Under your feet.

Joshua gave us an example after his victory at Makkedah. The battle victorious, he demanded five captive kings be brought before him. "And it came about when they brought these kings out to Joshua, that Joshua called for all the men of Israel, and said to the chiefs of the men of war who had gone with him, 'Come near, put your feet on the necks of these kings'" (Joshua 10:24).

What humiliation. Laying prostrate, face in the dust, with the boot of your opponent on your nape. Signaling not only defeat but also disgrace.

It's time we take this same stance over the enemy of the soul. After all, Christ already rendered him powerless (Hebrews 2:14). Jesus "disarmed the rulers and authorities (hostile to us and) triumphed over them" (Colossians 2:15).

And yet, our enemy still seeks to devour us (1 Peter 5:8) and disguise himself as an angel of light (2 Corinthians 11:14). Scheming, lying, manipulating, he is bent upon distracting, disabling, and destroying. Isn't it time we take a stand and tell him, "No!"?

We have authority, for "the grace of God … teaches us to say, 'no' to all ungodliness" (Titus 2:11–12 NIV). In fact, Christ is waiting on us to step up and stand on our enemy. Jesus is now seated at the right hand "of God, waiting … until His enemies be made a footstool for His Feet" (Hebrews 10:12–13).

He fully expects us to tread upon our enemies.

But where is our holy anger? Where is our divine passion?

The Father not only promised to make Christ's enemies a footstool for His feet (Psalm 110:1) but also vowed to crush Satan underneath ours (Romans 16:20).

What are we waiting for? Let's shake off our passivity in prayer and put our foot down—right upon the very neck of our enemy.

"Father, You have given me authority to tread upon all the power of the enemy without injury (Luke 10:19). You finished Your work by one sacrifice and are now awaiting my alignment with Your holy will (Hebrews 10:12–13; Romans 5:19). Like my holy Joshua, You have called me near to put my foot on the neck of our adversary (Joshua 10:24).

"I confess to You that I have been a fearful warrior and shrink back in taking my victorious position over my defeated foe. I have forgotten that the Holy One within me is actually greater and more muscular than my opponent in this world (1 John 4:4). Forgive me, Lord.

"Surge Your power within me by bringing all Your promises back to my memory (Colossians 1:29; John 14:26). Thank You for sending Your Son to free me from fear and destroy all of the enemy's works (Luke 1:74; 1 John 3:8). Praise You for being faithful to strengthen and protect me from the evil one (2 Thessalonians 3:3). Reveal Your accomplished work that I may faithe it into experience.

"Now, I put my foot down upon the enemy's work in (specific area). He has played the victor far too long. This (dissension, anger, addiction, rebellion—fill in the sin) has dominated lives long enough. In the name of Jesus, the enemy's work is over in this area. Realizing that the evil one will try to block Your prompt delivery, remind me to pray persistently until the emancipation comes (Daniel 10:12–13). I'm not moving my foot off his neck until You crush the enemy underneath (Romans 16:20). In Jesus's name, amen."

◆ ◆ ◆

Day 19

"I struggle with depression."
"My head loops with negative self-talk."
"Why can't I shake these feelings of inadequacy?"

These are comments I hear all the time. Although our lives are among the most prosperous on the planet, our thoughts swirl with famine and dryness. Why is this? The kingdom of fear is alive and well in our world today.

I first began to be aware of this realm of anxiety when we flew into Asian airspace for the first time. As we neared Taiwan, feelings of fear and despair overtook me. At that time, I chalked it up to my moving to a new culture and leaving my familiar. Yet, once flying to Asia became commonplace over the years, I found the feeling of dread and fear to be an expected part of returning to my home overseas.

I readily accept that God is the Supreme Ruler of both heaven and earth (Psalm 103:19). I believe that He has hosts of angels doing His bidding and carrying out His plans (Psalm 103:20–21; Zechariah 1:10; Matthew 25:31). The Bible makes it plain that some angels, like Gabriel and Michael, for instance, seem to have a higher position in the Kingdom of God than others (see Luke 1:9 and Jude 1:9). Considering the organization and numbers of these ministering angels, it is no wonder we are at a loss to understand the complexity of their administration (Revelation 5:11).

Despite this well-established system, the Bible testifies that all is no longer sympathetic across the cosmos. In fact, we are in a battle between forces of good and forces of evil, between a kingdom of darkness and a Kingdom of light (2 Corinthians 10:3; 1 Peter 2:9). This world has a "prince of the power of the air" (Ephesians 2:2). Yet as Christians, our war is not against flesh and blood but against these rulers, against these powers, against these world forces of this darkness, against these spiritual forces of wickedness in the heavenly places (Ephesians 6:12).

Yes, man was created to rule as governor over the earth (Genesis 1:26), but the first couple gave away that right to reign (Genesis 3:1–7). The devil realized this, admitting it aloud to Jesus (Luke 4:6). Before the cross, even Jesus Himself attested that this world was no longer held by His Kingdom (John 18:36). I'm so thankful that Christ's resurrection turned the tide.

But Satan still wars against us. He has scullions in our dominion to do his bidding. Some commentators, more scholarly than I, point to these being on God's left-hand side, using scriptures like 1 Kings 22:19 and Matthew 25:31–33 as proof texts. I'm not sure about this.

I can agree that the evil one has a territorial hierarchy with rulers, powers, world forces of darkness, and spiritual forces of wickedness (Colossians 2:15). Dominant spirits like fear, anger, hatred, and death not only work together but also have subjugated spirits working toward their purpose.

The spirit of fear, for instance, has lackeys like despair, doubt, anxiety, worry, and dread employed for his service.

Fear has always held a place in our society. But with the expansion of media in the horror genre as well as the melding of world beliefs into our education, we have welcomed spirits that whisper uneasiness, apprehension, phobias, and even suicide. Although counseling is often needed to begin truth building, it should always be coupled with warfare praying.

If you or someone you know struggles with feelings of fear and inadequacy, consider printing out a warfare prayer to pray daily until the deliverance is achieved. Christ is "far above all rule and authority and power and dominion, and every name that is named, not only in this age but also in the one to come" (Ephesians 1:21). He is now seated at the right hand of God, with angels and authorities and powers subjected to Him (1 Peter 3:22). Yes, this is a battle, but you are on the winning team. Know that I am fighting alongside you on your behalf.

◆ ◆ ◆

Day 20

I stared at the bucket suspended over the splash pool. It was empty now but wouldn't be for long.

Fed with trickles of water through two lemon-yellow pipes, the large pail hung slightly off-center. The water gradually filled the container to its tipping point, then dumped cool refreshment to anyone brave enough to stand below.

My individual prayer life often feels like a mere trickle of blessing—with a drip of an answer here and a dribble of a change there. On my own, my droplets of prayer are heard, but the principle of filling limits them.

When I joined corporately with others to pray, however, I noticed a sudden power feeding into the spring. United prayer fills the bucket of blessing much quicker than my singular drizzle could ever do.

John Chrysostom said, "What we cannot obtain by solitary prayer, we may by social ... because where individual strength fails, there union and concord are effectual."

Alone, you may toil in prayer for years before your God-glorifying request is answered. Ask a small group to join you, and the response comes within weeks. Ask a congregation to unite their hearts over the petition truly, and the Holy Spirit can't help but rush in with great power (Acts 2:2–4).

Consider Andrew Murray's illustration: "Nothing would be more unnatural than that the children of a family should always meet their father separately, but never in the united expression of their desires or their love. Believers are not only members of one family but even of one body. Just as each member of the body depends on the other, so Christians cannot reach the full blessing God is ready to bestow through His Spirit unless they seek and receive it in fellowship with each other."

Unity in corporate prayer unlocks the powerful spiritual principle of shared benefits. As we come together with one heart and one soul, all share the glorious blessings (Acts 5:32). Like the Israelites, we come together to collect our daily bread. Sometimes, I may bring a large container to prayer, ready to receive much from the Lord. On other occasions, I show up with only a small tote in hand.

Yet, the glorious truth is that "he who gathers much has no excess and he who gathers little has no lack" (Exodus 16:18). Corporate prayer distributes the wealth to all.

My individual prayer may seem very small. But amazingly enough, the Father has an abundant "matching gift" program. When I join my prayer alongside His saints' prayers, Jesus Himself increases the value of those prayers in a generous ratio. The pittance of our individual prayer multiplies into an abundant, billowing incense, which is pleasing to the Lord (Revelation 8:3–4; Romans 8:34; 2 Corinthians 2:15).

The heavens are bulging with His gracious gifts. Who can go with you to pick up His delivery? Believe me; it's far too much to carry on your own.

Day 21

What I saw took place beyond the dimension of physical eyes. Amidst the clouds of heaven, One "like a Son of man" riveted my attention. I could not see Him in His entirety, only His head, which peered out from the heavenlies with a perspective cutting across time and space.

This One who had been in the beginning with God stood with eyes wide open, seeing all and knowing all, scanning heaven and earth with just a glance (John 1:2; 2 Chronicles 16:9; Psalm 139:4). All things were open and laid bare to His eyes—eyes that flamed with the brilliance of fire, in purity and light (Hebrews 4:13; Revelation 1:14).

Mesmerized with the radiance of His glory, I realized that He looked precisely like His Father (Hebrews 1:3). Together, their light penetrated the expanse, extending like a rainbow in the clouds on a rainy day (Ezekiel 1:27–28). United as one, He spoke, and it was accomplished (Psalm 33:9). His Word, like an arrow that is always aimed precisely on its target, never failed, regardless of the purpose (Isaiah 55:11).

Despite my awe-inspired fear, it was His lovingkindness that extended throughout the heavenlies, not His terror. His faithfulness reached into infinity with color and brilliance (Psalm 36:5). The mountains I saw in the distance had been created through His righteousness, and the clear waters of bottomless lakes swirled with His unlimited plans (Psalm 36:6). His every character trait exploded into reality in this place where His perfection reigned supreme.

Then slowly, as if an unseen camera lens adjusted, my viewpoint panned out to expand my perspective. Breathless, I saw that this head, who saw all and knew all, had a body as well (Ephesians 1:22–23). Comprised of ligaments and joints, muscles, and sinew, His vast body filled not only the spiritual dimension but spanned into my time and space. My eyes scanned His form, and I realized He Himself was like Jacob's ladder, with His feet resting on earth yet His head reaching into the heavenlies (Genesis 28:12).

My gaze rested upon His feet and shocked into the realization that they resembled a mere human's. Like my feet. Like yours. Like those of the church, standing on earth while His head keeps the perspective of the heavenly.

There the vision ended, but it continues to influence my prayer life greatly.

We, who are many, are one body in Christ (Romans 12:5). He, as our head, has positioned each of us in His body to stand as watchmen wherever He has placed us (1 Corinthians 12:18). I in my place, and you in yours, our feet know well the trials and temptations of those around us.

But from our stance, we send petitions for resources upward to "Christ, Who is the head ..." (Ephesians 4:15 NET). "Truly, truly, I say to you, you shall see the heavens opened and the angels of God ascending and descending on the Son of Man," "sent out to render service for the sake of those who will inherit salvation" (John 1:51; Hebrews 1:14). "Devote yourselves (then) to prayer" "for everyone who asks receives and he who seeks finds and to him who knocks it shall be opened" (Colossians 4:2; Matthew 7:7).

◆ ◆ ◆

Day 22

Julia sent a quick text message to indicate that she would be arriving shortly. A busy woman with lots of plates spinning, Julia is a master at multitasking. Such a skill, however, has its mistakes. Instead of texting to say she would "pick me up," her phone autocorrected before she caught it. When she hit send, the text read that she would "slick me up."

We still chuckle about the value of proofreading.

This incident came to mind recently as I read about ancient Greek athletes. "Wrestlers strive to fasten upon some part of the body which will let them more easily throw their adversary. To prevent this, ancient wrestlers used to anoint their bodies before a match" (William Gurnall). In Turkey, wrestlers still practice the ancient sport of oil wrestling. Evidently, getting slicked up isn't a new idea.

When we wrestle against the enemies of darkness (see Ephesians 6:12), I wonder if getting "slicked up in spirit" wouldn't be a helpful exercise. God's Word often connects an anointing oil with His Spirit in both Old and New Testaments. Check out the following examples:

"Then Samuel took the horn of oil and anointed him ... and the Spirit of the Lord came mightily upon David from that day forward" (1 Samuel 16:13).

"The Spirit of the Lord God is upon me because the Lord has anointed me" (Isaiah 61:1; Luke 4:18).

"You know of Jesus of Nazareth, how God anointed Him with the Holy Spirit and with power ..." (Acts 10:38).

Think about it. If we are wrestling with a dark enemy, wouldn't a good rubdown of the Holy Spirit would be just the thing to keep our opponent from getting a good grip? What would it look like to utilize this powerful anointing oil during every temptation?

When a surge of offended anger rises within you:

"Father, anoint me with Your oil of forgiveness so the offense can't take hold."

When a burst of rebellion rears up on your child?

"Father, rub him down with Your oil of peace so that defiance can't pin him down."

When a wave of anxiety clamps down on your friend's demeanor?

"Father, smear her mind with Your oil of faith so that she will be anxious for nothing."

Whether we like it or not, we are in a daily wrestling match. Each contest is held to see who will pin his opponent to the mat and result as the victor. Despite our feelings in the heat of the bout, we can know we have the best Coach, which guarantees our ultimate victory. Let's go into today's contest well lubricated with this, our secret weapon, and remember to apply Him often.

Let's claim Isaiah 10:27 with faith: "And it shall come to pass in that day, that his burden shall be taken away from off thy shoulder, and his yoke from off thy neck; and the yoke shall be destroyed because of the anointing." Hallelujah

Day 23

I was in a cold, darkened room sitting next to a doorway. The doorway was covered over with blackout paper, causing no light to filter through. I realized that I held a straight pin, so I reached out to pierce its sharp end into the paper. There was no glass on the other side of the doorway, and my pin went straight through.

Immediately there was a pinpoint of light gleaming into the room.

I reached out again, perforating the blackness, first at this corner and then at the next. Each time, another small light broke through.

At some point, I realized that if I concentrated my jabs closer together, I could make the existing holes bigger. As I did so, my friends in the room reached out to help with their small pins. Together, we focused our movements onto the middle of the dark page, and soon the entire center broke away.

As the blinding radiance began to pour into the room, we realized that we weren't the only power weakening the filter, as the strength of the sun itself was wearing it away from the other side.

Working in tandem in this way, we soon found the opening large enough to step through into the warmth of the sunlight.

Then I awoke.

I've been thinking about how prayer is like those straight pins. As Christians, each of us holds power to puncture the darkness. Like my initial stabs, we often have no real direction and feel that our prayers have very little influence in the darkness around us.

Yet, when we begin to concentrate our prayers with specificity and importunity, even the tininess of effort reveals light. Our prayers then encourage others to join us, and soon we find that in that very pinpoint of light is the place that we can find even more light (Psalm 36:9).

Our world is in a very dark place. Will you join me in concentrated prayer today? Let's start by inviting His light to shine upon our own hearts. Ask that His Kingdom come, and His will be done inside of you just like it is already accomplished in heaven (Matthew 6:10). "All things become visible when they are exposed by the Light, for everything that becomes visible is light" (Ephesians 5:13).

And "If you will fear the Lord and serve Him and listen to His voice and not rebel against the command of the Lord, then both you and also the king who reigns over you will follow the Lord your God" (1 Samuel 12:14). Now that's light I'd like to walk into. How about you?

◆ ◆ ◆

Day 24

The words first pieced my heart when fear of the coronavirus appeared on the scene. I heard it again as our world began its journey with social distancing and sheltering in place. Then while tempers flared into riots and chaos, the apostle John's simple words pounded in my soul: "As He is, so also are you" (1 John 4:19).

As He is, I am?

I wondered, *How can this be?* Have you ever wondered the same?

The truth rests gently upon our souls: "Not as He was once, but as He is now."

Our childish hearts may thrill with a glimpse of our flannel-graph Jesus walking the dusty roads of Samaria and climbing the grassy knolls of Galilee. His brow damp. His clothes dirty, and His feet dusty. We relate to this body on earth that held "no stately form or majesty." We can identify with this One whose outer appearance drew no attention to Himself (Isaiah 53:2).

But our desperate need is to look at Him as He is now. To move past our Gospel depiction of Christ and see Him as He is today, in this instant. No longer disfigured and marred, He is now brilliant in glory and power (Isaiah 52:14; Revelation 1:12–17). Humanity no longer dims His light. His head glistens like snow, and His eyes look out at us like flames of fire. His feet radiate a dazzling brilliance like that of fine brass, while His face shines "like the brightness of the blinding sun" (Revelation 1:15–16 Passion Translation).

Here is Jesus as He is now: bright, luminous, intense, and resplendent. Dominant, powerful, majestic, and mighty. Pause to let His grandeur fill your view. Focus your gaze upon Him with wide-open eyes as His magnificence fills all you can see.

Now gradually look intently at His posture. No longer seated to wait, He rises, leaning forward toward our world. He stands, not upon clouds or even within heavenly realms, but stands—no, walks—amidst the lampstands, who are His church (Revelation 1:12–13; 20; 2:1). He is here among us. Not an absent fiancé, but an ever-present betrothed, consumed with His bride's well-being and moving among her in light, purity, and righteousness (meditate on other "as He is" verses—1 John 1:7, 3:3, 7).

Mere knowledge about Him cannot suffice. No amount of study will transform us into His image. We need revelation. As we "see Him as He is," then we shall be like Him. It is in the full vision of Him "as He is" that we transform to be like Him (1 John 3:2).

Exalt in the crisis you have experienced, for He can use our fear, stress, and uncertainty to stimulate His change. See Him as He is now, in His full splendor and power, because when we see Him, His glow within us reveals Himself to the world.

Our world desperately needs an outpouring of His Spirit. Will you turn your eyes upon Jesus to look full in His wonderful face? He is here in our midst, ready to make Himself known as He is today. Let's see Him just as He is so that we can be just like Him to this world.

◆ ◆ ◆

Day 25

"Your maidservant has nothing in the house except a flask of oil."

My eyes fell upon these words as the three of us bowed quietly in prayer.

On the table before us were pages of prayer requests, many of which we would never cover. Friends and family all around us were necessitous of our intercession, yet I felt impotent and overwhelmed. I could relate to this poor widow.

"Your maidservant has nothing in the house except a flask of oil."

In my Bible's margin, I noticed that the Hebrew word *flask* signified a tiny container of oil—used for anointing purposes and holding only a few teaspoons of the precious liquid. This destitute widow of Israel had used up every drop of oil for cooking. She now had only enough left to anoint a body for burial. Would it be hers or one of her two sons?

Her personal lack, like my prayer lack, seemed empty, exhausted, and hopeless. What prospect did either of us truly have?

"Then Elisha said, 'Go, borrow vessels at large for yourself from all your neighbors, even empty vessels; do not get a few.'"

More emptiness? That was God's answer?

As I looked at the requests recorded by our little group, I too saw much emptiness. A woman's depression. A crumbling marriage. A brain tumor. A loved one's death. The list stretched on before us. So much emptiness. So much sorrow. Yet the Scripture instructed us to gather even more.

> "Go, borrow vessels at large for yourself from all your neighbors, even empty vessels; do not get a few. And you shall go in and shut the door behind you and your sons, and pour out into all these vessels, and you shall set aside what is full."
>
> So she went from Elisha and shut the door behind her and her sons; they were bringing the vessels to her, and she poured. And it came about when the vessels were full that she said to her son, "Bring me another vessel." And he said to her, "There is not one vessel more." And the oil stopped. (2 Kings 4:1–5)

What glorious revelation!

Our hope is not in our few droplets of intercession but the abundant supply at the source! Because of Christ, we have within us a ceaseless flow (John

7:38). When we tap into His wellspring, "the Rock pours out for (us) streams of oil" (Job 29:6). He has anointed our heads with oil, so let's live with an overflowing cup (Psalm 25:5)!

O Father, thank You for being our everlasting fountainhead of plenty. For every need, for every weakness, You are always enough. How we need a fresh look at Your lavish source of living supply.

"As we gather all emptiness before You, we become very aware of the worthlessness of our resources. In and of ourselves, we are totally inadequate. We can barely keep up with our own needs, much less help others out of our insufficiency.

"But praise Your name that our supply does not depend on our pantry. Hallelujah! Our "adequacy is from God!" (2 Corinthians 3:5). "God's love has flooded our inmost heart through the Holy Spirit He has given us" (Romans 5:5 New English Translation). Because of Christ, "God is the source of my being" (John 8:42, New English Translation).

"So today we come, lugging our empty vessels as well as those of our friends. Begin the holy pour, O Father. Pour out hope into the emptiness of despair. Pour out healing into the void of pain. Pour out peace into the vacancy of discord. Give them a garland instead of ashes, the oil of gladness instead of mourning, the mantle of praise instead of fainting (Isaiah 61:3). We open our mouths wide so that You alone may fill (Psalm 46:10). Now, pray through us. In Jesus's name, amen.

Day 26

Our little prayer group agonizes week after week over devastation, divorce, and sometimes even death. New requests pour in, sometimes to such an extent as to overwhelm even our boldest prayer warrior.

Yesterday, as we prayed, the Father reminded us to cast all our anxiety on Him. He cares. He called us to give thanks and embrace all He allows in our lives to aid our reliance on Him. We were to be sober in spirit and on the alert because, He said, "Your adversary, the devil, prowls around like a roaring lion, seeking someone to devour" (1 Peter 5:7–8).

A roaring lion. Yes, we'd heard him often in our midst. A threat of cancer, a barrage of bankruptcy, a din of depression. Indeed, we were not ignorant of his schemes.

Then the Lord reminded us of an obscure story in Judges. Together, we turned to read an incident in the life of an Old Testament character. "Then Samson went down to Timnah ... and behold, a young lion came roaring toward him. And the Spirit of the Lord came upon him mightily, and he (Samson) tore him (the lion) as one tears a kid ... When he returned later, Samson turned aside to look at the carcass of the lion, and behold, a swarm of bees and honey were in the body of the lion" (Judges 14:5–6, 8).

The story resonated into prayer.

"Oh yes, Father," we agreed. "May Your Spirit stand face-to-face with the roaring lion in each of these situations—against the growl of bankruptcy, brain cancer, and court battles. Our hope is not in our own might or power but only in Your Spirit (Zechariah 4:6). You, O Lord, must deliver these precious ones before the lion of depression and disease tears their souls apart (Psalm 7:2). The evil one is lying in ambush to seize these afflicted ones and drag them away (Psalm 10:9). Come break out the fangs of these young lions, O Lord (Psalm 58:6)."

The Lord continued to speak, this time to another member of our little group. "I'm reminded of an African proverb, Lord: 'A roaring lion kills no prey.' In the savannah, the oldest and weakest lion is sent to lie in wait opposite the rest of the pride. With his eyesight dim and his teeth broken or missing, his roar is far worse than his bite. When prey comes to his scent, the old lion begins a ferocious roar, frightening the herd away from him and directly into the jaws of the awaiting lionesses.

"May we not be afraid of our adversary's roar but instead run toward it, knowing that the battle is not ours but Yours (2 Chronicles 20:15). Grant us faith, as we know that 'faith ... can shut the mouths of lions' (Hebrews 11:33). We can glorify You, knowing that when we begin singing and praising, You will set up ambushes against these roaring lions meant for harm (2 Chronicles 20:22). Hallelujah!

"Not only do we ask You to send Your Spirit to destroy these cougars, but that You bring sweetness out of the midst of death. The devil has intended these experiences for evil. But You, O Father, can turn it for Your good (Genesis 50:20; Romans 8:28). Reverse the outcome into opportunities for comforting others who have also walked these fearful roads (2 Corinthians 1:4). May we all taste and recognize that Your Word is sweeter than honey and the drippings of the honeycomb (Psalm 19:10)."

As a song of unified praise lifted from our lips, we were corporately aware that the peace of God was guarding our hearts and minds against the hostile ravage of our adversary (Philippians 4:7). He would continue to fight for us while we kept silent, feasting on His Word (Exodus 14:14; Psalm 119:103). Our eyes refreshed to pray another day (1 Samuel 14:29).

◆ ◆ ◆

Day 27

Nineteenth-century missionary Andrew Murray is one of my favorite authors. My introduction to him began when my high school mentor, Bobbie Trull, suggested we read *With Christ in the School of Prayer* together. In this classic, Mr. Murray ends every chapter with a prayer. Although a seasoned man wrote these prayers seventy-five years before my experience, my sixteen-year-old heart could repeat them.

Countless readers from all over the world have done the same. Talk about praying without ceasing! Written prayers like these continue to be a fragrant incense to God when they become the desire of another's soul.

When you write and send out printed intercession, you too are multiplying prayer. Most of the time, recipients of written prayers will immediately join their hearts to the words they read. These simple paragraphs may even be forwarded to others so that warriors across the miles can join together in unified intercession.

Sending out a prayer can also encourage persistence in someone who desires to pray but is too overwhelmed to know where to start. You and I can be an "Aaron and Hur" to our Moses, those people who desire to see victory but need additional support to press through (Exodus 17:8–13).

Is this the only way to pray? Absolutely not. But this is one way to pray, "with all prayer and supplication praying at all seasons in the Spirit" (Ephesians 6:18 ESV).

One way to order your prayer is by mirroring a segment in the Bible as your prayer template. Most of the psalms, much of Isaiah, Jesus's words in the Gospels, and Paul's prayers all contain an abundant harvest just waiting to be offered to God. The verses themselves will unfold to you how to pray.

Here is an example that I sent to a missionary couple returning to the States on furlough. Open your Bible to Isaiah 40 and follow along with the references to help you see this approach's simplicity.

Father,

(*Couple's names*) have been through so much in the last several years. Come upon them with the comfort You offer in Isaiah 40. Speak kindly to them, Father (Isaiah 40:1), revealing that their warfare will soon be over in these difficulties (v. 2).

Clear the way for Your entrance in this wilderness in which they live. May they be people who make smooth roads for Your Presence, no matter how dry and desert-like their environment seems. Lift every valley and bring low every obstacle (v. 3–4). Reveal Your glory, Lord, clearly speaking so they can hear (v. 5). Despite any personal weakness they feel, may Your Word prove more enduring than ever before (v. 6–8).

May their family life be one that lifts up what You can do (v. 9), pointing boldly to Your character. Be their Shepherd, gathering them into Your arms as they tend to their own little ewes (v. 11).

You are great and beyond comparison. Lead this family into the pathway You have called them into (v. 12–26). Thank You for never becoming weary or tired. Oh, how we need You whose understanding is inscrutable (v. 28). Give (*couple's names*) strength when exhausted and give them might when they lack power (v. 29). May they wait upon You even when they think they are waiting on a stoplight or a postal line. Grant them experience both to wait and see renewed strength. May they soar like eagles, run like cheetahs, and walk like camels (v. 31). In Jesus's name, amen.

Notice the freedom you have to skip verses you don't quite know how to pray. Over the years, I've found it better to keep moving than force elements that don't seem to fit. Since you ask the Spirit to do His praying through You, His living and active voice will guide you into the words you should say.

Will you accept the challenge of texting someone a prayer this week? Paul's prayers provide a great place to start. You will find yourself joining in prayers that have been prayed for God's people for at least two thousand years.

Paul's prayers:

Romans 1:9–11, 9:2–3; 10:1
1 Corinthians 1:4–8
2 Corinthians 10:3–5
Galatians 4:9
Ephesians 1:16–19, 3:14–20
Philippians 1:3–4, 8–9
Colossians 1:3, 9–12; 2:1
1 Thessalonians 1:2, 3–11; 3:9–10
2 Timothy 1:3
Philemon 4

◆ ◆ ◆

Day 28

Medicine proved no benefit. This once healthy young man was paralyzed, unable to move. The only thing that had changed was his family's future.

One of his friends caught wind that a teacher was in town. This carpenter turned rabbi not only healed lepers and cast out demons; He even tamed the weather on occasion. His stories kept people spellbound with authority.

"Maybe," someone suggested, "this teacher is the answer to paralysis."

Their first attempt to reach the Healer was simple enough. It took only one friend to carry the disabled man through the streets. Yet as they neared the house, crowds overflowed out the doorway and down the lanes, with standing room only. Every resident from Capernaum and its countryside must have been there that day. No amount of pushing and shoving gained access.

They needed to regroup.

Time was of the essence. With the door and windows blocked, the suggestion of the roof teetered on the ridiculous. Reason pointed out there was no opening from above.

"We'll make one," was the reply.

With the disabled man staring in unbelief, his friends rigged a simple rope system onto the corners of his sleeping mat. This scheme could not only haul him through the streets and onto the roof but also lower him into the house once the breach was made.

It was almost noon by the time the dig began. The four men unsheathed their knives and went to work on all fours to break up the tile. With a pallet-sized section of the terra-cotta removed, they began the tougher challenge of chiseling through the sun-hardened layer of mud. Once they reached the packed heather and reeds, the excavation went quickly, evidenced by dust filtering onto heads below.

Despite disrupting a vital parable, the four remained obstinate, tenacious, and unshakable. The inevitable grumbling from the unsettled crowd didn't halt their progress. Neither did the upturned eyes of the Master. Nothing stopped their bull-dogged determination.

With singular resolve, they had lugged, hoisted, and clawed their friend toward hope.

"And seeing their faith … (Jesus) said to the paralytic … 'Rise, and take up your stretcher and go home'" (Luke 5:20, 24).

"Seeing their faith." Their faith. It wasn't the conviction of the paralytic himself but the trust of his friends.

Who do I know too weak to get to Jesus? Will I scrap and fight to get them there? Charles Spurgeon said, "Smash or crash, everything shall go to pieces which stands between the soul and its God: it matters not what tiles are to be taken off, what plaster is to be dug up, or what boards are to be torn away ... the soul is too precious for us to stand upon nice questions."

Will I tenaciously bear their weight in prayer? Will you? Will we go around, over, and through whatever obstacles block our way? Will we seek others to join the effort?

Jesus can do "exceedingly, abundantly beyond all that you can ask or think." He doesn't need to be begged or convinced, but He does need to be faithed. Your faith can't save lives, but it can bear them into life-giving Presence.

———————————— ◆ ◆ ————————————

Day 29

While living overseas, I regularly received letters from my mentor, Bobbie Trull, who would often end her letters by writing out her prayer for me. I knew from experience that Bobbie's intercession always had power. So, I often kept this portion before me, praying her words as my own.

Each precious prayer had one thing in common: the Word of God. These weren't just Bobbie's words; they were God's! She was praying God's will for me. I discovered that "if we ask anything according to His will, He hears us. And if we know that He hears us ... we know that we have the requests which we have asked from Him" (1 John 5:14–15). This was powerful stuff!

At some point, I moved from just reading Bobbie's prayers to writing out my own. Something about the printed word extended the authority of what had been brooding in my heart. With fear and trembling, I too, began sending printed prayers to the struggling.

Today, most of my prayers are now typed rather than handwritten, but the value of God's Word has not lost His authority. My inadequate fumbling to pray His Word never negates the effectiveness of His desire. Ninety-eight percent of the time I send out a prayer written in weakness, I hear back from the recipient that the Holy Spirit has ministered in power.

I would like to challenge you to text or email a handwritten prayer to someone this week. I have found that having a prayer to refer to repeatedly helps the overwhelmed one know how to pray for themselves. Remember, a written prayer prays more than once.

As you begin, consider the following guidelines:

Begin short. What are one or two specific verses you can claim over their life? Find a highlighted promise in psalms or one that comes to mind from your pocket promise book.

Start your text with the words, "I am praying (*scripture reference*) for you today." Then, cut and paste this verse into your text. Follow it up with a simple description of your prayer. For example, "I am praying Psalm 46:1–2 for you today. 'God is our refuge and strength. A very present help in trouble. Therefore, we will not fear, though the earth should change and though the mountains slip into the heart of the sea.' Father, thank You that You are Martha's refuge and strength. You are present in the very midst of this trouble she is experiencing. I ask that she not fear, even though it seems like her world is changing and the very things she has relied on are slipping away. Give she and me both faith to trust You. In Jesus's name, amen."

Now send it out. Don't fuss about your wording. It is more important to get a timely message fastened around the carrier pigeon's leg than to worry about building an air freight carrier. The Holy Spirit, in the form of a dove, will minister His Word upon receipt. Your job is simply to send it on its way.

◆ ◆ ◆

Day 30

A written prayer prays more than once.

I love thinking about this. Not only do we pray as the Father unfolds His Word, but the recipient may also begin to pray as they read. That's already "two of you agreeing on earth about what they ask" (Matthew 18:19). Just think about what happens if they print out the prayer to pray again or forward it to friends. One simple prayer grows and expands into the hearts of many. Isn't that encouraging?

Let's explore yet another way to compose a written prayer.

For this exercise, you will need a pocket promise book. Start by opening the table of contents. No matter the publisher, each promise book is organized into topical sections.

Mine has a section that says, "Do you need peace of mind?" Who immediately comes to mind when you read this description? Turn to those verses, asking the Father to form them into a written prayer.

Pray the verses in order as they are listed. There is nothing super-spiritual about this. You are just praying God's Word. If one doesn't seem to fit, skip it and move to the next.

As you begin, do so with thanksgiving or praise to focus on the Who rather than the what. God is always bigger than fear. Remember, we are praying to the Promiser, not about the problem.

Here is how my prayer unfolded, using this one section as my guide:

Holy Father,

Thank You that Your peace can keep our thoughts and hearts quiet and at rest (Philippians 4:7). Every time I open Your Word, I find You speaking peace to Your people (Psalm 85:8).

Today, I come bringing _____ to Your throne. She is in dire need of Your peace, as the peace of the world hasn't panned out (John 14:27). You promised that if we come to You—even if we are bogged down and heavy-laden—You will give us rest (Matthew 11:28). I'm asking this restful peace for _____.

Despite all the panic that her thoughts suggest, You have not given her this spirit of fear. You have given her power, love, and self-control (2 Timothy 1:7). Thank You. I ask that You clear her thoughts so that she can see the power, love, and self-control rather than focusing on her situation. Turn her thoughts often toward You, for I know You alone are the place of perfect peace (Isaiah 26:3).

_____ needs hope and courage, Father. May she be able to lie down and sleep tonight, awakening in the morning with both courage and hope (Job 11:18–19; Proverbs 3:24). Remind me to pray for her often. In Jesus's name, amen.

See how simple this is? Yours will sound a bit different as the Word melds with your communication style, but the blessing of receiving a written prayer lasts for years. I believe in you.

Epilogue

I peered behind the curtained veil.
I held my breath to peek
On He whose heart had captured mine
With glorious mystique.

I'd known Him since my childhood.
He to my spirit came
Upon my invitation
And cleared my heart of blame.

With childlike faith of simple trust,
His Gospel, I believed.
Yet entered not into my soul
All for me He conceived.

"Take this my yoke upon you,
And thus, you'll learn of Me."
Misread to mean religion,
I changed to worker bee.

From mornings bright and early
To night times dark and deep,
I did for Him my duty
The jot and tittle keep.

Then gradually, I burned out.
My heart and flesh did fail.
My zeal was gone. My passion dim,
Consumed, fatigued, and frail.

And then one day I saw it,
With revelation speed,
That easy is His burden.
My toil He dost not need.

He did it all. It's finished.
My conscience has been freed
From dead works busy serving.
Deliv'rance guaranteed.

A once-for-all salvation
Includes His workmanship
Created in Christ Jesus,
Without one more guilt trip.

"You've done it all!" my soul exclaimed.
"So, what then is my part?"
He smiled and answered tenderly,
"Come see My work, sweetheart."

And so, with awe and trembling,
I gazed upon the throne,
Among the glowing cherubim
And radiance unknown.

There seated in His glory,
The Father and the Son,
With Spirit joining to them
Interceding for each one.

What is His job—this Jesus God?
Well, herein lies the key.
He's ever interceding now
To pray for you and me.

And this one thing He asks of us,
Our mission now of worth—
To hear His prayers, agree with them,
And bring them down to earth.

He lingers at the altar,
Our royal Priest. He stands,
Awaiting intercession
From fragile hearts and hands.

The import of our prayer life
Seems small to His compare.
Imperative, He's made them—
We're flint that starts the flare.

Before His golden censer
Can smoke with fragrant fire,
Our bowls must fill with incense,
Our groanings lifted higher.

We know not how to pray thus.
Which latchkey shall we use?
To open up His storerooms,
His pow'r and strength diffuse.

In might, His Holy Spirit
Helps weakness and defect.
Impotence and unfitness
Can never disaffect.

So, child, come boldly to Him.
Draw near to God this day.
Be strong and know your weakness
Is crucial when you pray.

When you and I can pray with Him,
And let Him bear the weight.
Then life and purpose—future, too,
Have cause to celebrate.

Additional Resources

Carré, E G. Praying Hyde: A Challenge to Prayer: Glimpses of the Amazing Prayer-Life of John Hyde, a Missionary in India, Whose Intercession "Changed Things". South Plainfield, N.J: Bridge Pub, 1982.

Gordon, S D. Quiet Talks on Prayer. Westwood: Fleming H. Revell Co, 1967.

Grubb, Norman P. Rees Howells: Intercessor. Fort Washington, Pa: Christian Literature Crusade, 1952.

Guyon, Jeanne M. B. L. M. Experiencing the Depths of Jesus Christ, 1975.

Murray, Andrew. With Christ in the School of Prayer: Thoughts on Our Training for the Ministry of Intercession. Old Tappan, N.J: Fleming H. Revell Co, 1972.

Nee, Watchman. Let Us Pray. New York: Christian Fellowship Publishers, 1977.

Peterson, Eugene H. Eat This Book: The Holy Community at Table with Holy Scripture. Vancouver: Regent College Pub, 2000.

Richard, Albert E, and Christian Unknown. The Kneeling Christian. Grand Rapids, Mich: Zondervan Pub. House, 1962.

Sheets, Dutch. Intercessory Prayer Study Guide: How God Can Use Your Prayers to Move Heaven and Earth. Ventura, Calif: Regal, 1996.

Smith, Hannah W. The God of All Comfort and the Secret of His Comforting. London: J. Nisbet, 1906.

Thomas, Lee E. Living the Exceedingly Victorious Life. Milford, Ohio: John the Baptist Printing Ministry, 2014.

Thomas, Lee E. Praying Effectively for the Lost. Milford, Ohio: John the Baptist Printing Ministry, 2003.

Tozer, A W. The Praying Plumber of Lisburn: A Sketch of God's Dealings with Thomas Haire. Harrisburg, Pa: Christian Publications, 1960.

Yun, and Paul Hattaway. Living Water: Powerful Teachings from the International Bestselling Author of the Heavenly Man. Grand Rapids, Mich: Zondervan, 2008.